NEW EYES

A Unifying Vision of Science and Spirit

Steve Treu

Cover design by
Randal S McKenzie

Illustrations by
Sarah Will
and
Randal S McKenzie

Quantum Revolution Inc.

CRANBERRY TOWNSHIP, PA

Steve Treu/Quantum Revolution Inc.
One Landmark North, Suite 205A
20399 Route 19, Brandt Drive
Cranberry Township, PA/16066
www.quantumrevolution.org

New Eyes/ Steve Treu. -- 1st ed.
ISBN 978-0-9973305-1-9

DEDICATIONS

To Kristen, with Infinite Love

The first time I ever saw The Light was in your eyes.

To Austin, Veridy and Aidan

Because of you I lost my hair, but found my heart.

To Kristina Grace, Alb, Faith and Nemo

I am forever grateful that there is no such thing as time.

To Mom and Dad

I am so blessed that I got to be "on your team."

To Kevin, Ramona and Marvin

Having you as role models was much more valuable to me than that Atari.

To Quantum Revolution Inc.

Thanks for everything you've done so far — this is just the beginning.

ACKNOWLEDGEMENTS

The Original *New Eyes* 'Fight Club'

Amara, Art, Bill, Chad, Elvis, Mike, Nicole, Sarah

Thank You For The Additional Financial Support (and more)

Dr. Sheila Balestrino, Chad 'Neo' Barnett, Babak Bazmi,
Chris 'Chippy' Boeh, Rich 'Al' Boeh, William Bremer,
Brad 'Anthony' Bulvin, Larry Coudriet, Lynn and Renee Ford,
Michael 'Magnum' Himpele, Debra 'Gabriel' Holz, Patrick Hooper,
Martin Irwin, Lynne Jones, 'Uncle' Peter Knebel, Craig 'Yang' Loop,
Robert 'Nate' Lozowski, Susan McGarvey, Ken McGettigan,
BJ 'Elizabeth' McLaren (My FMIL – Favorite Mother-In-Law),
Mary 'Jonah' Neal, Kathy 'Coffee' O'Toole, Doug and Christie Peel,
Christopher 'Cheech' Petronka, Brittany 'Zo' and Steve 'JB' Purvis,
Laurie Quattro, Kristin Rosenberg, Janet 'Grace' Schuch, Matt Sturgill,
Lauren 'Luna' Thompson, Mark 'Chuck' Tomkovicz,
Teri 'Peaches' Turconi, Brian 'Gil' Wright and 'Amara'

Thank You For The Additional Spiritual Support

Doc, John, Wayne, Ompah and Friends

Row row row your boat
Gently down the stream
Merrily merrily merrily merrily
Life is but a dream!
- NURSERY RHYME

"Everything we call real is made of things
that cannot be regarded as real."
- PHYSICIST NIELS BOHR

"Blessed are your eyes because they see."
- JESUS CHRIST, MATTHEW 13:16

CONTENTS

INTRODUCTION

"Imagination is more important than knowledge."
– Albert Einstein

Imagine you are living in a remote village of England sometime during the middle of the second millennium. One morning, you go outside and notice the sun rising over the lake. Twelve hours later, after working hard on the farm into the evening, you watch the sun set behind a distant hillside.

Just like every other sunny day of your life.

Would you think that the sun had moved across the sky? Of course you would, just like everyone else at the time.

Well, most everyone else.

One summer day a local villager returns from a semester at the University of Oxford and tells you he had read a book titled *De Revolutionibus Orbium Coelestium* by Nicolaus Copernicus, who was suggesting that the sun isn't revolving around the earth, that it was actually the other way around.

Initially, you wouldn't believe it, as it seems so obvious that the sun is moving around the earth. But something inside of you has been stirred. You awaken the next morning feeling inspired. A desire to learn more, a passion to know the truth.

So you go on your own inquisitive journey and come across the writings of Galileo Galilei, an Italian astronomer and physicist who championed the works of his Polish colleague Copernicus. It makes sense to you, and you are shocked to learn that Galileo was sentenced to house arrest for the last decade of his life due to his advocacy of heliocentrism (the astronomical model in which the sun is the center of the solar system).

Imprisoned for scientific inquiry? Unfathomable.

Your life goes on.

Understanding that the earth revolves around the sun was revolutionary, so you want to learn what else you did not know about the way reality works. You no longer assume that what appears to be true is actually true.

Something else beyond your own understanding was also sparked, as what it touched in your heart was much more important. Underlying your new insights lurked a truth that was now burning inside of you … and you yearned for all to know it as well:

The world isn't what we think it is!

***

This is not a science text. I am not a physicist, so this book is not intended to hold up to rigorous scientific scrutiny, though I have done my due diligence with more than a decade of research for *New Eyes*.

This is not a religious text. I am not a preacher, so I do not intend to convince you of anything, though I hope you are willing to be open-minded and read everything in this book before you render a final opinion.

This is merely a book written by a common man for common man. I am not trying to impress any PhDs nor persuade any pastors. I am simply painting a picture for my peers and will allow beauty to be in the eye of the beholder.

For 20 years, I was a sportswriter for a suburban Pittsburgh newspaper. I have authored a thousand columns and this book is written in that same casual, relatable style.

Now, as a licensed professional counselor, I have worked in the front lines with nearly 3,000 ordinary people in groups and individual settings, trying to help them help themselves. Over time I found out that these people were actually extraordinary … they ultimately were helping *me* by walking the walk of the talk I was talking … and it led to *New Eyes* for many of us.

They have been the players of this game; I've just been their coach.

The coach is rarely as interesting as the players, who have proven to me that the words written in this book are true, or in the very least, effective. I call this a "win-win" scenario: the concepts that yielded *New Eyes* are either true or effective … or both. Not only do you discover Truth, you experience the benefits of applying Truth in your life.

In this book, universal truth or spiritual wisdom that applies to all of us will be written as Truth, in contrast to relative truth. Capital-T Truth includes answers to questions such as "Is there life after death?" and "Does some kind of God exist?" and "Is there a meaning or purpose in life?" while little-t truth includes physical laws like gravity and facts such as "Pepperoni is the favorite pizza topping in America" or "The Pittsburgh Steelers have won six Super Bowls, the most in National Football League history." Those things are true at the moment, but not everlasting Truth.

I have found that learning and living Truth has profound healing power.

When someone has been struggling with heroin addiction or contemplating suicide off and on for a decade, you use any and all therapeutic means at your disposal to help. I wanted to be a good therapist, so I paid close attention to what seemed to work and what appeared to be a waste of their time, concentrating on the former while eliminating the latter.

In 2004, an inquisitive older gentleman named Jim brought a video into my office and asked to watch it during our session. It was a clip from a movie called *The Elegant Universe* by Columbia University professor Brian Greene. In it there was a discussion that, according to quantum physics, virtually anything was possible.

That immediately reminded of a saying by Jesus in the Bible.

"With God all things are possible."
- Matthew 19:26

That made me wonder, perhaps there was a link between science and spirituality?

Was there ever!

I began a group with clients called *Explorers*, during which we talked about new scientific discoveries and attempted to see how they could assist clients in improving their lives. Shortly after that I began a group called simply *Spirituality*, in which we discussed a wide variety of philosophies, including the world's greatest religions as well as other metaphysical and existential belief systems.

Soon the twain met.

Most of my insight-focused therapy with clients became about using quantum physics to understand the scientific nature of reality and then processing what it meant for them from both a physical (body) and non-physical (soul) perspective.

We were all hooked, a collective and healthy addiction. I loved going to work every day and my clients craved quantum spirituality sessions, frequently reporting rapid improvement in their symptoms and joking about withdrawing if they missed a meeting. Countless times I have heard things like, "I'm not sure what happened but I suddenly don't feel like using drugs any longer" and "My depression just faded away" and "What, me worry?"

My heart was full watching as clients healed their emotional, physical, mental and spiritual health. All things were indeed possible … with God and with quantum physics!

The approach seemed to be so effective that my wife and colleague Kristen suggested that we call our private practice *Quantum Counseling Services* with the tagline "Exploring Your Infinite Possibilities."

Possibilities such as being relieved of the symptoms of a condition, which is one definition for the word 'cure.' Possibilities that include one of the more intriguing Biblical verses ...

"Physician, heal thyself."
- Luke 4:23

We are all spiritual doctors, capable of healing our own souls.

These days I still help people explore their infinite possibilities, which includes them improving their lives through a variety of mind, body and spirit techniques.

They do the healing themselves.

I'm just their coach, an applied quantum philosopher.

While I do not fully understand all the intricacies of quantum physics, I do understand how to apply fascinating scientific concepts to the everyday lives of everyday people.

I do not need to understand all equations behind the law of gravity in order to know not to lean too far over a cliff. I do not need to understand the complicated thermodynamics of the sun in order to know that I should apply sunscreen on my child before she goes outside on a hot summer day.

It can be the same thing with quantum physics, as otherwise inaccessible concepts such as superposition, the observer effect and entanglement are used not just to secure government grants for doctoral students, but can also be made useful for common man. Quantum physics is indeed practically applicable, while at the same time it also provides scientific support for the profound wisdom of the world's greatest spiritual teachers ... and ultimately unites all spiritual perspectives. For many of us, this means *New Eyes*, seeing the world from a much different point of view.

So this is a book about the nature of reality. It's about science and spirituality and how they both are really revealing the same thing. It's about what works in improving your mind, body and spirit.

There are a lot of movable parts, but if you stick with it, *New Eyes* will come together like a jigsaw puzzle. Initially you might not know where any specific piece goes, then you establish the basics by figuring out where the corners are, followed by all the edges, then you group certain patterns together and finally … voila! The picture becomes clear.

When you understand the relevant physics, it's like putting on 3D glasses at a 3D movie … beforehand, you can make out what's going on but it's a little foggy. When you put on those specs, however, it pops out at you! As such, *New Eyes* is indeed a painting, relying on broad strokes across an even broader canvas.

Like most works of art, the whole is greater than the sum of its parts. There is a synergy within this book, as truth builds upon Truth, and understanding basic concepts leads to experiencing spiritual revelations.

Like most artists, I do not expect everyone to like the finished product. Art is ultimately a Rorschach inkblot test … it is what you say it is.

Same with this book … it is what you say it is.

Same with this universe.

***

There are two types of people in this world, *awake* or *asleep*, though there are many degrees in between.

Spiritually speaking 'sleeping' and 'dead' mean virtually the same thing. All of us have been asleep (or 'dead') at some point in this life, until you begin to awaken (or are 'raised from the dead').

In this book we will explain why 'waking up' is central to Buddhism (in fact, the word Buddha means "to wake up"), and why Christianity is really about Jesus trying to inspire a spiritual resurrection within all of us. Great revelations from Muhammad in Islam and teachings from Krishna in Hinduism, among others, will be included as well.

We will also show how science supports their teachings, often using the philosophical words of the world's greatest scientists themselves.

"Everyone who is seriously involved in the pursuit of science," said Albert Einstein, "becomes convinced that some spirit is manifest in the laws of the universe, one that is vastly superior to that of man. In this way the pursuit of science leads to a religious feeling of a special sort, which is surely quite different from the religiosity of someone more naive."

This book is about not being naive, not staying asleep. Awakening from naiveté can mean both understanding deep science and experiencing deep soulfulness by connecting to a "vastly superior" spirit.

How to do this? Let's think more about heliocentrism for a moment. It took hundreds of years for word to get around and for it to be commonly accepted that the sun does not revolve around the earth. Wouldn't you hate to be the last one to know the truth?

The earth does indeed revolve around the sun. But *how* do you know that? Unless you have been to outer space or studied the concept à la Copernicus and Galileo, aren't you simply taking someone else's word for it?

Truth is, it just sort of makes sense to us. Similarly, when we understand Truth, we simply *know* it to be true.

Max Planck was a mentor of Einstein's. As his teacher he

was basically an 'Einstein' for Einstein. That means he was a really, really smart guy.

Planck had a compelling perspective regarding science and spirituality.

"Knowledge is not gained by any process of reasoning," he said. "It is a direct perception and, therefore, in its nature akin to what we call faith. It is a metaphysical belief."

That's the Father of Quantum Physics comparing scientific knowledge to spiritual faith!

Actually he did more than compare the two. He basically stated that the acquisition of either knowledge or spirituality was precisely the same pursuit.

Planck continued, saying that theoretical physics can "satisfy the metaphysical hunger which religion does not seem capable of satisfying nowadays. But this would be entirely by stimulating the religious reaction indirectly. Science as such can never really take the place of religion."

Amazing.

Planck said his own life's work merely satisfied a "metaphysical hunger" *entirely* by stimulating a sense of spirituality. In just a few sentences, one of the smartest men in the history of the world undercut virtually every scientific argument against spirituality by suggesting that the pursuit of science is ultimately a pursuit of spirit in disguise.

An entire chapter of *New Eyes* (Level 20) is devoted to how science *needs* spirituality to be complete. Science and spirituality are not mutually exclusive, they complement each other.

Or as Einstein put it, "Science without religion is lame, religion without science is blind."

Science is ultimately a tool for spiritual growth, a very valuable one. Closing their eyes to incredible advances in science has limited the ability of many religious leaders to expand their audiences and, to be honest, they often end up sounding judgmental as a result. Science opens new avenues for spiritual insights.

We can go right back to heliocentrism for a perfect example. Galileo was sentenced to house arrest because he taught that the earth revolved around the sun, yet that is an ideal metaphor for spirituality!

The earth is all things flesh. The sun is all things light. The earth needs the sun to exist.

The body is all things flesh. The spirit is all things light. The body needs the spirit to exist.

It's perfect!

Of course the earth revolves around the sun, but the leaders of the Christian church in Galileo's time failed to see the beauty of the truth/Truth that was right in front of their own faces because they were blinded by dogmatism. They thought that it was somehow in opposition to God to support heliocentrism, preferring to believe that 'light' revolves around a physical body such as earth, which makes flesh the king. And yet it is the physical body that revolves around the sun, while our soul bodies revolve around the 'Son.'

Silly church leaders. They were so asleep.

Wouldn't you rather be the one who 'gets it' before everyone else? Don't you want to be one who helps others get it? Or would you rather be the last person to figure out that the sun is not moving across the sky?

There have been amazing new advances in science over the past century that have gone largely unnoticed by the mainstream, including the likelihood that we are living in a 3D hologram of some sort and that invisible energy fields are extremely influential in guiding our thoughts and behaviors.

We will go over why Einstein calls certain aspects of the world illusory, which is something Muhammad recites several times in the Quran, and why Krishna in the Bhagavad Gita calls our reality a delusion. We will review how the world operates as a mirror, which every major religion includes somewhere in its teachings, and why there is no such thing as time. And we will emphasize how reality is much like a mind game, an energy matrix in which we are only temporarily living.

New Eyes explains the applicable aspects of all that cool science during the first half of the book and links it to the meaning of life throughout the second half so that you don't have to go through life … dead. I certainly wouldn't want to be the last person on earth who understands why the world that we see is an illusion, that we are living in a hologram.

Your process of awakening has already begun, as it is highly unlikely that you would have picked up this book and read through this introduction if you were not already somewhat inclined in a 'science meets spirit' direction.

And better still, you are guaranteed to succeed on this journey. You are destined to see the world more clearly.

New Eyes await.

Seek and you will find.

THE BEGINNING

The End.

Successfully interpreting the following saying from the Gospel of Thomas may be the key to eternal life:

"The end will be where the beginning is. Congratulations to the one who stands at the beginning. That one will know the end and will not taste death."

Not tasting death? Sounds like a superb idea!

Now all we have to do is figure out what that verse means.

The answer is somewhere in the pages of this book ...

WE ARE ALL ONE

(or Un, Uno, Eins, Moja, Unum, Oneway, etc.)

How many different ways can you say the number 1?

In this chapter's title you can see it in numerical form, English, French, Spanish, German, Swahili, Latin and Pig Latin, with a list that could go on and on. All of them are different ways of saying the same thing.

So which way is the *correct* way to say 1?

You may have a second to think about it.

...

You're right! None of them is correct, because they are all correct.

Somehow we all know that the concept called '1' is true and there are many different ways of saying it. It's like that with a lot of things in life.

Think of a sunset. You could use poetry to describe it. Or simple prose. You could use a professional's photograph. Or a toddler's watercoloring. You could ask an astronomer to describe it. Or an orchestra to play it. Or a ballerina to do an interpretive dance of it. Or someone with closed eyes to simply imagine it.

All of them, different ways of describing the same thing. You might prefer one description over another, but really, would you argue with someone over their preference?

Welcome to *New Eyes* … where we do not argue over what anyone's preference for seeing reality is. (Though we might ask the question of whether their way of viewing reality is working for them.)

In Buddhism this is called the Kalama Sutta, where everyone has their own path to Truth. Over the course of this book we will show you how all paths lead to the same place, no matter how you describe it.

Similarly, Muhammad conveys in the Quran that "there is no compulsion in religion." In other words, do not force your way of seeing things onto others, much like Jesus commanding us to "judge not."

Good advice. *New Eyes* will not force anything on you, instead merely offering you a way to see things differently if you wish.

That's why the name of this first level is Incito Veritas, which in *my* Latin means "to incite" or "to inspire" Truth. (It may not be proper Latin, but it works for me.) We are all seeking Truth in one way or another, and what this book shares is just one road that gets there.

In Taoism, Truth is essentially a pathway (*Tao* in Chinese) that runs through each one of us. Walking that path is the goal of *New Eyes*, to stir up the very Truth that is already inside you by elevating your awareness of all the scientific and spiritual pieces of the mysterious jigsaw puzzle that is the universe, then by fitting them together into a pattern to reveal that Truth.

Level 0 (or Level Cero, Sifuri, Nulla, Erozay, etc.) introduced you to a riddle attributed to Jesus. You need to know the answer early, because understanding Truth is profoundly facilitated by comprehending that riddle.

What Jesus was referring to when he said, "The end will be where the beginning is," and what he and several other prophets were referring to in most of their teachings, is *consciousness*. As quantum physics has uncovered, consciousness is what makes this world go around.

Reality is all about consciousness. The beginning and the end, the Alpha and the Omega. We all begin as consciousness and we all end as consciousness. Alternatively, the answer can be called *soul* if you prefer that term. You begin as a soul and you end as a soul. What you are not is a physical body, you are not the *ego* aspect of yourself.

Adequately defining those terms is essential for *New Eyes*.

Consciousness and soul are interdependent, similar to your head's relationship to your body. They work together. The head feeds the physical body, both with electrical signals and with food. Spiritually speaking, consciousness is the mind of the soul. It feeds the spiritual body, guiding energy to all the places it can go, both positive and negative. Consciousness can provide nutrients or toxins. Just as the mouth can put healthy food or toxic food into the human body, so can consciousness put positive or negative energy into the soul.

Garbage in, garbage out. Spirit in, spirit out.

"For God's kingdom does not consist
of food and drink, but of righteousness."
- Romans 14:17

The soul consumes righteousness, not bacon double cheeseburgers. It's the ego that craves bacon double cheeseburgers.

You can think of your soul as an energy repository, or your 'spiritual personality' … in contrast with your 'ego personality.' Ego is whatever you associate with your physical body, an identity that correlates with the flesh world, including gender, race, age, sexual orientation, political affiliation, occupation, financial portfolio, etc. You are ultimately not any of those labels. Those are all features of a costume you are temporarily wearing (Level 18).

Your soul is your consciousness experience of your spiritual self, while your consciousness experience of your flesh self, or your False Self, is the ego. When your deepest desire is for materials, you are in ego mode. When your deepest desire is for Truth, you are in spirit mode.

"Those who live according to the flesh have their minds set on what the flesh desires; but those who live in accordance with the spirit have their minds set on what the spirit desires. The mind governed by the flesh is death, but the mind governed by the spirit is life and peace."
- Romans 8:5-6

That illustrates the answer to the riddle, for when the mind becomes governed by spirit and not flesh, it knows what it is (consciousness or soul) and cannot die as it is the energy that animates the body. If you were to smash a radio with a baseball bat, does the song that it was playing die? Of course not. It's the same with consciousness and the body. You can destroy the body, not the energy that animates it.

So you are the non-physical aspect of the physical experience that you are having. You may call it consciousness, soul, atman, awareness, True Self or whatever ... a rose by any other name will still smell as sweet.

Because they are so closely connected, the words consciousness and soul will be used interchangeably throughout this book. (Plus, 'soul' is nine letters shorter than 'consciousness' and over the course of this long book that may save us a few pages.) Whatever we call it, it is what you are. It's how you started and how you will end. Once you know this, once you decide to move beyond the material world of ego, you are standing at the beginning of your journey and you know you will never die. Neither consciousness nor soul can taste death.

Nearly all spiritual teachings, including "the end is the beginning" parable, are referring to you as consciousness/soul and not you as a body/ego. It is the same with quantum physics, which is largely a science of energy dynamics that also deemphasizes the material world as primary.

Therefore any discussion of reality really starts, and ends, with consciousness. It is who and what we are. Without it, there is no experience. You can lose an arm or a leg or your hearing or your hair or your championship game or your job or even your mind, and life goes on.

But when you lose consciousness, you lose yourself. There is no experience without it. In fact, as we shall see in Levels 8 and 9, there is no reality without it.

Think of it this way: If you separated your consciousness from your body, moving your consciousness out into the hallway while leaving your body in your favorite chair, where are you? In the hallway or in the chair?

At night when you are asleep and the dimmer switch on your consciousness is dialed way down, are you even aware of your body? When dreaming, don't you have 'experiences' that have nothing to do with your physical body?

I have asked these types of questions to hundreds of clients over the years and their answers are virtually unanimous: We, as human beings, recognize that we more closely identify with our consciousness than with our bodies.

With that in mind, there is practically no point discussing any 'big' philosophical questions before this one is addressed:

What is the origin of our consciousness?

Scientists are brilliant, and they have done so many things to advance civilization. From moon landings to heart transplants, from the Internet to smartphones, society has been greatly enhanced by their work.

Forget today's marvelous toys, where would we be without even more basic scientific and technological inventions such as plastic, refrigerators and, most importantly, soft toilet paper?

Science is awesome, and we are going to explore its greatest depths over the first portion of this book.

But there is one thing science cannot do … answer that nagging question:

Where does our consciousness come from?

Scientists may be brilliant, but they are not poets. Here is their best attempt of explaining where they are with the origin of consciousness:

"It's a hard problem," they say.

Just like most everything in this book, please google that and check it out for yourself.

The Hard Problem of Consciousness.

Discover its origin and you uncover the birth of humanity.

Why are we aware? Why are we aware that we are aware? Why are we not mechanistic robots? Why do you *know* that you are reading this book right now? Why doesn't the book *know* you are reading it? (Though perhaps it does. See the surprising 'behavior' of electrons in Level 9.)

The answer in each case is consciousness.

Most every debate on spirituality, religion, philosophy, ethics, morality, purpose, and meaning will all come back to the idea of consciousness. What is it? And what is its source?

It's a hard problem. For scientists.

Physicist David Chalmers coined the expression "hard problem of consciousness" and he asks a similar question: "Why are we not philosophical zombies?" A zombie in this sense is a being that resembles a human in form but lacks the consciousness of experience, like a robot.

Indeed, in many spiritual teachings, this is basically what is meant by being *dead* … lacking spiritual consciousness. Asleep to the spirit. Ego zombies abound!

At this point in our understanding, many people assume that the brain produces consciousness, so why haven't scientists figured out how it does that yet?

Why not?

Because they can't.

Because the brain doesn't produce consciousness.

Just like a computer doesn't produce the energy that runs it … and like a radio doesn't produce the song it plays ... nor does the phone produce the voices that it transmits … the brain is only fueled by consciousness, it does not create it.

Where's the proof of this? Keep reading the book. If you cannot see it yet, it will emerge. (And to any scientists who are searching for it in the brain, I admire your persistence. You will need it.)

Let's go ahead and think about the question of the origin of consciousness from the conventional, scientific point of view: There was a big bang. A bunch of light shot out into space. Stars were born. Many huge rocks formed. The light and the rocks whirled around each other and formed galaxies and our solar system. Over billions of years amoebas formed. Then dinosaurs. And then chickens (or was it eggs?). Then monkeys. Then humans.

Where in that process did consciousness as we know it arrive? Between the formation of stars and planets? Do amoebas or chickens have consciousness? Did it arise between monkeys and humans?

No one knows. The origin of consciousness is truly is the missing link.

Fact is, there is 'evidence' all over the place that consciousness is *the source* of this universe. The teachings of all of the major prophets are about it, and quantum science in particular points to consciousness as an essential building block of our physical world. It is the conductor of the energy symphony in which we live.

Indeed, there is mathematical proof that science is unable to answer all questions in its search (Level 20), and one of those questions is the nature of consciousness.

Saying No. 29 in the Gospel of Thomas puts it this way:

> *"If the flesh came into being because of spirit,*
> *that is a marvel, but if spirit came into being*
> *because of the body, that is a marvel of marvels."*

In other words, if the physical world came into being because of consciousness (which it does), that is incredible enough, but if consciousness came into being because of the physical world, that is beyond belief.

Jesus suggested that the physical universe is an amazing spiritual creation ... but the physical universe does not create the energy that fuels it. This is simply the first law of thermodynamics. Energy can be changed from one form to another, but it cannot be created or destroyed.

Well, that pretty much answers it right there, doesn't it? Energy can change form, from spirit into flesh and back into spirit, but energy is *not* being created, as in a physical brain producing consciousness. (See Levels 3 and 16 in particular to see how 'you' change from spirit energy form to physical energy form.)

Skeptics will argue most of these points, but there is no need to argue because, from their point of view, the skeptics are indeed correct! The world is an intricate, interactive inkblot test, you see what you see. Everyone, from their relative point of view, is correct about the way they see the world.

Prefer to say 'eins' instead of 'uno' when talking about the concept called 1? Fine. Enjoy a ballerina's interpretation of a sunset more than an astronomer's description? Can't argue with your preference.

Are you seeking God in this universe? Go for it, there are a lot of indications that what Einstein called "some spirit ... that is vastly superior to that of man" is out there. Do you believe there is no God? Seek that, and you will find no God. Reality is a mirror (Level 14).

As stated before, the only relevant question is whether your paradigm brings you peace. As a therapist, I often ask clients struggling with their perspective on life, "How's that working for ya?"

A sarcastic, but effective line. And delivered with loving intention, of course!

All mental health issues (depression, anxiety, anger, boredom, etc.) are at root a question of perspective, and that perspective is always a spirit vs. flesh paradigm (Level 17). This is where Jesus proves to be a savior, leading you out of Egoland into Soul World.

Christ IS the Way, the Truth and the Life ... as a consciousness shepherd.

Follow the leader.

***

Ultimately, there is no need to even debate the origin of consciousness, because as human beings, its origin is unknowable. Some things we will just not be able to physically prove (Level 20).

But as spiritual beings, consciousness is indeed knowable. And *that* is a major point of all prophets.

Gnōthi Seauton.

Those words were carved into the rock at the Temple of Apollo at Delphi in ancient Greece and they mean:

Know thyself.

Come to know yourself not as flesh, but as the consciousness that animates the flesh. You are not a body, you are a soul. And *this* is knowable.

From the Upanishads in Hinduism: "The Self, who can be realized by the pure in heart, who is life, light, truth … him I shall attain when my ego dies."

Your True Self is knowable and it is *not the ego*!

"When you know yourselves ... you will understand that you are children of the living Father. But if you do not know yourselves, then you live in poverty, and you are the poverty."
- Saying No. 3, the Gospel of Thomas

You will come to recognize your soul self as a child of God, but if you think you are merely a physical ego being, you are spiritually poor.

Aristotle said, "Knowing yourself is the beginning of all wisdom."

So know yourself!

Virtually everything in this book stems from this point.

You are not a body.

You are consciousness.

"Surely a man goes about as a shadow!"
- Psalm 39:6

Your body is a shadow of your soul.

There is a significant distinction between those two things and it makes all the difference in the spiritual world, as you shall see. They are both important, but one far more than the other.

Throughout this book, there will be countless references to the notion that physical reality is a dream-like experience of consciousness that ultimately renders physical reality relatively unimportant, save for this one concept:

Our mission on earth is to use physical reality to evolve our consciousness.

"Be perfect, as your heavenly Father is perfect."
- Matthew 5:48

Perfect? I sure hope he is not talking about bodies, as I am doomed by my hairline and my waistline!

Of course Jesus is not talking about bodies, nor behaviors. He is talking about spiritual development. We cannot attain perfect bodies, though many people try, but we *can* attain perfect consciousness. It's not as hard as you might think. It's what this book is all about.

To contextualize the "perfection" idea, I refer you to an interesting narrative regarding the many European secret societies that emerged during the Dark Ages.

In that time period, most of the people were peasants. They were born peasants and died peasants. They believed they were peasants. They worshipped kings and queens, whether they wanted to or not. It was indeed a dark era for many.

Common laborers did not have much freedom to travel, but highly skilled workers were permitted to roam from village to village and sometimes from country to country building castles and infrastructure for the ruling class.

In their journeying, the workers noticed that not all towns were the same. In those days, you could not check the *Drudge Report* or *The Huffington Post* online for updates on what was happening in neighboring communities nor did anyone ever tweet out breakthrough discoveries in science for all of their followers to see.

The traveling laborers noticed that some places operated differently than others, with differing cultures and practices. Some towns even had these things called books! Peasants were not particularly well-educated, if at all, so imagine what it must have been like for them to discover that learning was even possible.

One thing that peasants in the Dark Ages needed to learn was that things did not have to be the way they were. Each person could rise up out of his squalor and improve his life. Doing so, however, would require an expansion of consciousness. They had to think outside the dark box into which they were born.

Due to their unique access to information, skilled workers were on the leading edge of a new awareness that was, to put it mildly, not going to be very popular with the ruling elite. What do you suppose many kings commanded whenever word got to them that there were now commoners suggesting that things did not have to be the way they were?

That's right. Off with their heads!

Naturally, the workers had to keep it quiet, forcing their information-sharing operation underground.

Despite facing irrational persecution and spiteful resistance in one way or another, many of those secret societies flourished during the past millennium, including the Knights Templar.

The Templars were fierce Christian soldiers, the armed forces of the church at the time. They had several duties, chief among them protecting Jerusalem.

Another responsibility of theirs, according to legend, was that they were put in charge of finding the most sacred artifact in the history of mankind … the Holy Grail.

Now, most people have heard of the Holy Grail and many consider it to be the cup that Jesus drank from at the Last Supper. The Grail was thought to have special powers, providing wealth and eternal youth to anyone who sipped from it.

All true. Except one thing.

The Holy Grail exists, but it is not a cup.

Of course, the idea that finding and drinking from a magical chalice would give one eternal youth is clearly absurd. And also quite unfair, as there's only one!

At least every year a different group of professional hockey players gets a shot at drinking from the Stanley Cup … what if some loner got his hands on the Grail and kept it for himself? Perhaps he would eventually see what he could fetch for it on *eBay*, but once again, only the rich would have a shot at it.

Here's the good news, and ultimately the purpose of *New Eyes*.

There is indeed a cup … and we all have access to it because it is hidden inside each one of us … but it is not a material thing … it is a soul thing … called …

Christ Consciousness.

The Holy Grail is Christ Consciousness and it must be found inside yourself, as your soul is the 'cup' and for it to be 'holy' you must *fill yourself* with the light of Christ. Your physical body is designed to do precisely that (Level 4).

I will most often refer to it as Christ Consciousness, because I am an American with Christian conditioning. (It's also why I wrote this book in English, which is my conditioned language.) But you do not have to think of it that way. You may call it Krishna Consciousness. Or Buddha Consciousness. Or Muhammad Consciousness.

Or Optimal Consciousness. Or Unity Consciousness. Or A Rose By Any Other Name Would Still Smell As Sweet Consciousness.

You say uno, he says un, she says eins, I say one. We are all saying the same thing. Personally, I like the sound of Unity Consciousness. It rings true for me. We are all One (or Un, Uno, Eins, Moja, etc.) in perfected spirit mind.

New Eyes will draw a picture for you showing how the relevant science backs up all of the major prophets in the idea that the achievement of "perfect consciousness" is not only attainable, but it is our singular goal as a species.

"Congratulations to the one who stands at the beginning.
That one will know the end and will not taste death."

Consciousness is the beginning, and knowing that, you are now standing there. The end will be when you attain perfection in Christ Consciousness. Think that's radical?

Jesus, anointed with Christ Consciousness, did not taste death … he overcame it. And he tells you to do the same.

"If anyone would come after me, let him deny himself
and take up his cross and follow me."
- Matthew 16:24

If anyone wants to follow Jesus, he must deny the ego in himself and become the True Self of spirit through Christ Consciousness. Ego, the False Self, is the anti-Christ.

"Whoever finds his life will lose it,
and whoever loses his life for my sake will find it."
- Matthew 10:39

Whoever finds his ego life will lose his soul, and whoever loses his ego life via Christ Consciousness will find his soul. You use the consciousness 'mind' to fill the soul body with the Holy Spirit.

Just saying "Jesus is my savior" is not enough. He himself said that more was required, as you must deny yourself and carry your cross, too. There is more work to be done than simply declaring allegiance to Jesus. Thinking that way is the devilish ego trying to keep you from true perfection in Christ.

You must become enlightened to end the Dark Ego Age.

You must find the Holy Grail and fill it with spirit light.

A METHOD TO THE MADNESS

The world always appears to be in a state of disarray.

It is today, it was that way one thousand years ago, it will be that way one thousand years from now.

This is not a surprise, neither to science nor spirituality.

A fundamental tenet of Buddhism is that *suffering is inevitable* during our lives. If you are here on earth, you are going to experience suffering. That's the reality of this life.

It is indeed a universal Truth. Everyone goes through bad times, enduring a variety of physical, mental or emotional distress. Suffering ravages our world ...wars, famine, disease, relationship distress, financial instability, emotional unrest ... everywhere we look, pain reigns.

It's doubtful that anyone would argue with Buddha on his First Noble Truth regarding suffering, because it is so relatable. We've all been there.

In science there is a similar certainty called Chaos Theory, which indicates that the world is wildly unpredictable.

Call it the First Noble Truth of science: Chaos is part of the fabric of the universe.

Does turmoil play a large role in your life? Do unexpected events happen all too frequently? Best made plans gone awry? Life feel like a rat race? Busy as a beaver? Often feel overwhelmed? Join the club. It's supposed to be that way.

The world is just not designed to proceed smoothly and predictably.

The type of chaos we typically feel in our lives — complete disorder and confusion — is not exactly the same thing in science, which sees chaos objectively and non-judgmentally. A scientist would not call Chaos Theory 'suffering' or 'bad' as we might with our chaos.

The point of commonality between the chaos of our lives and the chaos of science is the element of surprise, the fact that random things just seem to happen, the reality that reality is unpredictable.

Scientifically, chaos means that many things cannot be calculated with any guarantee of accuracy. We cannot predict with certainty what is going to happen at the finish line based upon minor changes at the starting line. We just cannot know for sure what might happen next. Life is variable.

It doesn't take much to throw the world into turmoil, nor to radically change the direction of one's life, either bad or good. Chaos Theory happens to be the scientific basis for one of the most profound teachings of Jesus Christ, to be discussed at the end of this chapter.

The discovery of Chaos Theory even has a chaotic origin, in that no one was able to predict it. Half a century ago, meteorologist Edward Lorenz got his hands on a cool piece of machinery called a computer. The fancy new gadget was able to do things that weathermen were previously unable to do — crunch massive amounts of weather data very quickly.

The hope was that this would improve the ability of meteorologists to make forecasts. Turns out there's a very good reason why weather is so hard to predict, and you cannot blame weathermen for it.

It's because weather is inherently chaotic. Disorder is in its DNA.

Lorenz pumped a whole bunch of weather data — things like temperature, barometric pressure, dew point, etc. — into computers and carefully studied the results. At one point he reran a computer simulation with precisely the same numbers he had done before, save for one minor detail.

One model had the number .506 as a piece of data and the other .506127 in the same spot.

In effect, one computer model had a wee little bit more wind velocity than the other.

At first, the systems produced the exact same prognostications, as you would anticipate. But over a two-month period of time, something dramatic that you wouldn't expect happened.

What was going to be a sunny day, according to one computer simulation, morphed into a rainy day on the other.

Here's an example of Lorenz's data from that experiment:

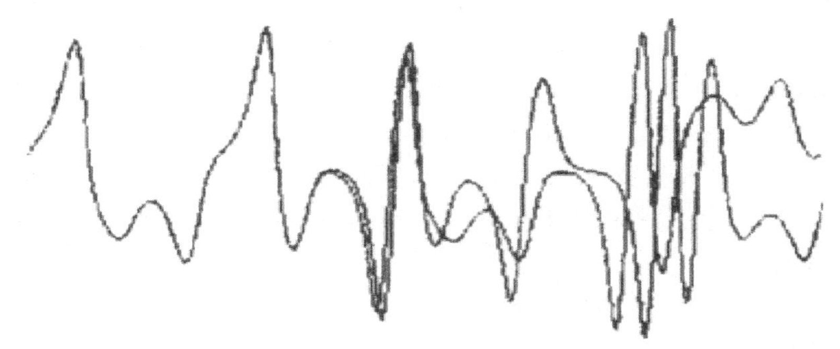

You can see how the computer model started out predicting the same course for both sets of data, but ended up varying wildly. Just by rounding one insignificant piece of data by .000127 the whole projection changed significantly.

A decade later at a major scientific conference, after this mathematical phenomenon had been retested and definitively verified, Lorenz gave a speech that a colleague entitled, "Does the Flap of a Butterfly's Wings in Brazil set off a Tornado in Texas?"

The Butterfly Effect was born.

(Lorenz originally referenced the flap of a seagull's wings to make his point, but was later convinced to swap protagonists in the concept to the more romantic butterfly. Also, Lorenz's first paper on the topic was called "Deterministic Nonperiodic Flow," joining the "hard problem of consciousness" as another example of science not being very poetic. But I digress.)

At the start of the Ashton Kutcher movie *The Butterfly Effect*, which is a much better Hollywood title than *The Deterministic Nonperiodic Flow*, this quote appears:

"It has been said that something so small as the flutter of a butterfly's wing can ultimately cause a typhoon halfway around the world."

The movie then basically has Kutcher time traveling (it's possible, see Level 15) and making changes in his life to affect future events. However, as the movie illustrates, those changes turn out to be wildly unpredictable.

It's like that in life. For example, if Kutcher hadn't starred in the movie *Dude, Where's My Car?* would he have ever married actress Mila Kunis? Perhaps, but such things are impossible to predict.

You also may have heard Chaos Theory simply explained another way in the blockbuster film *Jurassic Park*, when Jeff Goldblum demonstrated the Butterfly Effect to Laura Dern by dropping two drops of water on her hand and asking her which way they were going to roll off.

The droplets rolled in different directions.

Goldblum elucidates, "It changed. Why? Because tiny variations, the orientation of the hairs on your hands, the amount of blood distending your vessels, imperfections in the skin … vastly affect the outcome. That's … what?"

"Unpredictability," learns Dern.

Then Sam Neill jumps out of the car to chase after dinosaurs and Goldblum declares, "There, look at this! See! See! I'm right again. Nobody could have predicted that Dr. Grant would suddenly jump out of a moving vehicle."

That's Chaos Theory applied to our lives.

Here's how Lorenz described it in more academic language: "When the present determines the future, but the approximate present does not approximately determine the future."

That is chaos. If you don't have 100 percent of the data correct, you cannot predict the future with 100 percent accuracy. Far from it.

Whether it is the infinitesimally small amount of wind added to the air by the flap of a butterfly's wings or a single hair on Laura Dern's hand altering the flow of a water droplet, how often do you have all the variables in any given situation? Virtually never. As such, without all the information, chaos takes over.

And that is exactly why meteorologists cannot predict the weather as accurately as we would like. If only a small amount of their data is off, a major shift in the weather might occur. They need to account for all the butterflies ready to take flight out there.

There is a fascinating and ironic twist to Chaos Theory.

Think of a toddler playing a game of "Connect the Dots." At first, she cannot make out the picture. But the more dots she connects, the more an image emerges. Eventually, what was just a bunch of unrelated dots to a 4-year-old becomes something recognizable and distinct.

Similarly, if the trajectories of differing data sets are played out over time, recurring patterns emerge in the shape resembling … butterfly wings! (Though it is formally called a "strange attractor.")

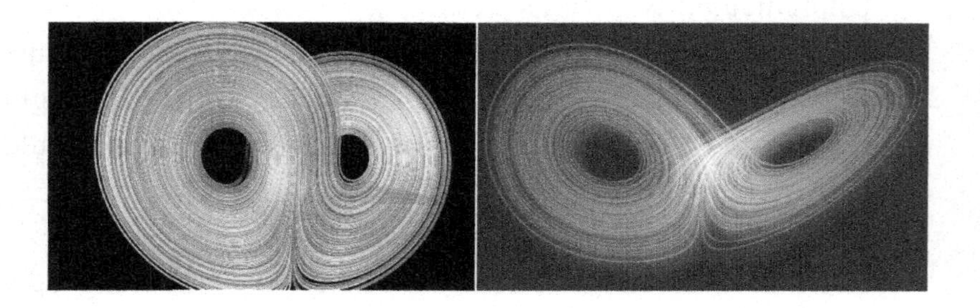

Digging deeper into this concept you can find the work of Benoit Mandelbrot and fractals, which are complex but self-replicating patterns that are byproducts of dynamic systems.

Amid all the chaos, there appears to be some sort an underlying order going on, a method to the madness. A beautiful structure underneath reality, actually. This is true in all systems, including societal behavior, ecosystems and the stock market — in addition to the weather.

Quantum physicist David Bohm calls it "Implicate Order" in which the fundamental feature of the universe is an *unbroken wholeness* that is actually quite organized. You might call this Oneness (Level 10).

Thus, the main aspects of Chaos Theory are:

1. Systems have a sensitive dependence upon initial conditions, meaning that small changes can lead to big changes

2. Systems are ultimately deterministic, following patterns that can be mapped out

It's worth repeating that you do not need to fully understand how or why scientists came to their conclusions, you just need to grasp the practical application of them and why the science matters to you.

Beyond not being annoyed at flawed weather forecasts any longer, here's a perfect example. Let's assume you have a brain. It operates as a very, very complex system. Not surprisingly, predicting the human mind and behaviors are accordingly very, very difficult to predict.

That's chaos.

Despite the apparent madness inherent in the human psyche at large, however, there is amazing new research that suggests an underlying organization to the structure of neuronal activity in all of our brains.

Which is order amid chaos.

At Carnegie Mellon University in Pittsburgh, neuroscientists have teamed up with computer scientists to map what they call "brain activation patterns."

Dr. Marcel Just, who is the director of CMU's Center for Cognitive Brain Imaging, was featured on the TV newsmagazine *60 Minutes* during an interesting piece called "Mind Reading" that can be watched online. (Just is a "D.O. Hebb" Professor of Psychology at CMU. Much of Level 6 is dedicated to one of Hebb's ground-breaking and mind-bending discoveries).

In the segment, Just calls his functional magnetic resonance imaging (fMRI) scanning work that measures and maps neural activity "thought identification" because, as he says, "We're identifying the thought that's occurring" in their subjects' brains.

Incredibly, if you are thinking of a hammer and if I am

thinking of a hammer, the same neural areas of our brains light up. Just and his team have also uncovered brain signatures for love, kindness and hypocrisy.

Which means a *brain scan* can now potentially identify if you are being a hypocrite … if you are being nice … or even if you are in love! (That's the *Twilight Zone* theme music you hear playing in your head.)

These high-tech fMRI machines have also had success in determining whether you have been at a particular location before, based upon your brain 'lighting up' if pictures of that location are shown to you, and whether you are lying about it (see the website noliemri.com).

How can they do this?

In my words — not theirs — it is because we all have basically the same underlying brain structures, we just use them differently.

There are neural pathways for love and hypocrisy, for hammers and celery, for here or there. Sounds like neural preprogramming, if you ask me.

Like a computer, we are essentially born with the same hardware and, depending on the software we use in our systems, varying parts of the motherboard are activated. If you never use iTunes, for example, it just sits there … waiting for you to use it.

Similarly, our brains appear to be 'pre-loaded' with an amazing array of thoughts and experiences, right down to the nitty gritty details such as the mathematical functions of addition and subtraction.

This is very valuable information. Let's say you have a friend who is feeling hopeless. Well, hope is up there in the brain, pre-loaded as a neural pattern, you merely have to find it!

As a therapist, I have found this to be an invaluable concept in working with clients, who are encouraged to know that hope is not something elusive — it's right there in our brains. When you do find something like hope, feel-good neurotransmitters called endorphins get released, which makes this type of information very important to anyone who wants to … feel good.

It's a neurochemical game of hide-and-seek.

And it demonstrates order amid chaos.

Here is where we really need *New Eyes*, where imagination becomes more important than knowledge.

This is not scientifically proven nor do I think it will ever be for reasons described in Level 20, but based upon the above research, it seems certain that Christ Consciousness is a brain signature. It's a particular pattern of neural activity that requires the achievement of a variety of spiritual virtues (Level 17) to experience. When you acquire mental and emotional skills such as patience, forgiveness, gratitude and hope — all of which are brain signatures — in addition to learning Truth, you evolve toward a higher state of consciousness.

But, like a needle in a haystack, you may need to sift through a lot of other stuff before you find it! Alas, as always, seek and you will find. If you find it and I find it and he finds it and she finds it, we have Unity Consciousness.

Buddha's First Noble Truth is that suffering is inevitable, but his Third Noble Truth is that suffering can cease. Order can rise up out of chaos.

In Buddhism, that is done with a clear mind or "bodhi," which is very similar to Christ Consciousness and serves to organize a chaotic mind through awakening and insight. We are all preprogrammed with the ability to do precisely that … so says Buddha and relevant modern research coming out of the lab at CMU.

The outwardly egoic physical world is chaotic, but higher consciousness is the underlying organizing principle found in our inner world. Once you understand that suffering actually guides you along in your spiritual journey, it ceases to be suffering. Once you understand the nature of chaos, it begins to transform into order. Uncertainty and unpredictability in the outer world are then felt as peacefulness and transcendence in the inner world.

Chaos Theory and the Butterfly Effect also perfectly support the wisdom of Jesus.

"Truly I tell you, if you have faith as small as a mustard seed,
you can say to this mountain, 'Move from here to there,'
and it will move. Nothing will be impossible for you."
- Matthew 17:20

Mustard seed-size faith? That's as delicate as the flap of a butterfly's wing.

Move a mountain? That's transforming something huge like chaos.

A tiny little shift in consciousness can move a mountain of ego pain from your life.

EVERYTHING IS ENERGY

Quick, name an equation other than the one listed above.

Sure, $2 + 2 = 4$ counts.

Name another that's not basic mathematics.

The Pythagorean Theorem? $a^2 + b^2 = c^2$? Good!

Name just one more.

Waiting …

C'mon, there are hundreds of them!

Such as Euler's formula for polyhedra: $F - E + V = 2$.

Or The Fourier Transform, which has too many squiggly lines for this book's typesetter to decipher.

Or the legendary Navier-Stokes equations, which seem to include upside-down triangles and some hieroglyphics.

Yes, I had to google 'famous equations' because I don't know any others, either. I was more interested in studying Major League Baseball statistics in high school than learning actual math.

Not many people know more than a few equations, and for good reason. They rarely come into play. Unless you are on *Jeopardy* and Alex Trebek tells you that the answer in the category "Things only Sheldon knows" is "$dS \geq 0$" and you are required to say, "What is the equation for the second law of thermodynamics?" in order to earn $500, you will never need to whip out a fancy formula to impress a girl on a first date. Hopefully.

But this one — $E = mc^2$ — changes all that. Everyone has heard it, yet few really *get* it. While you do not need to understand how Einstein determined it, you probably do need to grasp the implications of $E = mc^2$ for the purposes of this book. It will certainly help when considering why so many scientists and prophets called the world an illusion and why the great spiritual traditions are not referring to behaviors or bodies in most of their teachings.

Plus, understanding it *might* even impress a girl on a first date.

We've all heard of $E = mc^2$, but do we all know what it really means? Einstein himself didn't think we would.

He said of the world's most famous equation, "Mass and energy are both but different manifestations of the same thing — a somewhat unfamiliar conception for the average mind."

Did you hear that? Mr. Smarty Pants called us *average* minds! We'll show him. By the end of this chapter, you'll get it. Or at least you'll get why it really matters in ways that he might not have even understood.

Let's review the essential part of Einstein's quote:

"Mass and energy are both but different manifestations of the same thing."

!!!!!

?

Do you know what mass is? That's right, it's stuff. Mass is stuff.

Do you know what energy is? Correct, it's non-stuff. Energy is stuff that isn't massy stuff.

And Einstein is saying that stuff and non-stuff are really the same stuff after all!

One quick way to understand that concept is to consider H_2O H_2O. In liquid form, it is H_2O. In solid form, it is H_2O. That means water and ice are "different manifestations of the same thing."

Similarly, mass and energy are different manifestations of the same thing. So what is that thing? Keep reading, the answer is at the end of this chapter (no peeking).

Still confused? Probably a little. So let's get to work.

Einstein gets most of the credit for $E = mc^2$, but like most scientists he was expanding on other ideas that had already been conjectured.

In 1717 Isaac Newton theorized, "Are not the gross bodies and light convertible into one another?"

Rephrased: "Are not mass and energy really the same thing?"

In 1734 Emanuel Swedenborg speculated that all matter is ultimately made up of "dimensionless points of pure and total motion."

That's a fancier way of saying that matter is made up of massless moving stuff called energy.

In the early 1900s Einstein picked up on experiments done by Michelson and Morley regarding light not seeming to act in a consistent manner, which became the inspiration for his theories on relativity (see Level 7). During this time period, $E = mc^2$ emerged while he was exploring the nature of light and reality as we know it would never be the same.

Because, well, reality as we know it turns out not to be reality as we know it.

$E = mc^2$ means that EVERYTHING is made up of energy. Not some things are energy. Not many things are energy.

Everything!

Is!

Energy!

The sun, the stars, this table, that ham sandwich, music, your mind, your brain, your right thumb, you … everything is energy!

(Am I emphasizing this enough? There will be no complaining come Level 13 that it wasn't clearly asserted how the world is made up of just energy.)

On the surface, $E = mc^2$ indicates how much energy anything with mass has, simply illustrated by the nuclear bomb. The "E" stands for energy and the "m" represents mass, of course, with "c^2" equating to the speed of light squared. It essentially means that if you mess with mass a whole lot, a whole lot of energy gets released.

(There is a point to why the E is capitalized while the m and c are not, but that's beyond the scope of this level. Plus, I don't really understand why.)

Once Einstein figured out the equation, it was only a matter of time before the nuclear bomb was created. All the energy that destroyed Hiroshima came from about two pounds of enriched uranium inside the bomb.

Just two pounds.

That was world-changing stuff right there. But digging even deeper reveals soul-inspiring, perhaps even soul-identifying, non-stuff.

Let's dig deeper.

Take a tree, cut it in half. What do you have? Two halves of a tree.

Now chop those halves into halves. What do you have? Yep, quarters of a tree.

Now keep chopping. You have a bunch of 2x4-sized tree parts. More chopping, smaller pieces of the tree. Down to sticks, then toothpicks, then sawdust. A huge mound of sawdust.

So what if you keep cutting the sawdust in half?

Well, reduce anything down to its constituent parts and you reach the level of molecules, which are composed of atoms, which when I was younger I conceptualized to be just smaller parts of the original tree.

But that's far from the facts! On the atomic level, the tree stops being a tree, much like a cookie isn't a cookie prior to mixing the butter, sugar and eggs together. Just as similar parts that make up a cookie can go instead to making a cake, similar parts that make up a tree also make up other things.

Wood is comprised largely of carbon, oxygen and hydrogen. You know what else is also comprised largely of carbon, oxygen and hydrogen? Your body. Yeah, that's right, increase the amount of carbon in your body from 19 percent to 50 percent, decrease the amount of oxygen from 65 percent to 44 percent and tweak the amount of hydrogen by removing a bit and presto chango!

You just became Pinocchio.

Like cookies and cakes or human bodies and wood, physical matter is all about how you combine the same basic atomic ingredients into different forms.

That's very interesting, but we can dig deeper, as young George Washington isn't even close to finishing chopping up that cherry tree.

Atoms, you may recall from high school unless you were memorizing George Brett's career batting statistics like I was, are comprised of electrons, protons and neutrons. Those particles are made up of even smaller particles of things like quarks, leptons and bosons. Included somewhere in that mass of stuff are gluons, which help "glue" it all together.

We are now down to the quantum level, which is nearly the smallest unit of matter that anything physical can be reduced to … but we still aren't finished slicing and dicing our Giant Sequoia!

What's beneath the quantum level? This is where it gets *really* interesting.

With math, you can keep cutting numbers in half. Start with the number 16, cut it to 8, now 4, then 2, and so on. See how far you can get. Return to reading once you understand the point ...

I knew I'd see you again soon.

With matter, this is not so. You cannot keep chopping it in

half. You eventually reach a limit, or a scale that is called "Planck length" after the man (Max Planck) who figured out that things could only get so small before they hit a wall of nothingness.

Keep cutting sawdust in half and eventually you reach:

.00000000000000000000000000000000001616199 of a meter.

In standard notion it is 1.616199×10^{-35} and in standard language it is "impossible to ever see."

Take a piece of sawdust and cut it into a trillion pieces. Then cut that trillionth of a piece into a trillion pieces. Repeat one more time and you're there … Planck length. This is the scale beyond which our normal idea of "size" becomes incomprehensible, as shorter lengths do not make physical sense. Basically it would be like trying to measure the size of zero. That does not compute.

Down at the depths of Planck length arises one of my favorite concepts called quantum foam, theorized by physicist John Wheeler in 1955. This "space-time" foam is the fabric of which our universe is comprised, essentially tinker toys of energy from which consciousness manifests form. Like soap on the surface of bath water, consciousness "bubbles up" through quantum foam to create physical reality.

It is down here in the world of the infinitesimally small where we reach our ultimate destination of understanding the importance of $E = mc^2$. Using math and physics, super-human intellectuals have taken that trillionth of a trillionth of a trillionth of a piece of sawdust and made it dance.

They developed a model of the universe called String Theory. It's complicated, but it's brilliant and crucial to comprehend so I'll make this simple and practical as possible.

Strings are vibrating loops of energy. Just think of the energy that comes off of a guitar string when it is strummed. It's like that.

Some strings are *open* loops, which are sticky on their ends and clump together. Then there are strings with *closed* loops, which are not sticky and therefore do not clump together.

According to String Theory, which is by far the most popular type of physics taken up by our young geniuses of today because of its elegance, everything in the world is made up of these vibrating loops of energy.

As Einstein said, “Mass and energy are both but different manifestations of the same thing.”

String Theory was not even around when Einstein was alive, but he called it right. Mass and energy are both different manifestations of vibrating strings!

Sticky open loops create particles such as photons, which give light to our visible world, while the Higgs Boson is the particle that gives mass to the light in our physical world. The Higgs Boson is nicknamed the “God Particle” due to its seemingly omnipotent nature — it is everywhere all the time and has a ‘mystical’ property of being able to ‘transform’ energy into matter. Its existence was scientifically confirmed in 2012. (Many physicists do not like the term “God Particle,” but it is appreciated by *New Eyes*.)

As for closed loops, check this out: Since they are not sticky and do not clump together, closed loops do not need to hang around this physical universe. They can leave it and come back. One such closed loop string is called a graviton, which plays a major role in allowing gravity to work in our universe.

What?! Did you catch that?! *They can leave our universe and come back!*

Where have the smartest minds in human history taken us? To a place where we have two primary, practically invisible ‘things’ called strings, one of which leads to the emergence of the physical world and the other that can go beyond this universe to the great beyond.

String Theory has not been proven (hence, they call it a theory), but I've seen enough in it to know that it is true. If you want to wait for it to be "String Fact" before you keep reading, feel free, but I suspect that you will be waiting a long time (see Level 20).

Like a contestant on the *Wheel of Fortune* game show shouting out the answer to Vanna White before she turns the letters, sometimes you can complete the puzzle before others can.

It's similar to walking up to a cave and seeing a lion's tail wagging around by the entrance, but not specifically being able to see the lion.

"Nature shows us only the tail of the lion," Einstein said. "But I do not doubt that the lion belongs to it even though he cannot at once reveal himself because of his enormous size."

Basically, some things just become obvious after a while and need no further proof. The fact that it works is proof enough.

Remember that Einstein said, "Imagination is more important than knowledge."

So use your imagination.

Open loops of strings are the vibration of your body. Closed loops of strings are the vibration of your soul.

When you die, the open-looped body is "stuck" in this universe, but the closed-loop soul can travel freely to other dimensions.

Together, both the open and closed loops allow consciousness to permeate everything.

"I regard consciousness as fundamental," said Planck in 1931. "I regard matter as derivative from consciousness. We cannot get behind consciousness."

We can chop trees in half again and again, we can dig and dig and dig, and eventually we get down to the level of String Theory where we find pure consciousness, which creates everything. And we cannot get behind consciousness. That's where the story of science ends and where you really begin.

A few years before his death in 1947, Planck had not changed his tune. At a speech on the nature of matter in Italy he said, "As a man who has devoted his whole life to the most clear headed science, to the study of matter, I can tell you as a result of my research about atoms this much: There is no matter as such. All matter originates and exists only by virtue of a force which brings the particle of an atom to vibration and holds this most minute solar system of the atom together. We must assume behind this force the existence of a conscious and intelligent mind. This mind is the matrix of all matter."

You may think of "this mind" as God. The one who, in Genesis 1:3 said, "Let there be light," and then there was light. (He probably should have said, "Let there be energy," but let's not quibble over semantics, God was too busy in that moment creating everything to worry about word choice.)

We are created in God's image, as pure beings of consciousness manifested into this seemingly physical universe, a world that is nothing but energy. One part (open loops) is flesh, one part (closed loops) is spirit.

Heaven is a state of being that has nothing to do with this world. In fact, it is not even in this universe. Ask a hundred Americans to point to heaven and 99 of them will point up, as if you could blast off on a rocket ship, soar into space and smack into the bottom of heaven somewhere.

No, heaven is not in this universe. Heaven is 'outside' this universe, found by going within yourself. Heaven is a place where the closed loops of your very soul can vibe with others who get there through being perfect (Matthew 5:48) by attaining Christ Consciousness.

And I thought it was more important to memorize baseball stats in high school than explore $E = mc^2$ …

That equation, which is the scientific brain and spiritual heart of *New Eyes*, was also something that helped Einstein and many of his colleagues to develop a unique vision of reality nearly a century ago.

Reflect upon Max Planck's words again: "There is no matter as such. ... We must assume behind this force the existence of a conscious and intelligent mind."

He did not use the word "God" there, but he implied God. Not a physical God, but an energy God.

We will further clarify what God actually is during the course of this book, as He might not be what you think He is. Just as the world may not be what you think it is.

God is E. The world is mc^2.

THE MAGIC OF 137

You have a glass and 50 percent of it is filled with water.

Is it half empty or half full?

Before you answer that question, ask yourself this one: How free do you want to be?

***

When my daughter Veridy was 4 years old, I was reading a bedtime book to her when she raised her right arm and asked a most intriguing question.

"Why do I have a hand?" she inquired, shaking it a few times in disbelief. "It's just so … weird!"

Not really that weird from the perspective of *New Eyes,* something that will hopefully be made more clear by the end of this Level.

Seven years later, Veridy started experiencing something else that she considered to be strange … she was seeing the number 137 all over the place. Those three digits kept popping up everywhere she looked, especially on the clock when it just happened to be 1:37. She also noticed it on street signs (say, Route 137), sports scores (like 13-7) and even answers on some of her math homework (perhaps 1.37 or .137). You get the idea.

Veridy never mentioned any other number except for 137 and she even wrote a school paper on the topic of "recurring numbers" because of her interest.

Most of us do mildly idiosyncratic things like this, so I thought it was just a quirky little musing from a unique pre-teen girl. But since 137 also happened to be our house number on the street we lived on at the time, my wife tuned into our daughter's insistence that this was an important number and suggested that I investigate whether there was anything to it.

When I googled "the meaning of the number 137" one link quickly captured my attention, an article called "The Magic of 137" by Billy Phillips. Although all of what he processes in his article (and his entire website) is quite interesting, what specifically caught my eye was a revelation.

Here's the most important line:

"137 refers to electrons and the odds of an electron absorbing a single photon."

Epiphany!

In physics, this number (which is actually 1/137) comes from something called the "fine-structure constant" and is often denoted as alpha. It gets pretty complicated, so this is all you need to know about alpha — it's why you are here, at least in the flesh.

"It's one of the greatest damn mysteries of physics: a magic number that comes to us with no understanding by man," said Richard Feynman. "You might say the 'hand of God' wrote that number, and we don't know how He pushed his pencil."

Feynman, who figured out how the space shuttle Challenger exploded in 1986, is consistently ranked among the most influential physicists of the 20th century, right up there with Einstein. He is one of many who consider 137 to be magical.

"Alpha sets the scale of nature ... the size of atoms and all things made of them, the intensity and colors of light, the strength of magnetism, and the metabolic rate of life itself. It controls everything we see," said Frank Close, a physics professor at the University of Oxford. "In 137, apparently, science (has) found Nature's PIN Code."

Nature's personal identification number is 137 … Veridy was right!

If you trust Wikipedia writers more than Oxford professors, this number "is the threshold between the physical dimension and the utterly spiritual dimension. In other words, at the boundary of the physical world, the number 137 emerges."

Sounds familiar, as it fits in with Level 3 and Planck length. Somewhere way down deep in the quantum foam, there is a *threshold* where energy becomes matter. This boundary is where alpha is found.

"If alpha were bigger than it really is, we should not be able to distinguish matter from ether," said Max Born, another German genius who won the 1954 Nobel Prize in Physics. "It is clear that the explanation of this number must be the central problem of natural philosophy."

Natural philosophy is a centuries-old attempt at trying to unify science and spirituality … just like this book. Natural philosophy was ultimately what led Einstein to say that he believed in "Spinoza's God," based upon the work of Dutch philosopher Baruch Spinoza, whose conception of God was simply nature itself.

According to Born, the "central problem" of that philosophy is explaining the meaning behind the number 137. The explanation, from the perspective of *New Eyes*, has both scientific components and spiritual implications.

1. Everything is made up of atoms.
2. Within those atoms are electrons.
3. Electrons absorb and release photons.

4. Photons are particles of light.
5. So atoms absorb and release light.
6. And you are entirely made up of atoms.
7. Which means *you* absorb and release light!

In fact, as you are made up of *a lot* of atoms, approximately a trillion times a trillion atoms, that means you absorb and release *a lot* of light.

This should make a few of Jesus's sayings more clear.

"If therefore your eye be single,
your whole body shall be full of light."
- Matthew 6:22

"You are the light of the world."
- Matthew 5:14

"I am the light of the world."
- John 8:12

Jesus was not being metaphorical; he was being spiritual ... and *quantum physical*!

Within the body of an atom, electrons move up or down in their orbital states. Whenever an electron absorbs a photon, it jumps up. Whenever it emits a photon, it drops down.

In quantum field theory, which suggests that individual particles can be likened unto *force fields* that permeate throughout space and time, this absorption and emission of photons within the particles of an atom is fundamental.

So what exactly are photons, what is light, and how is energy involved?

The best way to think of a photon is basically like a little car, with energy as its passenger. Clump a bunch of photons together and you have a 'train' of energy called a light wave, which can be seen whenever that train is moving.

According to Einstein, light travels as both the entire train and the individual cars at the same time. He called this wave-particle duality, since light has both wave-like and particle-like properties at the same time, much like an ocean wave is just one thing comprised of many little things (droplets of water) at the same time.

So light is the vehicle that Mother Nature uses to shuttle energy throughout space. It enables our souls to tangibly interact with each other. Essentially, light is 'visual' energy. It allows us to 'see' consciousness, or at least see its projected effects (Level 16).

Imagine the pure, vibrant consciousness of all of us. Now add a bunch of quantum physics equations ... and in a flash, we have the physical universe.

Play with the equation $E = mc^2$ and make it $E/c^2 = m$. That means if you 'slow down' or 'reduce' energy by dividing it by the speed of light squared, our physical world materializes. Our world is condensed energy. Your body is an extension of your soul, a manifestation of consciousness.

And it happens because of the Magic of 137.

"Alpha," said Jean-Philippe Uzan, research director at the National Centre for Scientific Research in France, "characterizes the interactions between matter and light."

"It allows atoms to exist," said author Sam Kean. "This just-right balance has led many scientists to conclude that the universe couldn't have hit upon its fine structure by accident."

Well said. Either you see it, or you don't.

Spiritually speaking, 137 is magical as it is the threshold that opens the doorway for all forms of energy to pass through, ranging from full ego to full spirit. Not only is everything energy, but *everything is an exchange of energy.*

It's what life, and spirituality, is all about. Souls in an energy exchange. Like a multi-dimensional Wall Street for the Holy Spirit.

In the next chapter, we are going to discuss the exquisite balance of the universe, which makes possible an equitable energy exchange between sentient beings.

One way to characterize that exchange is by asking yourself the following question: What is better, giving or receiving? If you take just one second to think about it, you will say "giving." But take five seconds.

What if the person you are giving to refuses to receive? Then what? Imagine your child turns 16 years old and you are so excited to reveal a surprise that you have been saving up for, then the conversation takes an unexpected turn.

"Happy birthday, son. Here's your new car!"

"No thanks, Dad. I prefer riding the school bus."

Your heart sinks. The gift transaction fails.

In all energy exchanges, there needs to be a giver *and* receiver for the transaction to work. Can you insert a plug into a wall without an outlet? (Try it, it gets frustrating pretty quickly.) In baseball, you need a pitcher *and* a catcher. In football, when a quarterback throws the ball and the receiver doesn't catch it, it's called an incompletion … or a failed energy transaction.

Even the human brain has giver and receiver qualities. Your brain is made up of 100 billion neurons, both with giving parts (axon) and receiving parts (receptors). Your mental processing — and ultimately human emotionality — is the result of the release of neurotransmitters through those axons into those receptors.

And you know how making babies works, right? Try *that* without either the giving or receiving component … again, a failed energy transaction.

Scientifically understanding the giving-receiving dynamic helps to clarify some deep spiritual teachings.

"God created man in his own image, in the image of God he created him; male and female he created them."
- Genesis 1:27

Which means that you are *both* male and female.

Not physically male and female, of course — *spiritually* male and female. You are a soul, your physical body is inhabiting an illusory world (Level 13) and is comparable to a costume (Level 18) that is comprised of atoms, which are just little bundles of energy that give energy and receive energy.

God created man in His image; God was not created in man's image. If you believe Genesis 1:27 is referring to men and women, that makes God a physical man and a physical woman. But if you understand that we were made in His image, and He is not a physical being and we are spiritual beings, then the context of "male and female he created them" is about giving and receiving energy (Level 28).

We have to stop putting a man's body on God, that is Him being created in our image. God is pure, perfect consciousness. We are created in His image, which means we are potential beings of pure, perfect consciousness.

You are not a body, you are an image of God, made spiritually male and female so that you have the ability to exchange love, ego, the Holy Spirit, dark inertia, peace, fear, or any type of energy that can be transmitted.

Every male/giving and female/receiving interaction has a point of exchange. This is the real Magic of 137, the threshold where the spirit (God the Father) manifests into the physical form (Mother Earth).

"To you it has been given to know the secrets of the kingdom of heaven, but to them it has not been given."
- Matthew 13:11

Here's one such secret.

When you see through Christ's (or Krishna's or Buddha's or Muhammad's) eyes, or when you perceive the world with Unity Consciousness, the secrets of the kingdom of heaven are revealed. That requires you thinking of yourself as a soul, not as a body. To those who see themselves as physical and separate from others, those secrets are not revealed.

"We speak the wisdom of God in a mystery,
even the hidden wisdom."
- 1 Corinthians 2:7

Hidden wisdom?

The world is an illusion, made up of nothing but energy. You are a being of consciousness with a soul that is both male and female, created in God's image.

Whether you are a man or a woman, we are all giving and receiving forces, we are all united in that pure, perfect consciousness.

When we are not united in perfection, when our *initial conditions* of this moment are not in sync with each other, things become chaotic. Just as refracted light can reveal all of the colors of a rainbow, separated spirit unleashes a tremendous array of energy with many different frequency ranges and vibrations. That leads to all the differences we see in the world.

The two primary types of energy are spirit and ego, or love and fear. One gets transferred when you are focusing on the spiritual world, the other gets transferred when you are focusing on the physical world. There are many degrees in between.

In either instance, you can be male or female. A giver of spirit or a giver of ego; a receiver of spirit or a receiver of ego.

Giving and receiving are what atoms do … and what souls do.

Adam, the original soul, was created in God's image, male and female.

It all started with Adam's atoms.

***

So is the glass half empty or half full?

A pessimist would say half empty, while an optimist would say half full.

But it goes much deeper than that.

Anyone filled with ego energy would answer half empty, be jealous of those whose glasses seem to be half full, be disappointed in himself for not being more like them, post his tale of woe on Facebook seeking sympathy, blame others for all the emptiness, and then stare at the void in the glass for days.

The aspiring soul in search of Christ Consciousness would answer half full, consider the void an opportunity for filling up more in the future, compliment others on how filled their glasses are, take a yummy sip from the glass while trying to find a way to click "thumbs up" twice for *Tillman the Skateboarding Dog* on Youtube, and would simply be grateful for having a glass in the first place.

So are *you* half empty or half full?

How free do you want to be?

If your eye is single — if you stay focused on spirit — your whole body will be filled with light. You ascend into pure, perfect consciousness. Christ Consciousness. Unity Consciousness. You see all as One.

You also see as children often see — the physical world as a strange, mysterious place for their souls to be.

When Veridy wondered about the "weirdness" of her hand, it was a sincere moment of philosophical inquiry. (At least from *my* point of view. She was just a giggling toddler.) It is indeed an unusual thing for a soul to perceive flesh.

It was also not surprising when you consider that young kids are often instinctively closer to Truth than ego-conditioned adults are. Jesus even preached such things.

"Truly, I say to you, unless you turn and become like children, you will never enter the kingdom of heaven."
- Matthew 18:3

As we grow in the physical world we absorb ego energy, which acts like a barrier to keep us out of the inner kingdom of heaven. When they are not being forced to share toys, toddlers are relatively egoless, free from the madness of the seven deadly sins. Not many babies experience lust, gluttony, greed, sloth, wrath, envy or pride.

Heck, babies don't care if they are naked in front of the world, they don't care what clothes they are wearing, they are not interested in popularity, they have no idea what money is, they don't notice their skin color nor yours, they don't have a religious affiliation … after their basic physical needs are met, they just crave affection. Give it to them and they are at peace.

Just like you, right now. Receive the spirit associated with higher consciousness and you will be at peace.

You have to believe this to be true, but no worries, we can all do it.

"For nothing will be impossible with God."
*- Luke **1:37***

It's possible if you pursue the path of Truth.

You can use consciousness to either follow the flesh or follow the spirit. Since your atomic body is an energy vessel, in Christian terminology, you are capable of receiving the Holy Spirit until your cup overflows. That's when you have discovered the Holy Grail, which is Christ Consciousness in you.

What did the disciples do when they were pointed toward Truth?

"They followed Jesus."
- John ***1:37***

And what did the disciples who were searching "in the dark" say when they found Christ?

"Everyone is looking for you."
- Mark ***1:37****.*

If you are in the darkness, look for the light of Unity Consciousness. The "dark" is a metaphor for the ego's obsession with the physical world, and everyone is looking for higher consciousness … whether they know it or not.

It's a magical mystery, brought to you by the number 137.

THE BALANCING ACT

What's the opposite of tall? What's the opposite of fat? What's the opposite of black?

Did you say short, thin and white?

Wrong, wrong and wrong.

Niels Bohr spent most of his professional life studying atomic structure and quantum theory. As such, he knew a thing or two million about the makeup of the world we live in.

In studying of quantum minds, you will find that most are also part-time philosophers. How can they not be? As Einstein said, "Look deep into nature and then you will understand everything better."

Bohr did just that.

So impressed was he on his findings on the nature of reality that he included what he learned in his family Coat of Arms, which the great Dane himself designed.

At the top, there's the Latin slogan:

Contraria Sunt Complementa.

Opposites are complementary.

There really are no opposites in the physical world. Things are better understood as complements to each other, one definition of complementary being “mutually supplying each other’s lack.”

Short is a complement to tall, as shortness is really just a lack of tallness. Thin is a complement to fat, as thinness is really just a lack of fatness. White is a complement to black, as whiteness is really just a lack of blackness. And so on and so on.

Bohr’s science went way beyond the philosophy and logic of the above examples. He developed a concept called the complementarity principle, which is deep and complex, but generally states that the more you know about some aspects of something the less you know about other aspects of it. (The more ‘short’ something is, the less ‘tall’ it is.) The underlying properties of such entities can be considered to be mutually exclusive.

Physicist John Wheeler, who popularized the idea of quantum foam as referenced in Level 3, said this about his colleague’s work: “Bohr’s principle of complementarity is the most revolutionary scientific concept of this century and the heart of his 50-year search for the full significance of the quantum idea.”

In physics, complementarity is used to describe properties such as position and momentum as well as the wave-particle duality that was mentioned in Level 4, but we are not interested in the details of complicated physics. We want to see the applicable aspects of the relevant science. The painter does not need to know the chemical composition of the paint in order to produce a beautiful painting.

We should think of the physical world in terms of its complementary nature, how most properties can be evaluated on a continuum and not as opposites. There isn’t an opposite for 93 degrees Fahrenheit, but if you remove some heat by slowing the vibration of molecules, you have cold.

Similarly, light and dark are not opposites. Add a little light and darkness diminishes by a corresponding amount.

Spiritually speaking, if you remove good from a situation what are you left with? Evil. Remove God, you get the Devil. Hell is simply an absence of heaven. Your physical life and your non-physical life — the ego and the spirit — are complements. We often slowly shift from seeing the world as material to seeing it as spiritual. It's a subtle change of perception within an energetic continuum.

This is why physicist/philosopher Bohr included that second prominent feature in his Coat of Arms — the ancient symbol for balance, the yin yang. It is most commonly known as a spiritual symbol (based in the traditions of Taoism and Buddhism), and yet has its own complementary aspects with scientific interpretations.

The universe is indeed all about balance.

There are dozens of fundamental physical constants that are so precise, were any of them to be slightly off, the universe as we know it might not exist (i.e. the anthropic principle). The fine-structure constant, or alpha, discussed in Level 4 is one such example, along with the speed of light, the Planck constant, and the varying masses of electrons, protons and neutrons.

If the values of these constants, such as alpha's 137, did not remain in perfect balance, this might be a strangely different world we live in. If at all. (Some proponents of intelligent design point to these numbers as evidence of the existence of a creator God.)

The human brain is also all about balance.

There are 100 billion neurons up there in your cranium, each loaded with neurotransmitters that are chemically comparable or complementary to many street drugs and certain medicines.

The reason why opiates such as heroin work is because the brain comes equipped with a natural counterpart called endorphins. Cocaine significantly increases the amount of dopamine in the brain, which is the reason for the high feeling associated with stimulant use. Sedatives such as alcohol and benzodiazepines imitate a neurochemical called GABA, while marijuana (anandamide) and even psychedelics (DMT) have natural mimics already in the brain.

Using drugs typically throws natural brain chemistry out of balance, which leads to all sorts of dysfunction, including withdrawal symptoms and sometimes fatal overdose.

Similarly, mental health issues are also linked to brain chemistry. When one is low in serotonin production, the resulting feeling is called depression ... and the pharmaceutical industry labels it *a chemical imbalance*. Low amounts of GABA have been linked to ADHD, hypertension and panic attacks.

In both addiction and mental health, restoring the brain to proper functioning is a balancing act, establishing harmony among those neurochemicals.

Thousands of years ago the renowned philosopher Aristotle recognized what Bohr later determined scientifically — that reality is loaded with complements (not opposites) varying by degree.

Regarding character traits, Aristotle described humans as possessing virtues that are either "deficient" or in "excess" until they reach the "virtuous mean," or the average between the others. It is the balance point.

Courage is a virtuous mean. If one is deficient in courage, he is a coward. If one is excessive in courage, he is reckless.

Discipline is a virtuous mean. If one is deficient in discipline, she is indulgent. If one is excessive in discipline, she is obsessive.

Aristotle gave many more examples, including the virtuous mean of forgiveness (deficient is resentful, excessive is enabling) and humor (prudish, buffoonery).

You might be a coward if you are afraid to take any risks, but driving 110 mph down the highway doesn't make you courageous, it makes you reckless. If you cannot forgive someone, you may feel resentful toward them, but if you go too far in the other direction, you may open yourself up for further victimization. And if you can't take a joke you might be called a prude, but that doesn't mean you should be cracking jokes in front of a judge or at a funeral.

Bottom line, as human beings we are only properly virtuous when we are balanced. This is what the yin yang is all about, the balancing of energies.

The symbol, called taijitu, is most closely associated with the Chinese philosophy of Taoism, but also with Buddhism, Hinduism and Jainism. Taijitu literally means "diagram of the supreme ultimate."

It would take hundreds of pages to sift through all of the varied interpretations of yin and yang, but among the most common — and my personal favorite — is the notion that yin (female) and yang (male) are two halves that ultimately make a complete whole inside each of us, an important concept in many spiritual teachings. The male-female halves are also represented by the eternal, revolving nature of the infinity symbol.

In my work with clients, I have found the most practical aspect of yin and yang to be grounded in Taoism. Tao, in Chinese, means "path" or "the way."

Let's say you are walking through the woods on a nice, clear path and you take a wrong turn, going deep into the forest and finding yourself lost in the dark. There, you might encounter a snake or a bear, perhaps brush up against some poison ivy. What would the negative aspect of the above situation propel you to do? That's right, head back to the path!

Similarly, if you are proceeding smoothly in life and then take a wrong turn, what happens? All sorts of chaos, such as emotional disturbance, marital discord, financial distress. What's the proper thing to do? Get back on the right path!

Borrowing from Aristotle's work, cowardice, recklessness, resentfulness and other imbalanced virtues are off the path, while courage, humor and forgiveness are right on.

In Taoism, that path is balance and it is a pathway that runs through each of us. You could say that the path to Truth is inside you, and each of us has our own way of reaching it, which is the essence of Buddha's Kalama Sutta.

Another way of thinking about this path is considering what a global positioning satellite does for you while you are driving. If you are lost, would you ever turn off your GPS? No, you would listen to its guidance.

It is the same with the Tao. Listen to it. Simply stated, the Tao inside yourself is your emotional state, the feedback loop for your spiritual development.

If the goal is Christ Consciousness, the primary clues to determine how close you are to getting there are your emotions. If you are at peace, you are on the path. If you aren't, you are off your path. (Relatively speaking, Level 7).

"Do not turn to the right nor to the left;
Turn your foot from evil."
- Proverbs 4:27

Imbalance is evil, energetically at least.

Simple examples make this most clear.

If you are in a burning building, you will feel fear, which motivates you to get out of the building. When you do so, your fear subsides, and you are again at peace.

If you are lonely because you don't have friends, that loneliness is a motivator to find friends. If that were your only issue, and you find friends, you will be at peace.

If you are nervous before a test, and that nervousness gets you to study so that you know the material, what happens when you know the material? Confidence replaces the anxiety and you are at peace.

If you are insecure because you worry too much about what other people think of you, the feeling of low self-esteem can be offset by learning how to focus only on oneself. Peace will soon follow.

More complicated situations get more complicated, but the Tao still works.

If you are feeling grief because a loved one died and are concerned about whether you shall 'see' them again, you will never feel peace until you learn the Truth, and you will be at peace.

And if you are struggling with politics and things like abortion, capital punishment, war and same-sex marriage, life circumstances and your emotional state will allow you to continually refine your perspective until you arrive on your peace pathway.

A shifting of perspective is the evolution of consciousness (Level 12), with emotions being the GPS system for your soul.

Bottom line, whenever you feel a negative emotion, it is nudging you in a different direction, a motivator to get you to change your perspective and get you back on the path toward higher consciousness. Positive emotions operate as a reinforcer, a good indicator that you are headed the right way.

Most of us spend much of our lives hoping for external events to make us happier, but relying on things to always go your way is clearly a low-percentage strategy, whereas shifting the nature of your consciousness guarantees success.

Buddhist teacher Ajahn Brahm illustrates this well, relating a parable of four old men who were outside of a house while it was raining, and the owner invited them in.

But the old men told him that they would not come in unless the family invited the correct one of them in first. If they chose wrong, none of them would come in.

The Four Old Men were named Wealth, Success, Peace and Harmony.

The father, a hard-working man who was struggling to make ends meet, demanded that Wealth come in first. His wife, wanting her husband to feel proud no matter how much wealth they had, insisted that Success would be the first to enter. So they argued and argued.

Disliking all the fighting, the older child said she voted for Peace because she just wanted it to be quiet, but soon she was sucked into the argument as well.

That left the youngest child to finally speak up. "All I want is for all four of us to get along," he said, "so I will invite Harmony in."

Harmony entered and told the family they had made the correct choice. Following close behind Harmony came Peace, then Success, then Wealth.

The way to establish the peace we all want inside ourselves is to strike that perfect balance, a harmony among a sea of vibrational energy in our lives. Success and wealth often follow.

"Be perfect, as your heavenly Father is perfect."
- Matthew 5:48

Achieving physical perfection is impossible, but achieving mental balance is not.

Energetic harmony, attaining the delicate union between yin and yang while mastering spiritual virtues, is perfection. It is your mission in life.

Be perfect.

PRACTICE MAKES PERFECT

It doesn't take a brain surgeon to understand the brain.

Let's say that you want to copy a movie or some videos and you open a pack of DVDs, all shiny and new.

Look at the laser side of a disc. Can you see anything there? Not yet, as no data has been placed on it.

After burning the video, look at the laser side again. Notice any changes? You should. There's now information on it, so a faint change in appearance is visible.

Easy to understand, right?

Now you know how brains work. You don't have to be a neuroscientist to comprehend basic neuroscience.

Perhaps there's *a bit* more to it, and grasping that simple concept doesn't qualify you to operate on someone's brain, but we're off to a good start for what you need for *New Eyes*.

As discussed in Level 2 regarding fMRIs, neuroscience has revealed that there are incredible similarities in all of our brains as it pertains to neuronal activity.

This chapter goes into greater detail on that idea and provides a scientific backdrop for a well-known Buddha quote out of his collection of sayings in the *Dhammapada*:

"Our life is shaped by our mind. We become what we think."

No, this does not mean that if you think you are a giraffe, that you become a giraffe.

"We become what we think" means that we gravitate toward what we are thinking about. If you think about becoming a doctor, you are more likely to become a doctor. If you think about how mad you are at someone, you become resentful. And if you think about a giraffe, you might find yourself at a zoo.

But the ultimate meaning behind Buddha's Truth is this: If you think you are a body, you experience things physically and ego grows inside of you. If you think you are a soul, you experience things spiritually and consciousness expands inside of you.

A sacred Hindu text emphasizes this as well:

"It is true what they say, 'You are what you think.'
If you think you are bound you are bound.
If you think you are free you are free."
- Ashtavakra Gita

There are physical factors and cultural influences to be mindful of, but it really is as simple as that. The depth and breadth of "we become what we think" is rarely fully explained or placed in the proper neurological and spiritual context, so let's go there.

In the beginning there was tabula rasa, which is Latin for "blank slate" and originally was a term used in Rome to describe wax writing tablets that were heated after use and therefore became blank again.

Over time the term was co-opted by philosophers, who debated the nature of mind by considering the apparent "tabula rasa" aspect of newborns. Instead of containing innate knowledge, they reasoned, the brains of babies are more like those of a blank slate.

Level 6 is not a philosophical debate, though — it's about

relevant neuroscience, and brain scans do indeed show that babies are fairly similar to a fresh new DVD or a heated wax tablet. There's not much there.

This is otherwise known as *logical.* It surely shouldn't come as a shock that newborn brains are basically blank, save for distinct instinctual wiring such as reflexes (rooting, stepping, startle response, etc.) and other 'preprogramming' such as sensory input processing, motor control and language abilities.

But those things come preloaded on every ~~robot~~ brain. Don't babies all do the same basic stuff? Sure, there are individual differences in the equipment, just as you can use a desktop, laptop or your smartphone to check your email, but the bottom line is very similar. Despite coming in different packages, babies just eat, sleep, cry, coo and poop.

It's not like they have decided on their favorite sport yet.

What makes us truly different, and what might surprise you, happens next.

The fact is, babies don't think much. As researchers Duan Xu and Daniel Vigneron put it in a review of Magnetic Resonance Spectroscopy, "For newborns, the brain is relatively immature and has much less neuronal activity in comparison to adults."

Thinking gets us into trouble. Early on, it creates division. Babies are pretty similar, until they start thinking about things. That messes them up, as their consciousness begins to separate from each other.

"Let the little children come to me and do not hinder them, for to such belongs the kingdom of heaven."
- Matthew 19:14

We hinder them, those young souls in development, when we force ego perspectives on them. Before they start thinking too much and adopting their cultural attitudes, children have virtually no ego identity.

New Eyes is not anti-thought, of course. This book is pro-unity and anti-separation. When our thoughts pull us apart, we believe we are fundamentally different. Physically we might be, but spiritually we are not. We are One in Unity Consciousness. It's fine if our lower-mind thoughts draw distinctions between us as long as we understand our connection in the higher-mind realm.

Here's how it happens neuroscientifically:

Your brain features 100 billion neurons — or little 'thinking' cells — with axons that are oriented in the manner that 'you' tell them. It is as if you had 100 billion foot soldiers in your head, all marching to the general's orders. Consciousness is first in command.

Your brain can also be likened unto a garden, with flowers and weeds both capable of growing there, pending the focus and habits of the gardener who tends it. Or if you prefer to be indoors, our brains are like computers. We are all born with the same basic hardware and software. While you use your computer to write poetry, co-worker Marty over there uses his to watch inappropriate videos. While you are receiving your Nobel Prize in Literature, Marty is attracting viruses and getting called into the HR office.

What you download, you become.

Not many people recognize that our brains are really about wiring, that portions of our brains are moving around … but those neurons are indeed wriggling and jiggling like the legs of the spider inside the *Old Lady Who Swallowed A Fly*.

In 1949, Canadian neuropsychologist Donald Hebb published a book entitled *The Organization of Behavior* in which he stated, "When an axon of cell A is near enough to excite cell B and repeatedly or persistently takes part in firing it, some growth process or metabolic change takes place in one or both cells such that A's efficiency, as one of the cells firing B, is increased."

Translated, it means "neurons that fire together, wire together."

Neurons that fire together, wire together. Neurons that fire together, wire together.

Neurons that fire together, wire together.

Now that you have read it a few times, the concept is wired together in your brain.

This is what is known as "Hebb's Law" and it may be the single most important piece of science to understand if you want to affect real change in your life.

Like a 100 billion-sided Rubik's Cube, there are nearly an infinite number of potential configurations for a human brain. The normal, six-sided Rubik's cube with nine squares per side has more than 43 quintillion possible configurations. Thanks to all of those wriggling and jiggling neurons, there are those who have calculated that the brain has more potential orientations than there are atoms in the universe.

That's a lot of variation!

As similar as babies are initially, they develop very uniquely as their minds begin to form while they experience different things. Whatever neurons of theirs that fire together will wire together, so as babies develop, their neurons create different patterns.

For example, remember how the fMRI could identify if you are thinking of an igloo because 'igloo' is located within the same neural set in all of our brains? Well, what if one child is raised in Alaska and another in Ecuador? Chances are good that the former child's brain will develop the neural pattern for igloo much faster than the latter.

And remember how brain scans can tell if you are performing addition or subtraction? Well, what if one child is born into an affluent family where both parents are mathematics professors while the other is born into poverty and never receives any formal schooling? Clearly, their brains will develop much differently.

Now repeat the same type of thinking for hammer. And basketball. And bunny rabbit. And language acquisition. And chili cheese fries. And displaying courage. Or cowardice. And feeling hope. Or hopelessness. And being in love. Or being in fear. And "My name is Shaquille." Or not. You get the idea.

It gets much more complex than that, of course.

If a child is neglected by his parents as a toddler, gets picked on in first grade, befriends a trouble-maker in sixth grade and then smokes marijuana as an eighth-grader, his brain will link all of those items together in a pattern. When he sees his mother and father guess what happens? His brain connects the neural dots and he feels like using some weed.

Neurons that fire together, wire together.

Conversely, if a child is treated well by his parents as a toddler, fits in well with the other kids in first grade and is popular in sixth grade what's the likelihood that he will smoke marijuana as an eighth grader? Less so. Will seeing his parents trigger a desire to use drugs. Probably not.

Those are greatly simplified scenarios, of course, but this is precisely how the brain develops. This is linked to that, which is linked to this and that ... all coming together to form a neural network, what we experience as *an identity*. Each time a particular pattern is reinforced, the electrical-chemical link between neurons is strengthened. If a particular pattern is not reinforced, or not discovered in the first place, it either fades or doesn't ever show up at all.

Use it or lose it.

We all quickly diverge into these differing brain patterns. Over time, brain scans can pick this up. Unlike the scans of babies' brains, which are very similar, teen brain scans are wildly divergent. They are a mess, really.

Science demonstrates that teens are really wired to not think clearly! Researchers at the National Institute of Mental Health and the University of California, Los Angeles (UCLA) revealed in a long-term MRI study that the prefrontal cortex, which is responsible for "complex" thinking, is not fully developed until the early 20s. (The spiritual reason for this is discussed in Level 18.)

Generally, teens are still figuring themselves out, they still have their futures filled with significant potential ahead of them, they can still think things such as "I want to be a professional baseball player" or "I want to join the military" or "I want to get married and have kids." They also think things like, "I can do this" or "I cannot do that" or "This is awesome" or "This is terrible" as well as "This is a hammer" and "This is an igloo."

All of those things are potential neural patterns for them.

During these years, some patterns get strengthened more than others. The strong ones appear on brain scans as thicker lines in denser regions, while patterns not attended to grow dimmer in sparsely lit regions. In neurochemistry, this is called pruning.

If a teen gives up on his dream of being president, the "I am going to be president" pathway fades, along with everything that would have been linked to that pathway. When one becomes hopeless, the hope pathway never lights up. If a teen focuses on "I can do this" then *that* neural pathway grows stronger and the "I cannot do this" pathway fades.

As Henry Ford said, "Whether you think you can or think you can't, you're right!"

Just as you trim a few branches off a tree so that the others grow stronger — pruning — the human brain does the same. If some neural pathways are pruned, the others grow stronger. Neural connections that are reinforced are retained, while those that aren't just fade to black.

Now let's move onto adults. For greater effect let's make them senior citizens, as their brains are the most experienced at Hebb's Law.

What happens to that crazy mess of patterns that teen brains display on scans? Pruning after pruning after pruning reduces the potential neural patterns so significantly that by the time the golden years come around the connections that show up are fewer in number, but very well established due to continual reinforcement of identity over the years.

The sweet little Grandma who bakes those awesome lemon cookies? Lots of practice! And when you think of her and her kitchen, bet you think of those cookies!

Conversely keep repeating, "I am angry" and "I am irritated" enough times, next thing you know you have a brain signature of a grumpy old man.

Creatures of habit, all of us.

Neurons that fire together, wire together.

You have heard that you can't teach an old dog new tricks? Well, you can, it just requires a great deal more effort. Imagine doing bicep curls with just your right arm for decades while neglecting your left arm, then you decide to get your left arm in shape. It will take a while, right? (I call it neurochemical karma.)

The brain works like that, very similar to how rivers are formed. Sprinkle a few drops of water in a dry field, nothing happens. Keep pouring water, a stream will form over time. Continually add water and a river results, now capable of grabbing more rain because of its increased size.

How do you dry up that river? Stop adding water.

In the brain, if you sprinkle a few thoughts around, nothing happens. Keep practicing those thoughts, a neural pathway begins to form. Continually focus on those thoughts and the result is a strengthened pattern with which the thinker identifies.

"Our life is shaped by our mind. We become what we think."

How do you change a strengthened thought pattern, an identity that you don't like?

You change the way you think! It's as simple as that.

"Be transformed by the renewing of your mind."
- Apostle Paul, in Romans 12:2

The New Living Translation puts that verse this way, "Let God transform you into a new person by changing the way you think."

Changing the way you think can be difficult because of all the mind muscle you developed by working out certain thoughts, whether it is "I like ice cream" or "I hate my boss."

If the river is mighty, it will be a challenge to divert its flow, but if you take a shovel and scoop a little dirt out of the riverbank, soon the water will go in a new direction.

Same with your thoughts. It's called neuroplasticity. The brain is not as hard and fixed as we once thought it to be, it is really more soft and flexible. It's not like steel, it's more like plastic.

If someone goes through a traumatic experience, such as being victimized in a crime, they have every right to perceive the situation accordingly and are justified in doing so.

But there are different degrees of consciousness (Level 12). It just doesn't feel good for many people to perceive themselves as victims over the long haul. After years of doing so, that's when they often come into a professional's office and ask for help.

"I feel terrible," they say.

"You can change that," I say.

There's no going back and changing the crime, of course, so what's left? Changing the perception of the situation.

It's ultimately what spirituality is all about — changing one's perception in the direction of perfection, or Christ Consciousness. It's why Jesus emphasized forgiveness and noted that those who are persecuted are blessed (as long as they do so with higher consciousness in mind).

Remember the stunning findings that brain scans have uncovered as discussed in Level 2? Amid a vast sea of differing brain configurations, there are precise neuronal patterns that match your brain to mine.

Everything you can think of has a corresponding brain pattern associated with it. Tabula rasa, much like the world, is merely an illusion. Hidden on the tablet under that wax is a matrix of thoughts, ideas, experiences and emotions, all of which are ready to be expressed, and we explore these patterns from different angles and perspectives (Level 7).

But at its most elementary, with few exceptions, we have the same potential brain configurations.

Think of it this way. You and I both have a Rubik's Cube and we both randomly rearrange it for a few minutes. Are they rearranged differently? Yes.

But what happens when we 'get it' and rework the cube so that we put it back in its 'perfect' form? Your cube and my cube look the same again.

That's our brains. They get messed up differently via Hebb's Law, but then when 'properly' rearranged via Hebb's Law they appear the same on brain scans.

Conventional wisdom suggests that our minds are all different, that we are psychologically as diverse as we are physically. We should call that Humpty Dumpty's Law … our minds get all broken up and separated, so we argue with each other and then struggle to put our minds back together again.

Christ's wisdom utilizes Hebb's Law. Practice makes perfect … and we must be perfect (Matthew 5:48).

What is the pathway to perfection? Follow Hebb's Law to establish Truth in your brain. That is renewing your life with your mind. Reinforce Truth and old dysfunctional patterns fade away.

Those neurons are merely privates in the army, they take orders from you. Tell them what to do often enough and they will do it.

"If you think you are bound you are bound.
If you think you are free you are free."

JUDGE CORRECTLY

If this book were to attempt to describe Albert Einstein's Theory of Relativity in its fullest detail, two things would happen.

I would fail ... and you would decide that it was much simpler to see the world through old eyes.

Comprehending the deeper complexities of this theory is virtually impossible for nearly all of us, but fortunately that is not necessary in order to reap major benefits from it. Do you need to understand all of the laws of physics to know not to step in front of a moving bus or speeding train? No. If you can grasp that leaning over the railing of a balcony is dangerous, then you are an expert in the application of gravity and will soon be skilled at applying relativity as well.

Truth is, you will only need to understand a relatively minor amount of relativity in order to put a big piece of the *New Eyes* puzzle in place. A mere surface comprehension of relativity is enough for a paradigm shift on the nature of this world and allows for a spiritual, therapeutic application of the theory.

One thing you don't really need to know about relativity is that it has two parts: special and general. Einstein figured out the special side in 1905, and 10 years later nailed down general. (There is a distinction between the two, but for *New Eyes*, not much of a difference.)

What you do need to know about relativity is:

1. The speed of light is always the same.
2. Neither space nor time is constant as all of us have our own individual relationship with the universe.

We will first focus on the latter, which suggests that the universe is not at all what it seems to be … and that everyone is observing it in a personalized way. For this book, that's relativity in a nutshell: Each of us has our own unique point of view, both scientifically and spiritually.

What we think of as space and time is really just one thing that Einstein called "spacetime."

That's right, the clock on your wall and what it measures are two aspects of the same continuum … the fabric of spacetime. It's not the physical clock over there in space measuring something non-physical called time, it's collectively just spacetime. The clock and the time it measures are cut from the same cloth (Level 13 and Level 15 will go into greater detail about how space and time are not what we think they are).

Spacetime includes a pair of effects called length contraction and time dilation.

In length contraction, physical objects get shorter when they move relative to each individual observer. Time dilation is the "slowing" of time or the difference of elapsed time between independent observers moving relative to each other.

Which means *an object changes size depending on whom is looking at it* and *time can pass at different rates of speed!*

How can objects get shorter and time get slower? Because the universe isn't what we think it is. Spacetime is flexible, altering itself for each of us individually.

Here's a way of visualizing this phenomenon:

Imagine you are on the side of the highway and a long flatbed truck drives by with a pitcher and a catcher playing catch on it.

The pitcher is throwing the ball, in the direction that the truck is moving, at 100 mph while the truck is driving at 50 mph.

How fast is the ball moving relative to you, the observer on the side of the road? Yes, 150 mph. You add the speed of the ball to the speed of the truck.

But how fast is the ball moving toward the catcher from his vantage point? You got it, only 100 mph. Because he is moving 50 mph along with the truck, the ball is traveling slower for him.

Think of it this way, would you rather be hit by the pitch while on the truck or if you were alongside the road? What hurts worse, getting punched by someone in a car or being smacked by a fist in a driveby? The force of the fist inside the car is only the force of the fist, but the force of the driveby fist is the force of the fist *plus* the force provided by the car the fist is in. So clearly it would hurt worse to be hit by a 150 mph pitch than by a 100 mph.

See the dilemma here? It is the *same* situation with *different* effects. How can *one* ball be moving at *two* different speeds at the same time? How can it be moving at *both* 100 mph and 150 mph?

The answer starts with the first line from "what you do need to know about relativity" above, that the speed of light is always the same.

If you were running 15 miles per hour and chasing after someone going 10 mph would you be able to catch them? Yes. Because you would be gaining on him at a rate of 5 mph.

Light, however, is constant. If you are running at 15 mph, light is flying away from you at a rate of 186,282 miles per second. So if you run 30 mph and were chasing a beam of light, would you fall behind at a lesser rate? No! Because the faster you run, light *still* travels away from you at 186,282 mps. If you were as fast as Dash from *The Incredibles* and somehow managed to get up to 185,000 mps you would fall behind at the same rate as someone running 15 mph … because light would still be traveling away from both of you at 186,282 mps.

Light is *always* constant, according to Einstein. If the pitcher were throwing a light beam, both the catcher and the observer on the side of the road would see it traveling at 186,282 mps.

So how can a ball be moving at *both* 100 mph and 150 mph? It's not a trick of light, since light is always constant. Einstein determined that it is because of length contraction and time dilation, as the ball is *smaller* and time flows *slower* for the guys on the truck than for the observer on the side of the road!

Please take a moment to contemplate that.

…

If the baseball is a different size for relative observers and time elapses at different rates for relative observers, this means that you live in *your own universe* because *the universe adjusts itself relative to you*!

That's all you need to know about the science of relativity. Light is constant, space and time are not. (To recap: The sun does not revolve around the earth, 12 inches does not always equal one foot and 60 seconds does not always equal one minute.)

Many studies have been conducted to test this, and all experimentally confirm Einstein's relativity revelations. Precise calculations from atomic clocks demonstrate that one will tick slower if it is on a space shuttle soaring above earth than another ticking in Slippery Rock, Pennsylvania.

It's also true what you have heard, if you could travel to Mars and back at close to the speed of light you will return having aged less than everyone else who remained on earth.

The universe is indeed not what we think it is.

While understanding this theory helps open our eyes to the illusory nature of the world, the practical aspect of relativity is infinitely more valuable.

Relativity indicates that we all have our own unique relationship with the universe. It is the scientific support for the Native American saying, "Don't judge a man until you have walked two moons in his moccasins."

Everyone sees the world the way they see it relative to the way they have experienced the world. Consider the following situation:

Person A was a child of loving German immigrant parents, who were born during World War II and whose earliest memories include receiving care packages with food and toys that were airdropped into their villages by American soldiers. As pre-teens, they were welcomed with open arms by the very country that liberated them from their dictator. The first thing Person A's grateful father did when he turned 18 was enlist in the United States Army.

Person B was a child of loving American-born parents, who became anti-war activists during the bitter Vietnam Era after having a close friend killed in combat. They both entered seminary school and became ordained ministers, frequently speaking passionately from the pulpit about peace and pacifism. No members of their immediate family served in the armed forces, as they were sincere conscientious objectors to military intervention.

Knowing nothing else, ask yourself this: What types of political discussions did these two people hear around the dinner table while growing up? If they ever met at a Pizza Hut restaurant on a double date with twin sisters during the buildup of the first Gulf War, what would their dispositions toward that conflict be? Would either be able to see the other's point of view very easily? Is either 'wrong' for his perspective considering their backgrounds?

(And did either of us notice our future wives rolling their eyes during our argument?)

On a surface level, Person A and Person B have both been shaped by their life experiences. In complicated physics, relativity is "the dependence of various physical phenomena on relative motion of the observer and the observed objects." In practical application, relativity is "the dependence of various human perspectives on relative experiences of the observer and the observed objects."

If your consciousness is physically focused and based in lower mind thinking, your perspective is fairly predictable, formed relative to your experiences. It is pretty easy to guess how Gulf War conversations between Person A and Person B go. One conversation, two differing viewpoints … an argument ensues.

Buddha, however, would call it "conditioned ignorance" when a person sees only his own relative point of view. It is limiting consciousness to do so, much like believing English is the only language for communication because that's what you were taught when you were young.

It does not have to be this way, of course. What if there is a simple little shift in consciousness and each person tries to see it from the other's perspective? Going from the lower ego tendency of division toward the higher spiritual focus of unity can dramatically change everything in the direction of order. What if each perceptually walked in the other man's moccasins? Clarity of mind and peace of heart begin to arise.

This is why the American political dynamic is so divisive. Two sides debating each other solely from their relative position — it's yin arguing with yang.

As Einstein said, "You cannot solve a problem from the same consciousness that created it. You must learn to see the world anew."

New Eyes.

No argument is ever going to be settled by debating from

each person's original, relative perspective. That's all ego identity stuff. Most people who were raised in racist homes end up being bigoted. Many young men learn violence from abusive fathers. Those afflicted with chemical dependence often grew up with a prevalence of drugs in their homes.

The best way to break such cycles is by seeing from above the ego lens, from a more lofty perspective … from a soulful place.

"My ways are higher than your ways
and my thoughts higher than your thoughts."
- Isaiah 55:9

In that context, "my thoughts" are coming from the consciousness of Christ while "your thoughts" are from the ego perspective. You join Christ when you see things from his thoughts, from his *higher* vantage point above earthly focus.

This is why we should not judge each other, neither politically nor interpersonally, based upon physical circumstances. We rarely have all the information. We haven't walked in the other person's shoes.

That doesn't mean you should *never* judge in the flesh, as "I think it is foolish for you to drink and drive" and "I don't recommend leaning too far over that ledge" are intelligent, helpful, practical judgments. Those are also easy judgments to make, though they can be short-sighted when you do not know the whole story.

Jesus clearly drew a distinction in that regard.

"Stop judging by mere appearances, but instead judge correctly."
- John 7:24

"Judging by appearances" is surface, ego-based judgment,

when someone is ignorantly conditioned, looking at things from the mere appearance of physical experiences. This is racism, sexism, ageism and physical discrimination of all kinds, including many behavioral judgments about what is 'good' or 'bad' for a person.

"You should break up with that guy, he's acting like a jerk."

Maybe, maybe not.

"Relying on medication-assisted treatment to get off drugs is still using."

Perhaps for some people.

"Do you think I should quit school?"

It depends.

What might seem obvious on the surface is, in reality, relative. All of the above situations require more information, of course, in order to offer a precise opinion. But even with a great deal of information, good people can disagree due to relativity.

"Judging correctly," however, is universal when it is based in Truth. It is looking at the big picture from a higher place, from the recognition that each of us is on a journey of the soul toward Christ Consciousness and the same spiritual rules apply to all. It is the essence of the famous quote by Martin Luther King, Jr. regarding not judging the color of someone's skin (ego appearances) but instead the content of his character (consciousness development).

Correct judgment would be an assessment of virtues, such as whether someone is courageous, compassionate, forgiving, disciplined and wise, which are spiritual characteristics that are not based in ego.

You can guess someone's age by an assessment of her physical body, but age tells you nothing about her spiritual development. Some preteens are wise beyond their years, while immature 57-year-olds are spiritual toddlers. (Many egomaniacal adults are the equivalent of spiritual fetuses.) You cannot judge a soul book by its flesh cover.

Here's another way to understand the soul journey within practical relativity.

Imagine you are a graduate psychology student about to observe two mice roaming around in a maze, looking for the cheese at the exit. One mouse is placed in a difficult spot, around many corners, far from the cheese. Obstacles abound, including a snake lurking nearby and several hopeless dead ends. Meanwhile, another mouse is placed near the exit, by the cheese, with nary an obstacle in sight.

As a neutral observer studying only what happens, you are watching from a detached perspective, recording data. But along comes your pet-loving girlfriend and she screams, "That's so cruel and unfair! Why don't both mice get to start by the cheese? And you better not let that cute furry little mouse get caught in that trap!"

Yet in the name of science and in spite of her furrowed brow, you persist.

While the 'lucky' mouse quickly finds the cheese and nibbles it gleefully, believing itself to be king, the poor unfortunate mouse struggles to find its way around. Every time it gets cornered by the snake, you place it back in its original spot. (It slowly figures out not to go down certain corridors again.) Starving, Miserable 'Missy' Mouse keeps going, in search of the holy cheddar.

After repeated trials, it staggers to the finish line, where it finds King Mickey asleep with a full belly.

So you do something radical. You place both mice in the middle of the maze. Missy, who has seen every inch of the map and knows it inside and out, heads directly for the exit. Mickey, however, is dazed and confused. He doesn't know where to turn. He stumbles down wrong corridors, gets chased by the snake, cries a lot, and ultimately takes twice as long to find the cheese as did Missy.

Even more radically, you then place Mickey where Missy initially started, and vice versa. Missy very quickly finds the cheese and is very grateful, while Mickey is horrified to find himself in such "unfair" circumstances! Accustomed to getting his way, he stops frequently, resents his unfortunate situation, and either quits or takes thrice as long to find the cheese from the 'bad' corner as did Missy.

So here's the question: In the big picture, which mouse was more fortunate after all?

Judging by "mere appearances," initially one would quickly say that Mickey had it best, that being placed near the finish line was the preferred position. But "judging correctly" from a higher place, over the long haul, it is easy to see that Missy was ultimately better off because she endured the obstacles and learned so much more over time. She developed her character with persistence, gratitude and wisdom. (Yes, despite her tough initial circumstances, she became less miserable than Mickey.)

This type of relativistic thinking is at the heart of Jesus's teachings.

"Blessed are those who are persecuted for righteousness' sake, for theirs is the kingdom of heaven."
- Matthew 5:10

You are *blessed* to be put in challenging circumstances, as long as you are in pursuit of the *righteous* goal of 'thinking' like Christ or developing Christ Consciousness, which is how you enter the kingdom of heaven. In the mouse maze it was Missy who was blessed, as she persevered and gratefully found her little slice of heaven.

Note that Jesus did *not* simply say, "Blessed are those who are persecuted, for theirs is the kingdom of heaven."

Persecution is only a *blessing* if it occurs along a *righteous* pathway, the Tao of optimizing consciousness. Off that path, when you complain and are bitter about life's circumstances? In that case, persecution is painfully meaningless.

If someone hurts you and you practice the virtue of forgiveness, you are blessed. If someone hurts you and you remain eternally resentful, you might be justified, but you are not blessed. The pain you feel from your resentment will not gain you admittance into "the kingdom." The relief of forgiveness, though, is heavenly.

Being right is something egos are concerned with; being righteous is something souls do.

Therefore, not blessed is Mickey, who was complacent and boastful with 'heaven' placed right in front of him, ultimately facing the same obstacles as Missy but being overwhelmed by them.

Blessed is Missy, who learned much more from the journey and still received her reward.

"It is easier for a camel to go through the eye of a needle than for a rich man to enter the kingdom of God."
- Mark 10:25

An ego-rich man will not find the kingdom, but the righteous man will.

Don't judge by appearances, judge correctly.

That often requires relativity.

If you started in the bottom left corner of a maze and your friend started in the top right corner, would your pathway out be the same? Physically, no. You might need to go right, left, right, left, right, up, left, up and out, while he might need to go left, right, down, left, left, right, up and out. If you told him to follow your directions, he would get nowhere, perhaps running in circles.

" 'Kindly let me help you or you will drown,'
said the monkey, pulling the fish up into the tree."
- Zen Master Alan Watts

Relativity! What's good for the monkey might not be good for the fish.

But spiritually, from a higher place, you can judge correctly. The same spiritual rules apply to everyone. Stay focused. Hang in there. Never give up. Learn from your mistakes. Tell your friend to find openings in the maze, places where the resistance is minimal, and go through those openings. That is much more pleasant than banging your head against a wall. Also you can tell him that adversity is to be expected, that running into a trap will only remind him not to go down that corridor next time.

You ultimately get out of the maze by walking a peaceful path, not a physical one.

It is similar to suggesting to a friend that forgiveness will provide more peace than resentment, as opposed to telling her that she should hug the criminal who harmed her and bake him a pie. The former is spiritual advice, the latter is physical. That is judging correctly — from an internal place and not from external appearances.

Spiritually speaking, relativity is the reason why there is no need for arguments, because everyone is 'right' from their physical point of view. People see the world the way they see it, and the only relevant question is whether the way they are seeing it is leading them closer to peace. The kind of peace that is found in a deep, meaningful connection to Christ … Buddha … Krishna … Muhammad … whomever you believe best embodied perfected consciousness.

Physicist Niels Bohr puts our religious differences in relative terms: "I can quite understand why we cannot speak about the content of religion in an objectifying language. The fact that different religions try to express this content in quite distinct spiritual forms is no real objection. Perhaps we ought to look upon these different forms as complementary descriptions which, though they exclude one another, are needed to convey the rich possibilities flowing from man's relationship with the central order."

Don't judge appearances. The majority of religious Westerners identify with Jesus, religious Middle Easterners with Muhammad and religious Far Easterners with Buddha. But what if your consciousness manifested in an Iraqi body? You would probably be Muslim. And vice versa, a Muslim would likely be Christian had his consciousness arisen in an American form.

Does that make either person wrong? No, that's just their relative experience, not unlike Americans saying 'soccer' when the rest of the world calls that sport 'football,' which is an altogether different game in the United States. Neither side is right, it's just ego-world conditioning.

As Bohr suggested, our differences are merely "rich possibilities" that stem from relativity. All of us must balance our relative experience through our own relationship with the "central order," which some would identify as God. Scientifically, all of us have to balance our own brain chemistry, no matter the situation we find ourselves in (and sometimes the more difficult the situation, the better).

Whatever your relative conditioning or experiences, it becomes your job to neurochemically balance yourself in order to feel peace. Children of racist parents will have to learn a new perspective, otherwise they will likely end up in a lot of arguments, or worse. Anyone who grows up in a drug-infested community will need to elevate consciousness in order to escape that poisonous trap. Whatever culture you were raised in, you will likely have to broaden your horizons in order to feel lasting peace and unity.

"Go from your country and your kindred and your father's house to the land that I will show you."
- Genesis 12:1

In other words, leave your relative physical conditioning behind so that you can discover universal spiritual growth.

It's the same with daily experiences, things like practicing patience (spiritual) in long lines (physical), hope in the midst of adversity and forgiveness when one has been victimized. Understanding relativity can help bring internal peace in spite of external circumstances.

A simple example: Did you ever feel road rage? Or anything approximating it, like being really, really irritated by ignorant drivers?

I certainly did, always assuming that other people should be smarter or better drivers than they were. (Like not turning right on red, c'mon!)

Every "road irritation" I ever encountered always ended with the same result — the other person driving off either unaware or waving a digit at me for blasting my car horn — and with me feeling more aggravated.

That would accomplish precisely what? Me moving closer

toward rage and completely unsure as to whether the other driver even knew what he did wrong … and likely not caring that I felt irritated. The net result was me feeling worse.

Then I remembered something. I was born in a car!

True story … my mother delivered me in the back seat of a 1968 Ford Station Wagon prior to arriving at the hospital. When they sold that car in 1975 my father removed that seat and converted it into a couch.

Now, when I relax on it and contemplate the meaning of life, relativity jumps out at me. How do I ever know what's going on in another person's vehicle?

I once had a client find out during a session that his mother was nearly fatally injured in a car accident. He sprinted out of my office and drove 110 mph to the hospital, racing by people who probably cursed him out for being inconsiderate and dangerous. And yet he was always a classy and respectful young man, though you wouldn't know that if he cut you off on the way to see his injured mother. (Happily, she made a complete recovery.)

If you had known that he was on the way to the hospital, what would you have done? If you knew a woman was giving birth in a car that was flashing its headlights behind you, you would likely pull over, let them go by and not hit your brakes in an attempt to slow them down. That is, if you were judging correctly and not by mere appearances.

This does not mean you should not beep your horn at bad drivers, but it does mean you should take relativity into account. Chances are the other person is not experiencing the world the same way you are. Now, when I hit my horn, I do it much more peacefully. To do otherwise is to create an unnecessary emotional disturbance within myself.

Judging by mere appearances creates emotional pain, judging correctly does not.

"And that servant who knew his master's will but did not get ready or act according to his will, will receive a severe beating. But the one who did not know, and did what deserved a beating, will receive a light beating. Everyone to whom much was given, of him much will be required."
- Luke 12:47-48

That's Jesus, oft-portrayed as a peacenik hippie who just wanted everyone to be nice to each other, threatening you with a "severe beating." His intention is only love, though, as he was trying to inspire your spiritual growth. A "severe beating" is the emotional pain you feel when you fail to judge correctly.

Those verses from Luke are relativity in action. If you have 'mature' consciousness and do not follow spiritual rules, you will receive a "severe beating." As Jesus was focused on soul development and was much less concerned with physical affairs, "severe beating" means anger, anxiety, fear and many other emotional issues that you might call 'hell.' (It does not mean that God is going to put you over His knee and give you a spanking.)

If you have been taught about forgiveness and understand that you need to forgive someone and do not do so, your resentment will run deep. If you know that you need to show courage to do something and hide from it, your sense of cowardice intensifies. If you have been walking a spiritual path and then diverge, the contrast will feel more severe than someone who hadn't been on that path.

"Everyone to whom much was given,
of him much will be required."

"Much" does not necessarily mean money or materials, although it can mean that. But it definitely means spirit. If you have *much more* spirit than others because of consciousness potential, it is expected that you will understand and apply Truth because you know better. The bigger the grail is inside you, the bigger the challenges in life. The bar is set higher on you.

However, if you have *immature* consciousness and do not follow spiritual rules, your "beating" will be lighter. Sometimes ignorance is indeed bliss. If you have *much less* spirit because of undeveloped consciousness, you are not held to as high of a standard.

So in Luke 12:47-48 we discover something fascinating.

God grades on a curve! It's spiritual relativity.

We are all going to have different experiences in the flesh, but we remain united by the spirit within us. While the material world is unstable and unpredictable, the spirit is permanent and reliable. Materials come and go, yet hope, forgiveness and wisdom are always there for you, differing only by degree. People are temporary, souls are eternal.

Time and space change for each of us.

Only *the light* is constant.

INFINITE POSSIBILITIES

It was a light-bulb moment, for sure.

No, that's a little too mild for the impact that it had on me. It was more of a supernova moment.

A decade ago, my client Jim brought the scientific documentary *The Elegant Universe* into my office and was eager to show me one clip in particular. In it, contemporary physicist Brian Greene stated these exact words:

"There's even a chance that I can pass through something solid, like a wall. Now, quantum calculations do show that the probability for this to happen in the everyday world is so small that I need to continue walking into the wall for nearly an eternity before having a reasonable chance of succeeding. But (in the quantum world) these kinds of things happen all the time."

I felt like actor Jim Carrey in his role as a giddy Lloyd Christmas exclaiming, "So you're telling me there's a chance. Yeah!!"

Perhaps quoting a scene from *Dumb and Dumber* isn't the ideal reference for such a high-minded concept, but you get the point.

I sure got it.

Our discussion in that session immediately turned to the story of Jesus walking on water. For the first time in my adult life, a story that I had largely dismissed because of its implausibility became relevant again.

Level 28 will reveal what Jesus "walking on water" means in relation to Christ Consciousness, but at the time it simply opened a new way of seeing things. If it were actually possible to walk through a wall, however remote, what else is possible?

Turns out a whole lot, according to quantum physics. Like, an infinite amount of things are possible.

There's a quantum term that represents this concept, one that cuts right to the heart of spirituality and shines light in *New Eyes*.

Superposition.

It's like Superman, but with the whole universe.

Superposition is the reason why the tagline of our private practice Quantum Counseling Services is *"Exploring Your Infinite Possibilities."* There are many aspects to the concept, but as with relativity, we will only go over what you need to know for the purposes of this book.

Most of us have been taught or are under the impression that atoms are miniature solar systems, with electrons orbiting around a nucleus akin to the earth revolving around the sun.

Not so.

A single electron actually exists in multiple locations around the nucleus. 'Super' positioning, you could say.

Just as Clark Kent seemingly appeared to be in more than one place at a time, particles were discovered a century ago to be much, much faster than a speeding bullet … so 'fast' that they appear all over the place in a single bound, so to speak.

Grasping the implications of superposition will be a quantum leap forward in acquiring *New Eyes*.

In actuality, an electron doesn't need to be super fast or

revolve around a nucleus because it is already 'spread out' within its orbit in a cloudy or wave-like form, much like how any one individual droplet of water can be anywhere along an entire wave in an ocean. Only when an observer (i.e. your consciousness) interacts with it does it present itself in one place. (Level 9 will review that aspect in depth as these two levels are inextricably linked.)

This is known as wave-particle duality, because instead of being a separate thing, electrons exhibit the qualities of both waves and particles. They are best thought of as *potential* particles, existing in multiple locations at once. They are *both* the water droplet and the ocean wave.

Physicist Werner Heisenberg has been quoted as saying that "atoms are not things, they are only tendencies."

To be precise, this is what he actually said, "One might call (an atom) an objective tendency or possibility ... so the physicists have gradually become accustomed to considering the electronic orbits not as reality but rather as a kind of potentia."

That means an electron has a certain potential for being anywhere within its orbit. Say, 11 percent likely to be there, 9 percent there, 7 percent there, 4 percent there, then 3 percent, 2 percent, 1 percent, .917 percent, .0518 percent, .0000137 percent, and so on, adding up to 100 percent. An infinite number of possibilities.

When the probabilities are put on a graph, they form a wavy pattern that is termed a wave function. When a scientist attempts to locate the electron, it shows up in just one spot and is called a wave-function collapse.

Heisenberg, Bohr and many of their colleagues debated the implications of these atomic findings and what emerged in the late 1920s was something called the "Copenhagen Interpretation." It is complicated, of course, but this is it in its simplest form: A particle exists in all of its potential locations until you observe it, when it appears in only one place. Prior to observing a particle, it is everywhere. When you observe it, it is just in that one spot.

The entire world, remember, is made entirely of those particles.

This interpretation led to a raging debate about its implications. If this is the way the micro world of quantum mechanics works, what about the macro world in which we operate? Does it work this way as well?

Einstein disliked the idea that quantum particles behaved in a probabilistic fashion, stating, “God doesn’t play dice with the universe.” That line was his hope — a prayer and not a declaration of fact. (Bohr has been quoted as responding to Einstein’s dice line by saying, “Don’t tell God what to do.”)

When Einstein died in 1955, nothing had changed. All these years later it is experimentally clear that “playing the odds” is precisely what God is doing in the quantum realm.

But the big question remains, if particles behave like dice and we are made of those particles, does that mean God plays dice with us?

Physicist Erwin Schrödinger famously illustrated the implications of the Copenhagen Interpretation if applied to the world we live in with his thought experiment known as “Schrödinger’s Cat.” In his example of macro world superposition, a cat that is locked in a box with a potentially toxic poison is *both alive and dead* prior to someone checking on it. At that point, when someone opens the box, the 50-50 wave-function probability collapses and the cat turns out to be either alive or dead.

Repeat: According to the Copenhagen Interpretation of superposition, when applied to the world we can see, a cat can be *BOTH ALIVE AND DEAD* at the same time!

If the notion of a half-alive/half-dead feline doesn’t sit well

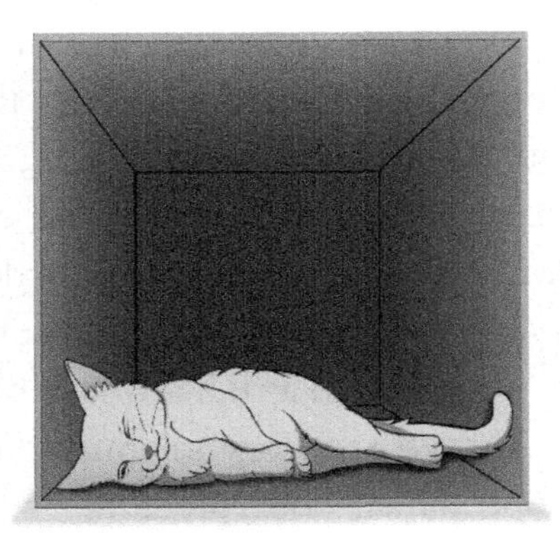

with you, reflect back upon Level 7 when we learned about the nature of spacetime. Since we must accept that space and time change for each individual observer, how much harder is it to believe in Zombie Cat?

While such applications of the Copenhagen Interpretation seem rather paradoxical, there is a certain logic to it as well.

Imagine what you might do tomorrow ... you could go to work as usual ... perhaps head to the gym instead ... or maybe just sleep in until noon. All of those exist as possibilities right now, correct?

If so, doesn't the universe have to allow for a 'pathway' for each of those possibilities to happen? Plans A, B and C all have to exist right now with a certain probability associated with each. Say, 75% likely you go to work, 15% you go to the gym, 7% sleep until noon (and perhaps 3% other).

When you wake up tomorrow, you will begin to head down one of the paths, increasing its probability while simultaneously decreasing the others. Eventually, the original wave function collapses and you end up at work, the gym or headed back to dreamland. The roads not traveled? Poof! They just disappear.

That's the Copenhagen Interpretation. All of the possibilities for tomorrow exist right now, then collapse into one when tomorrow comes.

Despite a consensus of opinion about the legitimacy of the Copenhagen Interpretation, the physicists were not fully satisfied. Many kept searching for a better answer. In the 1950s along came another potential explanation for superposition, as American Hugh Everett developed the *Many Worlds Interpretation of Quantum Mechanics.*

You read that right. *Many Worlds.*

Everett's theory maintained most of the elements of the Copenhagen Interpretation with one primary exception—instead of disappearing out of existence at the moment of wave-function collapse, the other potentials branch out in perpetuity. He noted that those branches are all 'actual' with none more 'real' than another.

In one universe the cat is alive. In another universe the cat is dead. There is no collapse of the wave function, just an infinite number of universes that exist in which all possibilities occur.

"Physical reality," Everett said, "is assumed to be the wave function of the whole universe itself."

Many physicists agree that Everett's many-worlds concept is the most mathematically sound explanation of the macro implication of superposition, and as Everett said, it is the "only completely coherent approach to explaining both the contents of quantum mechanics and the appearance of the world."

We are, once again, made up of a sea of tiny vibrating loops of energy. Why shouldn't the macro world operate like the micro world?

In actuality, by using real-world examples, the many-worlds interpretation is really not that hard to understand.

If a baseball pitcher is throwing a fastball, the ball is 99.999 percent likely to go in the direction that he throws it. The baseball is made up of a trillion atoms, all with a 99.999 percent probability of going in the direction it is thrown.

Guess what happens? Precisely 99.999 percent of them do exactly that, and the odds that the ball as a complete package does not go in that direction are astronomical. But does anyone notice the .001 percent of baseball particles that fly off in another direction?

In the lab, scientists do. They can detect peculiar behavior of quantum particles behaving precisely that way, most moving toward the target but some that go left, some right, some backward and some even disappear into an alternate universe!

Or consider free throw shooting in basketball. Steve Nash holds the NBA career record with a 90.43 percent success rate, followed by Mark Price (90.39%) and Stephen Curry (90.00%). Now imagine a million Steve Nashes, a million Mark Prices and a million Stephen Currys shooting one foul shot simultaneously. What are the chances they would all miss at that same time? Nearly infinitely low.

But cue movie character Lloyd Christmas again: "So you're telling me there's a chance!"

Like walking through a wall, it's possible that all would miss at the same time. Just not very likely, though according to the many worlds interpretation there is a universe in which they all missed.

This is why the micro world doesn't seem to translate perfectly well into the physical world, because of atomic probability clusters called matter. Most things in the physical world are grouped together and have a high probability of behaving in a certain way, and therefore that's what tends to happen.

When seemingly impossible things happen? Such as Jesus walking on water? Hey, there's a chance, and as we shall see in Level 9, consciousness influences the odds. Especially Christ Consciousness. God does play dice with the universe and you have a chance to affect the outcome … with your mind.

Understanding superposition in our macro world is best illustrated by likening reality to listening to a radio. How many stations can you listen to at once? Just one, because you can only tune into one frequency — one possibility — at a time. Yet there are many other options out there that you are not perceiving. (Although sometimes static interference can allow you to hear two stations at once, just like there are some people who tune into more than one reality at a time.)

Most radios have two bands, AM and FM, displaying a range of frequencies on each that typically go from 540 to 1600 kHz on AM and from 88 to 108 MHz on FM. If you are tuning into 93.7 FM and switch over to 1020 AM, does 93.7 FM disappear? Or are you just not tuned into it? Perhaps you only listen to hip hop music, but both country and hard rock stations exist, you just don't go there.

That's our reality. Everything is energy. Possibilities are infinite. You experience the energetic frequency that your consciousness is tuned into, given your Hebb's Law habitual history (Level 6) following your relativistic start (Level 7). What your soul has been practicing since birth, you are now living, leading you toward the goal of perfected consciousness.

Just as dogs can hear frequencies outside our normal range, people with expanded or higher consciousness can tune into things that others cannot. (It's how and why psychedelic drugs work, but that's a topic for another book.)

The superposition concept is sometimes misapplied, as proponents eagerly suggest that *everything* is possible. Perhaps everything is, but the notion of infinite possibilities is much easier to embrace.

For example, if everything were possible, then I could wake up tomorrow 10 years younger and 10 inches taller. I'd say, no, not possible. That's not what superposition implies.

However, with infinite possibilities, there are an endless number of things I could do tomorrow. I could do one pushup, I could do two pushups, I could do three pushups, I could do four pushups while wearing my pajamas, I could do zero pushups while wearing a tuxedo, I could legally change my name to Bart Savagewood, I could put my hand here, there, there, there or there. Or here. There is no limit to the number of things I can do tomorrow. It's infinite.

But does that mean I can hold my breath for three hours? Or flap my arms so hard that I can fly? I think not.

So could Jesus physically walk on water? I'll let you decide that one.

Here is another way of thinking about it. There are an infinite amount of numbers between 1 and 2. But that does not mean you can make the No. 2 become No. 1. That's impossible.

So it's a quantum yin yang — in the physical world there are an infinite amount of possibilities without everything being possible.

I'm not interested in a debate about whether *everything* is physically possible, anyways. I have no need to walk through walls as yet, and it really doesn't do much for me right now to think that Jesus actually physically walked on water. As this chapter hopefully demonstrates, perhaps he did. Thanks to the Copenhagen and many worlds interpretations, it's conceivable, and that makes it worthy of consideration.

But what has mattered to me over the past decade is whether people can change the things that matter to them — the normal aspects of their lives — not extraordinarily impractical "walking through walls" or "walking on water" ideas.

Can they alter the course of their addictions? Their diseases? Their mental health?

And the answer has been a resounding yes.

As the late great Dr. Wayne Dyer wrote, *Change Your*

Thoughts — Change Your Life.

That is what superposition permits. Each of us has an infinite number of possibilities that we can experience. It's just that many of us never shift and as a result we keep our consciousness tuned to the same frequency, repeating energy patterns again and again.

I've worked with hundreds of addicts who have been told by supposed experts that they have a disease for which there is no cure. Using superposition, that's completely false. There might be a low probability, but certainly there is a possibility of a cure and it is a disservice to not help them increase the likelihood of success using whatever means available to us.

The definition of 'cure' is to relieve a person of the symptoms of a disease or condition. Striving for Christ Consciousness can do precisely that for whatever ails you.

"Then the blind and the lame came to Him
in the temple, and He healed them."
– Matthew 21:14

People do get healthier in pursuit of higher consciousness. As peace is increased and stress is reduced, physical health tends to improve. But there is no guarantee. Not all addicts will be cured; clearly many health problems are fatal; life itself is a terminal disease; and I have still never met a 379-year-old. Everyone physically dies. Christ Consciousness did not allow Jesus to celebrate his 2015th birthday last year. Living physically long or physically well was never the point.

The Bible is a spiritual book about restoring health to minds and souls, not bodies. In the above verse, replace "Him" with *Christ Consciousness* and "in the temple" with *your mind*, then read it again. Christ helps the spiritually blind see Truth, which heals the mind. When the mind heals, the body often follows … but not always.

Indeed, a great many things are possible, but probably not everything. Jesus stated that very clearly.

"Humanly speaking, it is impossible.
But with God everything is possible."
- Matthew 19:26 (New Living Translation)

Many times when that verse is referenced people take it to mean that, with God, you can do anything in the flesh. While there is some truth to that, the deeper meaning is more essential.

On the human level, there are impossibilities. On the spiritual level, with God, everything is possible.

You are a developing soul. Superposition is about physical tendencies, and those are indeed impacted by consciousness ... but everything is possible *for your soul*.

Reread the definition of 'cure.' What might relieving a person of symptoms include? More hope? Less suffering? Greater feelings of peace, acceptance, forgiveness, gratitude, understanding and meaning?

'Cure' does not mean permanent avoidance of death. Physical healing comes in degrees, via tendencies. But spiritual healing? That's when your soul is perfected, freed from ego. Everything is possible for your soul.

Superposition makes the physical world an interesting place, that's for sure. It is the framework for the illusion (Level 13) and the hologram (Level 16) in which we live. Spiritually it plays the role of incentive. The more you consciously evolve (Level 12), the more you are going to be at peace in your physical world.

Eventually, the higher your consciousness climbs, the less you focus on the physical world anyway.

Superposition is a fertile, versatile playground in which souls move around. There are an infinite amount of things to do in it, all resting in a state of potentials, like a video game just waiting to be turned on and played.

It's consciousness — it's you — that makes reality come to life.

BELIEVING IS SEEING

This *New Eyes* puzzle piece begins with an oft-repeated narrative about a man named Mr. Wright and the power of the mind.

The story may be partially fictionalized, it may be fully factual. Several aspects are based on confirmable accounts, while others are debated or perhaps embellished. Doesn't much matter — it illustrates an important point, one with which most of us are quite familiar.

In the 1950s, Mr. Wright was a cancer patient. He had numerous tumors throughout his body, and his prognosis was grim. Doctors gave him an experimental drug called Krebiozen and suggested that it could be a cure. Mr. Wright responded very well to the medication and the tumors vanished.

A short time later, reports started coming out of the medical community disparaging Krebiozen as useless with no verifiable effects. Mr. Wright's tumors returned and so did he, right back to the hospital for what the doctors told him would be more effective, higher-concentrated doses of Krebiozen.

They deceived him. It was actually distilled water. They felt it would be in his best interest if he believed in the treatment he was getting.

Again, the disease went into remission … until the American Medical Association released an authoritative study discrediting

Krebiozen once and for all. Mr. Wright felt wronged. He no longer had faith in the medicine nor the doctors. His cancer returned and he died soon after.

Mr. Wright's story is detailed by German psychologist Bruno Klopfer in an article entitled "Psychological Variables in Human Cancer," published in 1957 by the Journal of Prospective Techniques.

Think what you will of the plight of Mr. Wright, but I believe we can all relate to that story in one way or another.

Have you ever played golf and stood over a tee shot on a Par-3 hole with a water hazard in front of you? During your backswing, if you are thinking about the lake, where's the ball likely to go? Yep, in the drink.

When an opponent is shooting a free throw, why do the home fans at basketball games attempt to distract him? Because if it changes the shooter's focus, it works. (See "the legend of speedo guy" on YouTube.)

If a teenage boy is going to ask his crush out on a date for the first time, is she more or less likely to say 'yes' if he is confident … or if he seems insecure, with his head down, kicking at the dirt?

Or how about this: There once was a long train that asked to be pulled over a high mountain. None of the big engines were up to the task, but when asked if he could do it, the Little Engine replied, "I think I can."

It was an arduous chore indeed! Struggling to get up a high peak, the Little Engine repeated his mantra to himself, "I think I can, I think I can, I think I can."

Sure enough, he did it. He got the train over the big hill and basked in his success, "I thought I could! I thought I could!

Perhaps you've heard that one?

Although that story is a bald-faced lie (c'mon, no engine can even think, much less talk!), parents have been reading that story to children for nearly a century now. Why? Because it's based in Truth!

There is no historical accuracy to *The Little Engine That Could* ... just tons of anecdotal evidence and plenty of research that supports the moral of the story. There's science behind confidence.

It's called the observer effect.

The way you look at things affects those things.

On the quantum level, this is a sure thing. The observer effect is tied directly to superposition, as it is observation that collapses the wave function of possible outcomes.

"The mind is like a television set with hundreds of channels. Which channel will you turn on?"
- Zen Master Thich Nhat Hanh

"The mind" is the observer and the "hundreds of channels" represent the many possibilities of superposition.

The technical aspects of the observer effect are complicated, with many hieroglyphical equations. For *New Eyes*, we can disregard squiggly lines within math formulas and just address the fun, practical, enlightening aspects of quantum physics. The life-changing, reality-altering therapeutic implications of this science have been kept from the mainstream far too long.

The observer effect started with something called the double-slit experiment. You can see excellent explanations of this on the internet by searching for "dr. quantum double slit experiment" (from the eye-opening *What The Bleep!?: Down The Rabbit Hole* movie) or "the original double slit experiment" (by Veritasium, a superb science site).

Originally conceptualized by Thomas Young in 1801, the double-slit experiment has since been replicated, analyzed, re-analyzed and reformulated in countless numbers of ways, including the Delayed-Choice Experiment and the Quantum Eraser, until it has been proven to be The Way Quantum Things Work. It's also how most (if not all) things throughout the universe work.

And here's how things work, as simply as possible.

Light, which is responsible for everything we see and makes all of our experiences possible, travels as both waves and particles. It is a wave when you are not directly 'observing' it and it becomes a particle when you directly 'observe' it.

A few excerpts from the Dr. Quantum's educational YouTube video:

"The granddaddy of all quantum weirdness (is) the infamous double slit experiment."

"When we throw things (i.e. matter) through two slits we get two bands of hits and with waves we get an interference pattern of many bands."

"The very act of measuring, or observing, which slit (the electron) went through meant it only went through one ... the electron decided to act differently as though it was aware it was being watched."

In other words, similar to time dilation and length contraction in relativity, light and sub-atomic particles behave differently depending upon what you are doing.

Taken to the fullest, as scientists must do, superposition and the observer effect lead our smartest human beings to debate things such as, "Is the moon there when you are not looking at it?" (The answer, in Level 20, may surprise you!)

Now imagine you are standing over a golf ball, facing 50-50 odds of hitting the green. You can't get that lake in front of you out your mind … so you just increased the chances of getting wet.

"All things you ask in prayer, believing, you will receive."
- Matthew 21:22

Splashdown!

I realize you weren't "praying" for a two-shot penalty, but remember — reality isn't what you think it is.

"Praying" is whatever you are focusing your conscious energy upon, not whatever you might say when your hands are folded while you are kneeling beside your bed. When Jesus refers to praying in Matthew 21:22, he is coming from a spiritual place. He is not promising you a big bag of gold or a pony if you ask for it — that would make him Jesus Claus — he is guaranteeing you a sense of spirit if you believe in it.

"Believing" is demonstrated by the degree to which you have practiced certain thoughts, reinforced by Hebb's Law. One momentary idea isn't enough to counteract years of bad swing thoughts. Beliefs are thought patterns. Practice makes perfect. If you practice worrying about hitting a bad golf shot, you become perfect at it. If you practice thinking about how bad your life is, you become depressed. But if you practice gratitude, you receive it.

Ultimately, prayer and belief combine to form an energy field that emanates from each individual consciousness and affects material reality.

"If we consider what matter really is, we now understand it as much more of a mathematical thing ... I think that matter itself is now much more of a mental substance."
- Sir Roger Penrose, mathematical physics professor at the University of Oxford

Penrose is another really smart guy. His comment — "matter is more of a mental substance" — implies that our physical world is basically a mind game, which explains Mr. Wright's story.

Medically, this explains the placebo effect. A placebo is a 'fake' medicine or procedure and a placebo effect is when a treatment using a placebo benefits the patient in a way that cannot be attributed to any medicine or procedure, therefore must be due to the patient's beliefs.

According to the American Cancer Society (from the website www.cancer.org), "The placebo effect even plays a role in mainstream medicine. There's evidence to suggest that what a patient expects about real medicines can influence how the patient feels after the medicine is taken. Even though responses from real drugs aren't typically thought of as placebo effects, some short-term effects are affected by expectations — good ones as well as bad."

This is *not* to say that we physically cause diseases and achieve cures with our minds, although that is possible. What the observer effect clearly indicates is that there is an *influence* involved, that you can *influence* the outcome of a disease (or a golf shot or job interview, etc.) by what's going through your mind.

Confidence matters. Belief matters. Expectation matters. Imagination matters. Because as Penrose suggested, matter is really just a form of confidence, belief, expectation and imagination.

"With imagination," says imaginary philosopher SpongeBob SquarePants, "I can be anything I want." And that's pretty close to the Truth.

Having worked with thousands of opioid addicted clients, this is eminently clear. If a client believes what he has been told far too often — that he has an incurable disease and that he is likely to relapse because statistics demonstrate that — then that is precisely what tends to happen.

Let's say that current data indicate that 90 percent of addicts nationwide relapse within a year; what is that also saying? That 10 percent do not. What number is the professional going to focus on? The 90 percent or the 10?

I have been flabbergasted to witness that most in the field of addiction treatment focus on the 90 … and the addicts typically buy it.

"I think I can't, I think I can't."

When relapse happens, the 'experts' can then say, "See, I told you so."

And the client can respond, "I guess you were right."

Gee, thanks for the help ...

Every addict faces an infinite amount of potential futures. They could be sober for a year. They could use once. Or twice. Or three times a day, but not in July. They could overdose. They could substitute with another drug. They could never use again.

The list goes on and on, and there is a certain probability associated with the occurrence of each.

This is where the butterfly effect comes into play, as it only takes a small shift in initial conditions to dramatically affect outcomes. If it is emphasized to a rehabilitating group that 10 percent of people in recovery are succeeding and conscious attention is shifted toward the reasons for their success, they are more likely to find themselves making progress as well. What might have been a relapse just turned into sobriety.

A wide array of studies have illustrated the "what you believe, you receive" concept, including being able to improve muscle strength by participating in imaginary exercises … to affect a random number generator by meditating on certain digits … and to increase the likelihood of making a putt or free throw by displaying confidence in yourself, as (ego alert!) my senior project at Allegheny College demonstrated with statistical significance.

In sports this is sometimes called 'the zone' where an athlete feels as if he cannot miss a shot. Physical abilities can only take you so far, but those with the extra gear in their heads and hearts are most likely to take it to a higher level.

Ask any poker player if there is something to having a 'hot hand' and most will say yes. Even the slightest mental edge typically gives someone an advantage in any competition.

There are studies that discount phenomena such as 'the zone' and 'hot hand,' though the observer effect may play a role in that as well. Researchers themselves can influence the outcomes of experiments.

Even Jesus wasn't able to perform miracles in front of cynics.

"He did not do many mighty works there because of their unbelief."
- Matthew 13:58

Taoists say that the pathway to Truth runs through you. In the Kalama Sutta, Buddha challenges you to judge Truth for yourself. So trust your own experience. Science only takes us so far, anyway (Level 20).

Virtually every client I work with understands that, on a deep level, the way they look at things affects those things. And virtually every one of them stops short of utilizing that concept to the fullest because of fear, doubt and cynicism.

Skeptics will say that anything approximating the New Age "you create your own reality" maxim does great harm to people who have been victimized, but it does *greater* harm not to let people pursue their own Truth. Cynics see what they see through their own paradigm, as do believers.

Naysayers don't see it *specifically because* they don't believe it, thus supporting the "Believing Is Seeing" concept. You must first *believe* in order to *see* many things. Like golf shots, first dates, disease remission and the presence of God. The emphasis must be on *believing*. Seeing comes later, if necessary, but belief is primary. It's the essence of the observer effect.

"Blessed are those who have not seen and yet have believed."
- John 20:29

Levels 8 and 9 are the scientific core for why virtually every major spiritual philosophy refers to reality as a mirror (Level 14). Superpositional possibilities collapse based upon the way you are looking at things, providing a reflection for you to see what you are believing.

This is otherwise known as *logical,* and we know this instinctively.

Say you receive a cancer diagnosis and your doctor gives you a 50-50 probability for survival. Your first reaction is the same as most everybody's … you think you are going to die. So you spend the next year thinking about death.

In your gut, what do you suppose happens to that 50-50 probability? Of course it shifts in the direction of dying. Like Schrödinger's Cat from Level 8, you open the probability box … and you find yourself in a wooden box.

But what about the alternative? What if you hear the 50-50 diagnosis and then make a commitment with all of your mind, body and soul that you are going to live? And you spend the next year doing precisely that, pursuing mental, physical and spiritual ways to heal?

In your gut, what do you suppose happens to that 50-50 probability? Of course it shifts in the direction of healing. You open Schrödinger's box and you are a cool cat let out of the bag.

Are either the pessimistic or optimistic scenarios guarantees? No! God plays dice with the universe, remember. The 'I'm going to die' patient might lower survival odds to 25 percent, while the 'I'm going to live' patient might increase hers to 75 percent. There will still be pessimists who live and optimists who die. No one is at fault for dying and no one gets all the credit for living.

But, hello! If the odds changed at all because the mind affects the body, that is of major importance … and should always be told to every patient in every physician's office everywhere. Confidence, belief, expectation and imagination matter. If you can see it in your mind's eye, you increase the likelihood of it happening. With consciousness, you *influence* the odds of physical outcomes.

So why does God play dice? Why do only some optimists live, while others die? Why do bad things happen to good people?

Because the observer effect only plays a secondary effect on the body. Its true, deeper application is for the soul.

"Whatever was written in the past
was all written for our instruction."
- Romans 15:4

The physical world is indeed impacted by the combination of superposition and the observer effect, but the intended purpose is definitely NOT to improve your golf game. Events happen to give opportunities for our souls to develop. The Holy Grail is not winning a championship or making that first million or being elected president, it's establishing Christ Consciousness.

"Do you not realize about yourselves that Jesus Christ is in you?"
- 2 Corinthians 13:5

Jesus Christ is in you. Pretty sure Apostle Paul did not mean that literally.

That's because he meant it spiritually.

It's in the world of consciousness that superposition and the observer effect really apply, the non-physical world of souls — which is what you really are.

I might heal myself from addiction or disease or become a better athlete through belief, but that's not the ultimate purpose of life (Levels 11, 12, 33). When you believe something, while it manifests into physical form through superposition according to certain percentages or potentials, there are no guarantees. However, in the process of experiencing those physical things with which God plays dice, we learn something much more valuable about ourselves.

We learn patience. We learn hope. We learn courage. We learn persistence. We learn compassion. We learn discipline. We learn faith. We learn love.

We learn that *Christ is in us*.

No dice there. That's a 100 percent guarantee.

Like falling in love, there's no need for scientific evidence when you experience that type of higher consciousness.

"I can do all things through Christ who strengthens me."
- Philippians 4:13

Some physical things.
All spiritual things.

EVERYTHING IS CONNECTED

Good Vibrations.

It's such a relatable experience that it became a No. 1 song by two different music groups in two different generations.

There's the Beach Boys version that topped Billboard in 1966:

"I, I love the colorful clothes she wears
And the way the sunlight plays upon her hair
I hear the sound of a gentle word
On the wind that lifts her perfume through the air
I'm pickin' up good vibrations
She's giving me excitations
I'm picking up good vibrations ..."

And 25 years later, we had Marky Mark and the Funky Bunch's chart-topping hit:

"I command you to dance
I wanna see motivation
So come on now feel the vibration
It's such a good vibration
Come on come on come on
It's such a sweet sensation
Feel it feel it"

Can you feel it? I'll break it down for you.

Good Vibrations are very, very real. Of course, so are Bad Vibrations. And Everywhere In Between Vibrations.

Remember String Theory? Vibrations make up everything in the universe. Brian Wilson and Mark Wahlberg, meet Albert Einstein and Max Planck. All of you got it right.

Whether it is described by singers or scientists, poets or prophets, it is the same thing. Everything is energy, and we are all exchanging that energy all the time.

A significant part of why the world is an illusion happens to also be the most understandable reason. It's why we love songs like *Good Vibrations* and *Good Vibrations*. We get it. Deep down, we really get it. Because we feel it all the time.

Even though we cannot see it, there is something connecting us. We get vibes from each other.

If you have ever been inside a stadium during a big sporting event, you can feel it. Players all say they feed off the energy of the crowd. Teams sometimes rally or choke based upon the vibe running through the field and the stands, a perfect storm of collective observers influencing the field of superposition.

If you are in a movie theater during a particularly tense scene, you can feel it. After watching *The Silence of the Lambs* on opening night and experiencing such a shared common bond with everyone who was there, I thought group therapy was warranted afterward. The collective vibe was intense. (All these years later I can't watch Buffalo Bills football games without getting creeped out.)

We all know that fun-loving groomsmen and a dancing bride set the tone for a great party at a wedding reception, but what if the deejay is lame and that makes the groom grumpy? You can tell as soon as you walk into the party hall.

And have you ever been in a hospital? Is there a different vibe in the air in the maternity ward than there is in the

Emergency Room? Of course there is.

Try calming a fussy infant when you are stressed. Anyone who has been around a baby knows that they respond to your mood, and in return they can feel good vibrations. It's the same with animals and plants. Most every pet lover or green thumb gets a sweet sensation when around the objects of their affection.

Wilson, one of the founders of the Beach Boys, said that the inspiration for their hit song was a canine connection that came from his mother.

"She told me about dogs that would bark at people and then not bark at others," he said, "that a dog would pick up vibrations from these people that you can't see, but you can feel."

We all know this is true based upon experience, but there is a science behind all of this energetic interconnectivity.

It's called entanglement.

Wilson said the idea of vibrations "scared" him when he was a child, which is ironic, because Einstein called the science of vibrations "spooky" as well!

Erwin Schrödinger called entanglement "*the* characteristic trait of quantum mechanics, the one that enforces its entire departure from classical lines of thought." (One might say a good definition of *New Eyes* is "a departure from classical lines of thought.")

So what exactly is entanglement?

Simply put, it's when two things are linked together in such a way that when one moves, so does the other … simultaneously.

Imagine this: Wherever you are in the world reading this, if I were to raise my hand right now, is there any way you could know to also raise yours? Like, instantly? One would think not.

Except that's what happens in the lab with elementary particles that are energetically paired with each other. When one spins, the other does so at the exact same time, no matter how far apart they are.

According to conventional physics, there is no possible way a message or signal can be sent from one particle to the other without some passage of time, as travel even over a short amount of space has to take a nanosecond or two.

"Spukhafte Fernwirkung!" declared Einstein.

Spooky action at a distance.

It is bizarre behavior, to say the least. Particles become inextricably linked, as there is an immediate, permanent connection between them.

French physicist Alain Aspect was able to confirm entanglement in 1982, showing subatomic particles instantaneously communicating with each other regardless of the distance separating them. Whether it is 10 millimeters, 10 miles or 10 light years, particles are able to send information of some kind to each other immediately.

But surely this is limited to just the quantum world, you say? Nope. Scientists have been feverishly studying entanglement for decades and it keeps creeping up from the micro world into our macro world. Quantum physicists have performed experiments that demonstrate entanglement between diamond crystals that are large enough to be seen with the naked eye.

One researcher, Xian-Min Jin of the Centre for Quantum Technologies, said that such results offer "a glimpse into the transition between the quantum and classical realms."

Another contemporary physicist, Andrew Cleland from the University of California at Santa Barbara, called the experimental evidence "clear and convincing" that entanglement occurs in our macro world.

But you already knew this … if you've been to a football game … or to a wedding reception or hospital … or held a baby … or had a pet … you know, if you have been alive.

There is clear and convincing evidence that energy connects

us, instantaneously and permanently. Knowing this, and applying this with *New Eyes*, can change your world.

In Level 4 we established that we are all vessels of light, now with this level we are seeing how those vessels can exchange light during each and every moment of our lives. It supports the potential of prayer, it backs up the power of compassion, it can help explain inexplicable mood swings and it gives credibility to superstitious baseball teams wearing 'rally caps' in the dugout.

It also would explain how someone like Jesus could heal people using energy as he distributed the Holy Spirit to believers via entangled particles … and how Christ Consciousness can impact you right now, merely by connecting to it.

In order to best understand entanglement and all of its implications, it helps to understand the nature of reality and the concept of oneness by considering an example to visualize. David Bohm, who in Level 2 noted an "unbroken wholeness" of the universe, came up with an excellent illustration to describe our entangled reality.

Imagine two television monitors, A and B, both displaying goldfish — Fish A from the front and Fish B from the side. When Fish A turns to the right so does Fish B, and now you are looking at the side of A and the front of B. Then when A turns back to its original position, so does B. This continues on and on, with B moving simultaneously every time A moves, and in a corresponding direction.

Something fishy is going on here ... Is Fish B receiving some sort of mysterious, instantaneous signal from Fish A? Are A and B reading each other's three-celled brains?

Or could there be a much simpler solution? Indeed there is.

There were two independent cameras both viewing the *same fish* from different angles, each displaying the images it captured on different monitors. So of course when A moved in one direction B did as well, being that it was just one fish. It's not that hard to transmit messages between two things when it is actually one thing. (Your brain does this all the time, firing entangled messages around in a coordinated and instantaneous fashion.)

Bohm's goldfish example is a revolutionary concept when applied to the world we live in. Reality is just ONE THING and we are all viewing that ONE THING from different perspectives!

Imagine a dozen monitors on the same fish, all showing Goldilocks from a different angle. When you walk into that room and see all those screens, it would take a lot longer to realize that it was the same fish, right? Now imagine seven billion cameras and seven billion monitors! No way you would ever be able to tell that it was the same fish, with each camera focusing on a microscopic part of one scale. It would be way too much to process.

That's our world. Seven billion of us all viewing reality from seven billion different angles and many trying to convince others that their perspective is the correct one. You know, sort of like saying that uno is more correct than eins.

Fact is we all come from the same universal consciousness, the same source energy, and we are all variations of that same energy, different aspects of consciousness.

Put another way, we are all *ONE*. Just like all the great spiritual philosophies say. Entanglement is ultimately the science of that oneness, which all of the most prominent religions feature within their doctrines.

In Buddhism there is a concept called esho funi — which links together 'e' for environment and 'sho' for life and calls them 'funi' or inseparable. The environment and life are inseparable. Another way of defining funi is 'two but not two.' We think things are separate from each other ('two'), but in reality they are *ONE* ('not two').

In Hinduism there is a proverb from a sacred text that says, "The moon is one, but on agitated water it produces many reflections. Similarly ultimate reality is *ONE*, yet it appears to be many in a mind agitated by thoughts."

The most important belief in Islam is Tawhid, which emphasizes that God is *ONE* and that everything in existence originates from that *ONE* source.

Jesus says the same thing in Mark 12. After being asked "Which commandment is the most important of all?" he answers in verse 29, "The most important is, 'Hear, O Israel: The Lord our God, the Lord is *ONE*.'"

That is Jesus quoting the Old Testament and Judaism's Torah, from Deuteronomy 6:4, which says, "Hear Israel, the Lord is our God, the Lord is *ONE*."

Unity is also a fundamental tenet of Taoism, in that there is no separation from nature and its observers. "These all emerged from oneness," it says in Chapter 39 of the Tao Te Ching.

Clearly a theme has emerged. You may interpret any of the above in whatever way you prefer, but it is all ONE with *New Eyes*.

"The oneness of God means that all that exists, all forces and all powers, are an expression of a greater, transcendent Unity that is the source of their existence as well as the source of any power or influence they seem to exert within existence."
- Jewish author Rabbi Shimon Apisdorf

Science is showing us that reality is *ONE*. Spirituality is showing us that God is *ONE*.

I don't care what you call it — God, Universe, Reality, Source — it's all transcendental unity. It's all the same goldfish. We are all part of the same fishbowl. We are all *ONE*, which explains entanglement perfectly. Like different neurons in a human brain, seemingly separate but actually acting in synchronicity.

Comprehending this affords a great many applications, from helping sports teams rally to being a dog whisperer to tackling some of the big questions of religion.

Author F. Scott Fitzgerald said that "the test of a first rate intelligence is the ability to hold two opposed ideas in the mind at the same time, and still retain the ability to function." Understanding entanglement can certainly facilitate first-rate intelligence because it helps answer some long debated questions, things like the Trinity and the apparent incompatibility between monotheism and polytheism.

What is the chemical composition of water? H_2O. What is the chemical composition of ice? H_2O. What is the chemical composition of steam? H_2O.

H_2O is 'one thing' in three different forms — liquid, solid and gas.

The Trinity — the Father, the Son, the Holy Spirit — is the same thing in different forms as well. God is one thing (monotheism), manifested in many forms (polytheism), encompassing the entire universe (pantheism) while including no thing (atheism).

Those are mystical questions. As a counselor, I often face practical questions, such as, "Why do I get so nervous around other people?" and "My daughter seems depressed, how can I help her?" and "Is it possible to move past this grief since my father died?"

There are many therapeutic approaches to those situations, but what I have found to be the most effective is when clients learn how science and spirituality work together to produce a solution for them.

Using entanglement as a foundation, many clients have come to understand that they *absorb* the energy of other people, often parroting symptoms of Bipolar Disorder with up-and-down mood swings. When left to themselves, they are at peace, but feeling the vast array of emotions coming through energetic interconnectivity throws them for a loop.

"Above all else, guard your heart."
- Proverbs 4:23

We have to learn how to protect ourselves from the negative energy of others. Failure to do so leaves us vulnerable to energy thieves.

"Be on guard against the world. Prepare yourselves with great strength, so the robbers can't find a way to get to you."
- Gospel of Thomas

Set up a strong defense, because others can steal your spirit.

"Do not be anxious, which of you by being anxious
can add a single hour to his span of life?"
- Matthew 6:25

Family members and friends often agonize over how to help struggling loved ones, and they all typically agree that worrying about their loved ones never does any good. That's because worry is felt as negative energy and helps no one, typically only causing pain for the worrier. Accordingly, the idea of sending good vibrations in someone's direction clearly makes more sense. Prayer has been shown to bring peace to both the giver and receiver.

As for death, as you will see in the spiritual levels, the separation between this realm and the next is also merely an illusion. Life and death are also part of Oneness.

"Whoever discovers the interpretation
of these sayings will not taste death."
- Gospel of Thomas

Third grade and fourth grade are different, but really they are just a part of the same educational system called elementary school, differing only by degree. Similarly, death is merely 'graduation' from this life, a transition of your soul to the next part of the same system. The soul is the same here as it is there, and you are energetically connected to souls that are currently there just as you are here.

You live in a system of Oneness. All of the science points to it, as well as all of the spiritual teachings. There is an energy that runs through it, a universal force that unites us all.

That force is with you.

"IT'S GOTTA BE MORE THAN THIS"

Tom Brady is a champion in my book.

Not for winning football games, but for one moment of sincerity and vulnerability that perfectly captures the intention of *New Eyes*.

For 24 years, I followed the National Football League as a sportswriter covering the Pittsburgh Steelers. My first season as a columnist was Bill Cowher's first as their head coach. I was fortunate enough to attend four Super Bowls that the Steelers played in, two of which they won.

Along the way, perhaps the most impactful moment of my journalism career occurred while Brady … was giving a TV interview.

Brady, as most every NFL fan knows, burst onto the scene in 2001 as a quarterback for the New England Patriots. That was at a time in my life when I needed the Steelers to win a Super Bowl in order to heal an old emotional wound of mine. As a child living in Pittsburgh during the 1970s, I was a passionate fan of the Los Angeles Rams. In sixth grade my Rams played the mighty Steelers, already winners of three Lombardi Trophies that decade, in Super Bowl XIV.

Amid all the Steelers' Black-and-Gold paraphernalia throughout Sloan Elementary School, my teacher let me decorate a corner with the Rams' Blue-and-Gold. I hung up a Pat Haden poster and a Vince Ferragamo picture. I wore a Rams jacket just like the Jets version that Kevin Arnold rocked in *Wonder Years*. And I spent hype week before the game talking like Joe Namath before Super Bowl III, guaranteeing victory for the underdogs.

Oh, the folly of youth.

Do you have any idea what it's like to be 11 years old and have no defense against being teased by first graders? I mean, little kids fresh out of kindergarten were calling me 'loser' the day after the Rams lost that one to the Steelers. To each taunt I defiantly … whimpered like a wounded kitten.

Fast-forward 22 years to early 2002, long after I had wisely converted to being a Steelers fan in college (if you can't beat 'em, join 'em) and a full 10 years into my career as a sportswriter. As a journalist you do not root for outcomes, but tell that to the juvenile boy inside of me who was desperate to balance a little football karma by being present when the Steelers won the Super Bowl.

After a decade of near misses in the '90s — Pittsburgh had lost two AFC Championship Games and one Super Bowl in that time — the Steelers were on the verge of another shot at the crown as hosts of the conference title game in January of '02.

Enter: Tom Brady. Exit: Steelers.

Ever present: My childhood demons.

Three years later the same scenario played out all over again and blah blah blah to heck with not being biased I now officially hated Tom Brady.

By the time the Patriots had claimed their third Lombardi Trophy in four years, I was suffering from PTSBD (Post Traumatic Super Bowl Disorder) and my resentment of Thomas Edward Patrick Brady, Jr. was at a fever pitch. I used to grumble his name 'TomBrady' as if it were an eight-letter word (which is *twice* as bad as a four-letter word, grumble grumble).

Fortunately I had started transitioning out of my career as a writer and into counseling, so I had already begun my own journey of trying to liberate myself from the poisonous clutches of the ego. Buddha and his idea of detachment were quite helpful in that process, but dang that TomBrady was making it difficult!

For a few years I did what every normal person would do, I bought a lot of Red Sox gear and became a Boston baseball fan as tangential therapy. It was my 'Opposite' strategy, borrowed from neurotic sitcom character George Costanza, figuring if I could root for a Boston team my loathing of TomBrady would subside. (Didn't work.)

Just as I was reaching my most pathetic *Seinfeldian* self, that's when it happened.

I was watching TomBrady give an interview on *60 Minutes* in 2005 and he was asked by Steve Kroft what he had learned about himself.

"Why do I have three Super Bowl rings, and still think there's something greater out there for me?" he said. "God, it's gotta be more than this. I mean this can't be what it's all cracked up to be. … What else is there for me?"

It's. Gotta. Be. More. Than. This.

Those words are now tattooed on my heart, a permanent reminder to stay focused on what really matters in life.

Thanks, Tom Terrific!

Here we have The Golden Boy, while living the quintessential American Dream, suggesting that he felt a void inside. *It's gotta be more than this.* Such a sincere, authentic moment, more valuable than any touchdown pass that he has ever thrown.

A switch flipped inside of me. It all crystallized. Somewhere deep in my soul, I knew then I would be writing this book one day.

Green Bay quarterback Aaron Rodgers expressed similar

sentiments after the Packers won Super Bowl XLV, noting that he felt something was missing.

"I'm sitting there with a semi-empty feeling because I accomplished everything I wanted to do since I was a kid, and I kind of had a moment," said Rodgers, noting what inspired him to take part in a movement called *Raise Hope for Congo*. "I said to myself, 'Is this it? Is there more to life than this?'"

Brady: "It's gotta be more than this."

Rodgers: "Is there more to life than this?"

New Eyes: There is much more to life than this.

Among the thousands of questions I addressed to athletes during my career, I never asked this one: "Have you ever read Leo Tolstoy?"

No, not *War and Peace*, that's way too long … *The Death of Ivan Ilych*, which makes its point with 1,000 fewer pages.

In the book, Ilych lives a good life — as an intelligent and accomplished lawyer with a typical family — but when he faces his own mortality he experiences an emotional breakdown. He ultimately asks: "What if my whole life has really been wrong?"

It's a heartfelt existential question, expressed in the same spirit as Brady and Rodgers.

After hearing his "gotta be more" statement, Kroft then asked Brady, "What's the answer?"

Brady replied, "I wish I knew. I wish I knew."

Rumi knew!

In his 13th Century discourse *It Is What It Is*, the Muslim poet provided the answer for all of us.

"There is one thing in this world that must never be forgotten. If you were to forget all else, but did not forget that, then you would have no reason to worry. But if you performed and remembered everything else, yet forgot that one thing, then you would have done nothing whatsoever.

"It is just as if a king sent you to the country to carry out a specific task. If you go and accomplish a hundred other tasks, but do not perform that particular task, then it is as though you performed nothing at all. So, everyone comes into this world for a particular task, and that is their purpose. If they do not perform it, then they will have done nothing."

We human beings are so very good at accomplishing those hundred other tasks.

We pursue jobs. We build roads. We make money. We buy cars. We get married. We have children. We get new hairstyles. We tweet. We sing songs. We write books. We fight wars. We win Super Bowls. (Well, not the 1979 Rams, grumble grumble.)

All of that worthless, according to Rumi, unless you perform that one specific task. You must overcome the temporary False Self of the ego world and come to understand your True Self as a spiritual being.

Gnōthi Seauton.

Know thyself.

"You must be born again."
- John 3:7

You are born once in the flesh. You must be born a second time in spirit.

You are not white, nor black. You are not young, nor old. You are not Republican, nor Democrat. You are not thin, nor fat. You are not straight, nor gay. You are not a Super Bowl winner, nor a loser. All of that, and more, is ego.

Believing that you are anything but a soul is a case of mistaken identity, which Rumi declared was the origin of pain for anyone who is emotionally struggling: "They do not know their own self."

The one task we must perform requires finding and filling the Holy Grail within ourselves. With lower consciousness, we strive to fill ourselves with physical experiences. With higher consciousness, we come to know our True Selves and are born again, filled with *the light*. It is everyone's quest, whether they know it or not.

Buddha won the equivalent of a dozen Super Bowls in his days as a wealthy prince, but he was not fulfilled until he became enlightened. Despite all of his successes, Brady revealed that he felt the same inner void that we all do at some point in our lives when he said, "It's gotta be more than this."

Whether it is money, championships, possessions, power, food, drugs or alcohol, we all spend much of our lives trying to fill that void with something in the flesh, to no avail. Succeeding at accomplishing earthly goals is, as Buddha emphasized, temporary at best.

Influential psychiatrist Carl Jung referred to such physical cravings as indicative of a "spiritual thirst of our being for wholeness."

As Brady, Rodgers and Jung suggested and as all of the prophets teach, that search for wholeness does not come with physical fulfillment.

A millennium ago there was another phrase that exemplified this. Coming after the time of Classical Antiquity in which *nunc est bibendum* was the theme — 'now is the time to drink' — the Dark Ages had a more somber motto.

Memento Mori.

Remember your mortality.

Or ... you are going to die!

As legend has it, the more enlightened kings and queens of that era would appoint a court jester to remind them of their mortality on a daily basis, lest their lust for physical power get the best of them. Some royalty knew that being nicer to their subjects would spare them a revolt and having their heads served on a plate, while others were more aware that there might be an afterlife in which they would meet their Maker.

Either way, it's a Truth that haunted Ivan Ilych and affects us all today.

We are all going to die.

The first 10 Levels of *New Eyes* were primarily concerned with explaining the laws of the physical world, which clearly demonstrate that the most vital force in the universe is consciousness — for without it, there is no universe.

And yet, many of us live most of our lives without actively trying to develop consciousness. Ignorance of our essential nature leads to philosophies such as Absurdism, which basically states that *life is absurd* because human beings seek meaning when they are inherently incapable of finding it.

The Absurdist concept is symbolized by the story of Sisyphus.

In Greek mythology, Sisyphus was punished for his deceitfulness by being forced to push a heavy boulder up a hill, which would then roll back down the hill, and he had to repeat this action throughout the rest of time. As such, Sisyphus spent eternity pursuing useless efforts and experiencing unending frustration.

If you look closely, you can see yourself in that Sisyphean mirror. That's us, spending our whole lives doing things and accumulating stuff and then dying. For what physical purpose? You can't take it with you.

Oh sure, you say, "But what about the kids? How about future generations? Don't they benefit from what we are doing now?"

Here's a little story I like to tell. There once was a husband and a wife and their two happy children, one boy and one girl, who all lived in a little house on a prairie during the 1850s. The mom and dad worked really hard to give their kids a chance to grow up and experience a better life, which they did. The boy became a rich doctor and the girl married a rich doctor. They each had a few kids of their own and at Christmas they all gathered at their grandparents house for a joyous and memorable occasion.

Now they are all dead.

Memento Mori!

I don't care how good you have it, how wonderful of a life you have built, it is all going to be taken away from you. And it will be taken away from your children, grandchildren, great-grandchildren, great-great-grandchildren, etc.

It's really Absurd, when you think about it.

You say you want to keep evolving humanity? News flash — we are ALL doomed. Humanity schmanity. Do you know what scientists predict will happen in about five billion years? The sun will grow in size, burn up planet earth, then collapse into a white dwarf and our corner of the solar system will freeze into a snowball.

Good times, good times.

You say, "But wait, we will learn how to travel to other galaxies and populate their solar system by then …"

First of all, good luck with that. Secondly, ever hear of the *Big Crunch*? You may populate whatever distant planet you wish, we're all gonna be reverse Big Banged in the end. Will the last one to leave the universe please turn off the lights? Oh, too late — the light is putting itself out.

Even the universe cannot escape Memento Mori, which makes Absurdism spot on: there is no way for a human being to fulfill himself. Good thing we are not human beings!

"We are not human beings having a spiritual experience.
We are spiritual beings having a human experience."
- French philosopher Pierre Teilhard de Chardin

Put another way, Tom Brady is not a guy who might seek a soulful experience, he is a soul having a Tom Brady experience.

As Brady told Kroft, "I love playing football, and I love being a quarterback for this team, but, at the same time, I think there's a lot of other parts about me that I'm trying to find."

He's trying to find Unity Consciousness. We all are. We're wired to do so. And that's accomplished by you, the soul.

How to find your True Self? How to be born again?

Rule No. 1: You must stop sinning.

Rule No. 2: Learn what it really means to sin.

The Bible has been translated, in one way or another, countless times. A few things have been lost in translation, including what a sin really is.

The original Hebrew Bible was first written in Greek, and the primary Greek word for sin is *hamartia*, which is an archery term for 'missing the mark.'

When an archer is shooting an arrow but does not hit the bullseye, it is because his perception was off — he missed the mark due to his misperception. That is sinning, aiming at the wrong spot.

This is an extremely important point for the rest of this book. You are aiming at the wrong spot if you think you are your body, if you set your sights on the physical world and neglect the spiritual. That's it. That's sinning.

Recall Levels 8 and 9. Superposition is a world of infinite possibilities and the observer collapses the wave function or 'selects' one of those possibilities on a probability basis, based upon the way you are perceiving it.

If you believe yourself to be a physical being, first and foremost, you will have one set of experiences. If you understand that you are actually a spiritual being, you will have another set of experiences.

This is easily demonstrated. An addict who has lived a difficult life due to many childhood traumas will experience a shift toward abstinence and recovery when she discovers her True Self. It takes all the pressure off when you learn that you have not been hurt, that you do not need to feel shame or guilt, that everything is fair, that we are all learning the same Truths. With new insights, your feelings and therefore behaviors and experiences automatically change.

I see this happen with clients regularly, as virtues such as forgiveness and mercy and wisdom and courage greatly reduce cravings for addictive substances. Soul attributes such as hope, remember, have been shown to produce endorphins, an opiate-like substance in the brain. It's why pursuing a 'higher power' works so well in Alcoholics Anonymous, because a spiritual connection affects an alcoholic's mood and thereby affects his drinking behavior. But when an alcoholic thinks of his life as absurd due to its profound lack of meaning? Bartender, he'll have another.

Such soulful attributes have also helped Tom Brady win several Super Bowls. He is clearly hopeful, courageous, disciplined and persistent with excellent leadership qualities — all fruits of the spirit. Imagine if he had the same physical skill set but played with hopelessness, fear, recklessness and quit every time the going got tough. Those are not attractive qualities in any quarterback or any man, so as a hopeless, fearful quitter he probably wouldn't have any Super Bowl rings … nor would he have been allowed to put a diamond ring on the finger of his supermodel wife. (Hi Gisele!)

Another definition of hamartia is 'a tragic flaw.' Rumi would say that it is a tragedy for people to go through their whole lives without learning who or what they really are, a tragic misperception that leads to volatile behaviors counter to one's peaceful inner nature.

This is an essential puzzle piece for *New Eyes*. Sinning has very little to do with behaviors — it has everything to do with misperceiving reality. Your behaviors come from your perceptions, or the way you perceive the world. If you want to change your behaviors, you must change your perceptions.

In fact, the only way to effectively and permanently change any behavior is through an evolution of consciousness (Level 12). In the original Greek Bible, the word for repentance is *metanoia*, which means 'a change of mind.' If you are sinning you are misperceiving, but when you repent you have changed your mind.

Life is not about behaviors or bodies, it's about consciousness. When you see yourself as physical first, as ego, you will judge behaviors by mere appearances and will stay in the dark. But when you see yourself as a soul, you can see the spirit light of Christ and will renew your life with your mind.

That's the meaning of life, and there is nothing absurd about it.

Thanks to Tom Brady's moment of sincerity, I started pursuing a spiritual perspective on life with a passion. I stopped being Sisyphus and letting NFL boulders knock me down. I had been sinning, missing the mark by overemphasizing materialism. I had been suffering not because my teams had lost, but because of jealousy and resentment. I wanted to win my own Super Bowl, a championship that is claimed within my soul.

Over the past decade, winning and losing have become

balancing features of the physical world for me, just like everything else in the flesh. There are highs and lows to material life, but everything is a spiritual opportunity. We can always grow our souls. Winning is a chance to practice gratitude and humility, while losing gives you a reason to be respectful and keep things in perspective.

Gold medals are great. Medals of honor are greater.

"Whoever loves money never has enough; whoever loves wealth is never satisfied with their income. This too is meaningless."
- Ecclesiastes 5:10

Physical success is meaningless. It makes the ego happy, but it is temporary and ultimately empty. Hollow.

Brady: "It's gotta be more than this."

Rodgers: "Is there more to life than this?"

"What good is it for someone to gain the whole world, yet forfeit their soul?"
- Mark 8:36

You cannot take money nor trophies nor anything physical with you. Far better to make spiritual progress.

Once I started to shift my perspective, I released myself of negative perceptions. Instead of being resentful of Brady, different thoughts started to emerge, more peaceful thoughts such as "I respect that guy's talent" and "It is only a game, after all."

It worked. I felt more connected. I felt more spirit, less ego. By the time the Steelers won the Super Bowl the very next season, my silly childhood demons had vanished.

"In all thy works remember thy last end and thou shalt never sin."
- Ecclesiasticus 7:40

That apocryphal verse is the essence of Memento Mori. When you remain mindful of your pending death, you will not miss the mark. You will always perceive yourself as a spiritual being having a human experience.

You can throw a football to wide receivers, but the most meaningful target is aiming for your soul.

THE MIND GAME

IT has long been a great debate: What's the meaning of life?

An eternal question with an elusive answer.

Being able to derive a satisfactory response to that inquiry requires a careful examination of those words. Where are you putting the emphasis in that sentence?

What's the MEANING of life?

Or what's the meaning of LIFE?

It all depends upon the meaning of life ... what you *mean* by life ... or how life is defined.

Is life the outer world, one that includes matter and bodies and all physical things? Or is life the inner world, featuring consciousness and soul and all things non-physical?

Believing that life is the former is a vote for ego and is a cause for all the war, all the separation and all the suffering in the world.

Believing that life is the latter is a vote for spirit and is the reason for peace, unity and healing.

The first third of this book is mostly dedicated to science, an emphasis on physical laws that operate in our universe. You can use such science to enhance your physical world, to improve your health, to fatten your wallet or sharpen your athletic skills. Indeed, you can get financially rich by successfully combining Hebb's Law and superposition with the observer effect while paying careful attention to entanglement.

But most of us know already that improving your golf game is not the meaning of life.

Death will have the final say over your body, and the physical laws that were once so important, that we used to promote wellness in our physical lives, will be rendered meaningless. Whatever you achieved or acquired on earth stays here, you cannot take it with you.

Thankfully, life isn't about that outer world. That would be depressing. And Absurd.

But that doesn't mean there is no purpose to those physical laws, not by a long shot. The physical world is the canvas upon which consciousness can be displayed. While the paint makes the painting, where would it be without the canvas? (In a bucket somewhere, unused.) Conscious energy requires physical laws so that souls can have a physical experience.

It says in *A Course in Miracles* that "what you use the body for, it will become to you."

If you use it with physical intent, if you think that's the meaning of life, then the final purpose of the body is as a vehicle for death. But if you use the body with spiritual intent, for the development of the soul, it is an altogether different thing and you can have eternal life.

A Course in Miracles also states that "we can change the purpose that the body will obey by changing what we think that it is for."

We can shift from believing the body to be for physical purposes toward understanding that it is a spiritual vessel.

The next 11 Levels will move us in that direction, to help bring clarity to what the purpose of the body really is. The middle portion of this book still features plenty of science, but the emphasis will shift more towards concepts and ideas that will facilitate the ultimate goal, the reaching of the type of higher consciousness that is explored over the final 11 Levels.

Throughout these pages, *New Eyes* transitions its focus from body to mind to spirit. The link between the body and the spirit is indeed the mind — it determines what you use the body for, a tool for expanding consciousness and pumping life into the soul.

In the Gnostic Gospel of Mary, Jesus was asked by Mary Magdalene about seeing him in this physical world. Jesus, whose perspective was always spirit-focused, answered:

"Congratulations to you for not wavering at the sight of me.
For where the mind is, there is the treasure."

Jesus was praising Mary for not seeing him as flesh, for not wavering from the Truth that he was a spirit-filled soul. With that, Mary received the treasure of Christ.

Mary then inquired how one sees the "vision" in this world, with the soul or the spirit? Jesus replied:

"He does not see through the soul nor through the spirit,
but the mind that is between the two."

To Jesus, the body that we see as physical is actually an energetic vessel that needs to be linked to the Holy Spirit, via the mind. The purpose of the body (i.e. cup or grail) is as a home for the soul … and the mind fills it with spirit.

"Be like a wise man who built his house upon the rock."
- Matthew 7:24.

The "house" is the soul-body structure and its foundation should be solid like "the rock," which is Truth.

The purpose of your mind is to learn Truth, so it operates as a tour guide for your soul. If the tour guide is clueless, the soul will get lost. But if the tour guide is sharp and knows its way around, consciousness will expand and your whole body will be filled with light.

The mind is also a traffic cop for the soul, directing positive energy and negative energy to different parts of the body. Traffic jams can occur when the cop doesn't do his job well — resulting in needless stress and a nagging headache.

Through this lens, the meaning of life becomes clear. We learned from quantum physicists that there is no external world without the inner world, unless you consider fuzzy probability waves to be more real than the special energy that animates it.

Life must be the inner world.

"The kingdom of God is within you."
- Luke 17:21

Although many religious people tend to be obsessed with physical events and behaviors, their prophets are unanimous in teaching that reality isn't about your body ... especially because the reality we think we see isn't really real.

In Islam, Muhammad revealed the practical meaninglessness of our physical lives in the Quran.

"You should know that the life of this world is only play and amusement, a show and boasting among yourselves, a quest for greater riches. The life of this world is nothing but delusion."
- Surah 57:20

In Hinduism, Krishna used similar words to emphasize that the world is not a physical place.

"All forms of life are in delusion by the illusions of duality."
- Bhagavad Gita, Chapter 7, Verse 27.

In Christianity, Jesus put it another way in the Bible, yet clearly downplayed material reality.

"The spirit gives life, the flesh counts for nothing."
- John 6:63

And Buddha pointed out the power you have in determining the meaning of life.

"Our life is shaped by our mind. We become what we think."
- The Dhammapada

If you think you are a body you are deluded, according to Muhammad and Krishna ... because as Jesus said, the flesh counts for nothing.

But if you think this is a spiritual world, it is. If you think you are capable of Buddha-level consciousness, you can become a Buddha … according to Buddha.

All of that, remember, is supported by the words of quantum visionary Max Planck: "I regard consciousness as fundamental. I regard matter as derivative from consciousness. We cannot get behind consciousness. Everything that we talk about, everything that we regard as existing, postulates consciousness."

That says it all.

You are not your body, which counts for nothing … you are not ego, that is a delusion … you are consciousness, you are a soul, you are light, you are spirit.

So what's the meaning of life?

To evolve your consciousness, ultimately to perfection. You may call that Christ Consciousness, Krishna Consciousness, Muhammad Consciousness, Buddha Consciousness, Unity Consciousness, reaching heaven, achieving nirvana, whatever you wish.

You use your mind as a firestarter on that journey toward perfection, a booster rocket for the soul.

"Do not conform to the pattern of this world,
but be transformed by the renewing of your mind."
- Romans 12:2

The mind is fundamentally important in transforming us from ego focus into our spiritual destiny. The mind is "between" the two. As the mind learns Truth, consciousness expands and fills the soul with spirit light.

If you embrace that concept, everything that happens in the the world will eventually make sense and all of the spiritual teachings in Levels 23-33 will ring true as the prophets preach to your spirit body, not your physical body. Science and religion, when correctly comprehended, both point to the evolution of consciousness as our mission.

In Level 1 we noted that "Alpha and Omega" is a reference to consciousness, specifically, Christ Consciousness.

"I am Alpha and Omega, the beginning and the end,
the first and the last."
- Revelations 22:13

This is the essence of Christ … and your essence. You begin and end as a being of consciousness. The *beginning* of your conscious experience on earth is Alpha and the *end* of your conscious experience on earth is Omega. What goes on in between is the expansion of your consciousness.

Like the universe starting with a Big Bang, you exploded into this physical reality as consciousness 'within' a physical body and, like the universe, are capable of expanding or evolving in all directions.

Dr. David Hawkins laid out that journey of consciousness evolution in his book, *Power vs. Force*. The guideposts of progress are your emotions. Lower levels of consciousness include the experience of shame, guilt and grief, then slowly shift toward neutrality, willingness and acceptance. Evolving souls are capable of reason and love, while the highest levels of consciousness involve joy and peace before finally reaching enlightenment.

It's like having a radio station in your head. If you are listening to 93.5 SAD on your FM dial and every song they play depresses you, would you tune into a different station? Probably. Does 103.7 JOY sound more appealing? Of course.

That is the function of the mind. It tunes the *consciousness dial* in your brain to a more suitable frequency, one that eventually delivers peace to the soul. The mind does so by learning Truth and focusing on it. (Learning about quantum physics can help!) Then, as illustrated in Level 6, it practices spiritual Truth within physical truth until consciousness is perfected.

That's learning wisdom within a physical world until you are filled with spirit light … which is accomplishing the purpose of life.

It's useful to think of Alpha as the lowest level of consciousness. We've all been there. Such as shame regarding insecurities about our physical appearance and impulses … guilt for things we think we have done wrong … or grief over the loss of a loved one whom we believe died and is gone forever.

But over time such emotions are unbearable and motivate us to alter our perspective. Instead of sinning or missing the mark by looking at things from the ego's point of view, we shift and begin to apply Truth. Thus begins our journey upward, toward willingness to embrace change and the ability to reason correctly during our circumstances instead of simply responding emotionally.

Inspired by this inner growth of consciousness, we seek more Truth and find more Truth, yielding the type of real spirit love (unlike codependent ego-based love) that even Jesus worked on throughout his life.

"Jesus grew in wisdom and stature,
and in favor with God and man."
- Luke 2:52

Growing in wisdom and stature? That's the same as expanding consciousness. "Growing in favor with man" makes sense, but "growing in favor with God?" How could Jesus grow in favor with God?

Because he filled his mind with wisdom and his soul with spirit. God is 'interested' in spiritual growth, not behavioral change. Jesus is the ideal role model for us, as one who perfected peace within and tamed the ego. While he matured in spirit, he grew in favor with God.

In *Power vs. Force*, the highest form of consciousness allows one to experience blissful emotional states such as love, joy and peace. Enlightenment is the full embodiment of Truth, the type of mind state that the prophets all attained.

That is the transcendental realm of pure consciousness, or Omega.

"Let this mind be in you, which was also in Christ Jesus."
- Philippians 2:5

This is an unambiguous Christian teaching from the man, Apostle Paul, who has been reputed to understand Jesus the best. *Let Christ's mind be in you.* It's the sense of being where Truth is personified, where unity between all of God's soul children is experienced, where separation and division fade away, where we only change form and never die.

If you seek it, you will find it.

The consciousness journey is like climbing Soul Mountain, going from body through mind to reach spirit.

At the base of the mountain, everyone is physically focused. It's all about bodies, money and material possessions. At times ignorance can be bliss down there, but life can also be pretty boring as it starts to feel like a rat race after a while. At least we have a lot of company — and misery loves company.

Eventually we grow tired of physical monotony and get the idea that we are supposed to climb this mountain, which requires developing some new cognitive skills. This is the area, in the middle of the mountain, where the mind is actively engaged. The cliffs get steeper and the air thinner, but we get wiser. There aren't as many people here, but you can look down below and recognize that you have done something, progressing out of your obsession with the flesh.

The top of the mountain is the most challenging as danger abounds, and the higher you go the fewer people there are to help. It remains physical, and the mental strength you gained along the way is helpful, but you cannot get to the top without that extra gear — a passion and a desire to reach Spirit Summit.

Life is like that, we all start at the base of the mountain (Alpha) and ascend to the top (Omega). The goal is clear.

"Set your minds on things above, not on earthly things."
- Colossians 3:2

Strive to reach the summit.

It's a heavenly view.

LIFE IS BUT A DREAM

Think of the best dream you ever had or, if it's more vivid, the worst nightmare.

One of my most memorable featured a Major League Baseball game, involving the Pittsburgh Pirates trailing by one run against Unknown Opponent in Game 7 of the World Series in some year very soon. It was the bottom of the ninth inning at PNC Park. I was a fan sitting in the stands behind third base.

Needing one run to tie and two to claim the championship, the Pirates' leadoff hitter walked and then Jay Bell (who is now in his 50s and retired a long time ago, but it was a dream so I didn't question it) stepped to the plate. With the fans chanting "Let's Go Bucs!" Bell hit an opposite-field flare down the right-field line that Unknown Opponent's right fielder dove for … and missed.

The ball skipped toward the outfield fence and the crowd erupted as the runner on first and Bell both took off, racing around the bases. The tying run scored and Bell cruised into third with a stand-up triple. He clapped his hands frantically as the fans began to party, anticipating the high probability of Bell soon crossing the plate to deliver a long-awaited World Series title back to the original City of Champions.

I can still hear the crack of the bat, see the roaring fans and feel the wild excitement. The euphoria was palpable. (I am getting chills just writing this.)

Except one problem. It didn't actually happen. It was just a dream.

I literally woke up from the excitement of that moment, never getting to see Bell crossing the plate. Which makes that one, in the end, a bit of a nightmare.

The most profound thing I took away from that experience was this: It sure felt real.

It definitely *happened*, but not in the 'this is reality' way I believed I was experiencing it at the time. When the dream was over, I realized that it wasn't what I thought it was. It was vivid, all right, but it was ultimately just images in my mind unfolding before me like a bedtime story.

Just like this world in which we are living.

It sure feels real. It is definitely *happening*, but not in the 'this is reality' way we are experiencing it. When this life is over, we will realize that it wasn't what we thought it was. It is vivid, all right, but it is ultimately just images in our minds unfolding before us like a bedtime story.

A dream might seem real, but that doesn't make it so. A dream is just an illusion, or by definition, "something that has a deceptive appearance."

Science has done a great job uncovering why the world is an illusion. A brief review:

- We do not know where consciousness comes from, as it's a "hard problem" for scientists. The very origin of our experiential existence therefore remains a mystery.
- Everything is energy. If you break any matter down into its constituent parts, it eventually transforms into light. Your body, which seems so real, is actually made up of tiny vibrating loops of energy, not flesh.
- Atoms are best thought of as energy vessels. Your body is not flesh, it is actually seven octillion cups of light.

(Yes, octillion is a number and that is an actual estimate of the number of atoms in your body.)

- The world exists in a state of infinite possibilities, and all but one of those possibilities "collapse" each moment … or there are an infinite number of realities existing right now alongside this one.
- Those possibilities are extremely sensitive to and perhaps even completely reliant upon each individual's perception. Reality is an external manifestation of an internal state of mind. It happens *in here* more than *out there*.
- Physically, we are seemingly separate beings. But in reality, we are energetically interconnected.
- Space and time aren't what we think they are, they change according to each individual observer. Reality is better thought of as flexible spacetime, where only light is constant.

"The distinction between past, present and future is only a stubbornly persistent illusion."
- Albert Einstein

"Everything we call real is made of things that cannot be regarded as real."
- Niels Bohr

Reality as we think we know it … is not real!

The fact that the world is all energy makes it an illusion, which means that you are vulnerable to believing it is something other than what it is. In spiritual terms, believing the world to be physical means you are sleeping. When you are asleep, you believe yourself to be an egoic avatar in the dream world instead of the consciousness or soul that manifests it.

All of the major religious traditions agree on this.

The man Siddhartha Gautama became known as the 'Buddha' upon his enlightenment. In Pali, an old language from India, the word Buddha means 'awakened' or 'to awaken.'

Awaken from what? The life dream we are experiencing.

"The world, indeed, is like a dream and the treasures of the world are an alluring mirage. Like the apparent distances in a picture, things have no reality in themselves, but they are like heat haze."
- Buddha

A mirage *seems* to exist, but it does not.

In Hindusim the world is maya, which in Sanskrit means illusion, as physical life conceals the nature of spiritual life. As such, we are in danger of misinterpreting the dream world as true reality. Similarly, in Kabbalah the world is a dream state in the infinite mind of the creator.

Christian teachings, when understood in the proper illusory light, are very illuminating on this concept as well.

The Bible gets to it early, in Genesis 2:21, when "the Lord God caused the man to fall into a deep sleep." The Bible never mentions Adam waking up. It's a long book, you would think that would be mentioned somewhere, unless it is deliberately making the point that mankind is still sleeping. (Which it is.)

Then there is this classic snoozing reference in Luke 22. The night before Jesus was crucified he went to the Mount of Olives to pray and he asked his disciples to do the same. He went for a while by himself to pray and when he returned, the disciples had fallen asleep.

Now, if you are a disciple and Jesus himself asks you to pray, do you instead hit the hay? Of course you don't. You pray feverishly and repeatedly until he returns and tells you to stop. But Luke 22:45 says that Jesus came back to the disciples "and found them sleeping for sorrow."

Do you sleep well when emotionally anguished? The disciples had just shared a Last Supper with their leader, who was preparing to die the next day ... you would think they might be pacing around and *wringing their hands for sorrow,* not sleeping!

Well, that *was* what they were doing. They were very worried.

If you focus on the flesh aspect of this world, you are *asleep*. Jesus wanted the disciples to be thinking spiritually, or wakefully. When he witnessed them pacing and feeling sorrowful over their belief that he was going to die, Jesus thought of them as sleeping spiritually.

In Matthew 26 the story becomes almost comical, if read

literally. First, Jesus "found them sleeping" and said to Peter, "Could you not watch with me one hour?" You can practically visualize Jesus shaking his head at Peter, who was clearly worried about Jesus's impending death instead of supporting him in the wisdom that he was in fact *overcoming* death.

Continuing, Jesus left the disciples again, prayed again, returned again and "again he came and found them sleeping, for their eyes were heavy." That's right, they had heavy old eyes and could not see straight. (Unless you believe they literally fell asleep *again*.) Jesus then left a third time and returned and said to them, "Are you still sleeping?"

Perhaps it's possible that the men who followed Jesus so passionately kept napping during his hour of need as if they had nothing better to do, but to *New Eyes* it is clear that the disciples were merely agonizing the fate of Jesus … and thus had slumbering souls. It was a great thing Jesus was doing, something that he expected his followers to understand, yet instead they were fearful.

The ego was awake in them — the soul was asleep.

"This place is a dream, only a sleeper considers it real. Then death comes like dawn, and you wake up laughing at what you thought was your grief."
- Muslim poet Rumi

When you sleep you dream, and in that time and space, it seems like reality. If you have a nightmare and are grieving in it but wake up, you may laugh as nothing actually happened. You were temporarily deceived into believing it was real.

Rumi stated that's how it is with our reality. If you are asleep to Truth, you think the physical world is real. Things that happen in a dream seem bad at the time, but after awakening ... not so much.

"A wise man, recognizing that the world is but an illusion, does not act as if it is real, so he escapes the suffering."
- Buddha

If you wake up from your sleep and realize your soul is having a physical dream, you no longer suffer. Our physical life is a temporary home, and any peace you achieve from the flesh is a deception.

"The life of this world is but comfort of illusion."
- Muhammad

"Foolish dreamers live in a world of illusion."
- Proverbs 14:18, The Message Bible

"You are from below; I am from above.
You are of this world; I am not of this world."
- Jesus, in John 8:23

Jesus was speaking as Christ, anointed with the Holy Spirit and beyond the flesh-obsessed ego world, aware that this place is just a dream. He was above it, fully awakened.

In the next verse, John 8:24, he added, "That is why I said that you will die in your sins."

Recall from Level 11 that the root meaning of the word sin is to 'miss the mark' by aiming at the wrong thing, or simply to misperceive. If you do not understand that this "below" place is just an illusion, you will indeed "die in your sins" because your misperception makes your body a deathtrap instead of a spiritual vehicle. But when you know that you can be one with Christ, you realize you are a conscious soul and are "from above" and are no longer sinning. As such, you overcome the grave.

In the Vedas, which are the oldest scriptures of Hinduism, it says this in Srimad-Bhagavatam 10.84.24-25:

"A sleeping person imagines an alternative reality for himself and, seeing himself as having various names and forms, forgets his waking identity, which is distinct from the dream. Similarly, the senses of one whose consciousness is bewildered by illusion perceive only the names and forms of material objects."

Someone who identifies himself as his body is dreaming of an imaginary physical world, believes he is his ego name as well as gender and age and race, and forgets that he is actually a soul that is not a tangible part of that imaginary world. Similarly, the sleeping consciousness can only see material objects.

So there you have it. Einstein + Bohr + Christianity + Buddhism + Islam + Hinduism + Kabbalah = reality is an illusion.

The 1999 movie *The Matrix* wonderfully illustrates the nature of the illusory reality.

The mentor to the protagonist Neo is Morpheus, the name for the Greek god of dreams and the root word of the opiate morphine. (The Roman god of dreams is Somnia. If you cannot dream because you cannot sleep, you have insomnia.)

In mythology, Morpheus would appear inside the dreams of man and deliver messages from the gods above. Early in the movie Morpheus does the same, delivering messages to Neo from the enlightened state "above" him.

"I imagine that right now you are feeling a bit like Alice, tumbling down the rabbit hole," Morpheus says. "You have the look of a man who accepts what he sees because he is expecting to wake up. Ironically, this is not far from the truth."

Not far indeed. He might as well be talking to us. We are awakening.

Morpheus continues: "The world ... has been pulled over

your eyes to blind you from the truth. You are a slave … like everyone else you were born into bondage, born into a prison that you cannot smell or taste or touch. A prison for your mind."

Perfect! That's what *New Eyes* wants you to see, that the world is a cognitive jail cell with a lot of cots for snoozers.

Morpheus tells Neo that once he commits to understanding the truth about the movie's matrix, he cannot turn back. In the spiritual matrix of life, once you know that you are a soul and not an ego, you cannot turn back. Doing so would be a sin.

Then Morpheus lets Neo know that he can choose to "believe whatever you want to believe" and also that he cannot simply tell him what the matrix is, for "you have to see it for yourself."

Just like life. We can choose to believe whatever we want to believe. We can believe it is physical (and that the sun revolves around the earth) or we can dive into the spiritual world, where we can help each other understand that the path to enlightenment exists and even tell each other where it is … but one must walk it alone.

"Work out your own salvation," Apostle Paul says in Philippians 2:12, an idea known in Eastern religions as karma.

"All I'm offering is the truth, nothing more," says Morpheus, his mirrored glasses reflecting Neo back to him.

Knowing that you have a mountain to climb is a lot different than actually climbing the mountain. Once you know Truth, the game begins, as you have to apply it in order to evolve and climb toward Christ Consciousness.

Later in *The Matrix* Neo meets an enlightened child who is bending a spoon using mind power, explaining, "Do not try and bend the spoon. That's impossible. Instead only try to realize the truth. … There is no spoon. Then you will see it is not the spoon that bends, it is only yourself."

You cannot change the outer world without first changing the inner world.

At the end, Neo puts it all together as The One and becomes impenetrable to the attacks of the enemy. It's an ideal metaphor for everyone's spiritual development, as the soul becomes impenetrable to the attacks of ego energy.

That impenetrable notion is essentially what makes the quantum spiritual approach so therapeutic. Once you know that reality is not what you think it is — that it is an illusion likened unto a dream — suffering diminishes. You still live your physical life, but you do so with your pathway enlightened by Truth.

"The righteous man casts off evil, and by rooting out lust, bitterness and illusion do we reach nirvana."
- Buddha

Therapeutically, reaching nirvana brings peace. It's the ultimate goal.

Spiritually, reaching nirvana brings peace. It's the ultimate goal.

Reaching nirvana, or entering heaven, requires the casting off of "evil" ego, which is made much easier by recognizing that it is only a feature of the physical illusion. Just as you have more wakefulness when you fully arise out of a dream that you were having at night, you have more consciousness when you arise out of the dream of life.

There's no simpler way to understand all this than through the old American nursery rhyme:

Row, row, row your boat
Gently down the stream
Merrily, merrily, merrily, merrily
Life is but a dream!

Repeatedly maneuver your vessel,
Peacefully as the stream of consciousness guides you,
Feel nothing but joy and good cheer,
As reality is merely an illusion.

Lewis Carroll, author of *Alice's Adventures in Wonderland*, penned a variation of that nursery rhyme in *Through the Looking-Glass*. This is the end of that poem, sometimes called "A Boat Beneath a Sunny Sky."

In a Wonderland they lie,
Dreaming as the days go by,
Dreaming as the summers die:

Ever drifting down the stream
Lingering in the golden gleam
Life, what is it but a dream?

That's us, drifting down the stream of consciousness in the *Wonderland* dream world.

You are capable of being aware of the dream, however, and an awakening might be found by following your path down the rabbit hole. There is light at the end of that tunnel.

Enlightenment promises to brighten everything — both dreams and nightmares.

A SPIRITUAL REFLECTION

Let's say you need to shave your scruffy face.

You look in the mirror, see all of the stubble on your chin and cheeks and want to see those little hairs gone. So, while looking carefully at the image, you apply shaving cream precisely where you are seeing it … on the mirror. You slide the razor across the smooth glass several times, wipe away the cream with a towel then look again … and … ?!?

You have done absolutely nothing. That scraggly beard is still there! Instead of addressing the actual issue at hand — yourself — you attempted to alter what you were seeing.

Welcome to reality, an illusion, where most of us try to change what we are seeing instead of trying to modify its source … our consciousness.

It's a radical concept, yet one that is supported by quantum physics and every spiritual discipline.

"We but mirror the world," said the venerable Mahatma Gandhi, one-time heart and soul of India. "All the tendencies present in the outer world are to be found in the world of our body. If we could change ourselves, the tendencies in the world would also change. As a man changes his own nature, so does the attitude of the world change towards him. This is the divine mystery supreme."

This is sometimes paraphrased as, "Be the change you want

to see in the world."

That reality is a mirror of our true selves is certainly a supremely divine mystery. It is also one of the most deeply therapeutic principles I have ever encountered.

The first time I came across a variation of the idea was in college. It was called psychological projection, or "the act of defending yourself against unpleasant impulses by denying their existence in yourself, while attributing them to others."

I thought it was the stupidest thing I ever heard. Blame others for your own issues? Who would do that?

I've since learned … absolutely everybody does that.

Until they wake up and realize that the world is merely a mirror for their souls.

The Mirror has solid scientific support. Superposition and the observer effect combine to indicate that reality exists in all possible states until an observer (consciousness) interacts with it. There is nothing to see (superposition), then there is something to see (observer effect). Physical mirrors are like that, too. They don't reflect anything unless there is something there to be reflected. Once something appears, however, an image appears as a reflection. Electrons, remember, seem to be *aware* that you are watching them, and they reflect back in accordance with each individual observer.

The Mirror is also a notion with relativity at its core, as the universe adjusts space and time for each individual observer. That means we all have our own unique view of the outside world; in effect, our own mirror. You and your friend might be standing next to each other looking at your outward appearances in the same conventional mirror, but you actually see things from a different vantage point. Very similar images, but nevertheless definitely different.

Images in a physical mirror are not reality, they are just *reflections* of the primary object (you), so if you don't like what you see in the mirror you must change the primary object (you).

This is our world. It appears to be the same basic thing for all of us, but really we are all looking at the illusion from varying angles and getting what we see reflected back at us. If we want to change the illusion that is the world, we must change ourselves, as Gandhi said.

It is not a new idea, long predating Gandhi, and it goes much deeper than you might think. It also receives broad-based support across all religious teachings.

At many weddings you hear the following Bible passage recited, though most people recognize only the "noisy gong" and "love is patient" parts. But there is an absolute jewel hidden in 1 Corinthians 13:

"If I speak in the tongues of men and of angels, but have not love, I am a noisy gong or a clanging cymbal._And if I have prophetic powers, and understand all mysteries and all knowledge, and if I have all faith, so as to remove mountains, but have not love, I am nothing._If I give away all I have, and if I deliver up my body to be burned, but have not love, I gain nothing.

"Love is patient and kind; love does not envy or boast; it is not arrogant_or rude. It does not insist on its own way; it is not irritable or resentful; it does not rejoice at wrongdoing, but rejoices with the truth._Love bears all things, believes all things, hopes all things, endures all things.

"Love never ends. As for prophecies, they will pass away; as for tongues, they will cease; as for knowledge, it will pass away. For we know in part and we prophesy in part,_but when the perfect comes, the partial will pass away._When I was a child, I spoke like a child, I thought like a child, I reasoned like a child.

When I became a man, I gave up childish ways._For now we see in a mirror dimly, but then face to face. Now I know in part; then I shall know fully, even as I have been fully known. So now faith, hope, and love abide, these three; but the greatest of these is love."

Beautiful. Memorable. We all relate to those noisy ego gongs and cherish patient love, but the most therapeutic line of that verse is typically overlooked.

"For now we see in a mirror dimly, but then face to face."

It's like Alice stepping *Through the Looking Glass*, climbing into a whole new world.

By now hopefully you can embrace the idea that the "we" in that verse does not mean human beings … it means consciousness or spiritual beings.

We are seeing "in a mirror dimly" when the reflection is faint and indistinct, when we cannot fully comprehend what we are seeing. We think we are seeing flesh, but in actuality we are seeing reflections of our own spiritual likeness. Most people are spiritually asleep and have no idea that this is true. It is a very, very dim mirror indeed!

Yet the world never ceases in its mirror imaging, constantly shining your own light back on you. Everywhere you look. In Buddhism this is the Three Jewels, multi-faceted gems of Truth that are always showing you who you are and what you are learning on the path of consciousness evolution.

"Everyday events start to mirror and more and more subtly and directly to confirm the truths of the teachings, as contemplation slowly unfolds and enriches what we have begun to understand intellectually and carries that understanding

down from our head into our heart."
- Buddhist teacher Sogyal Rinpoche in his inspiring book
The Tibetan Book of Living and Dying

Thanks to The Relentless Mirror, you eventually go from "thinking" to "being" as Truth goes from your head into your heart … from your mind into your soul. (In deep spiritual symbolism this is what is meant by a "beheading," which obviously has tragic consequences when misinterpreted. See Level 27.)

Life is constantly presenting circumstances and situations to each of us that challenge us to grow spiritually. Successful human relationships require a variety of spiritual attributes, especially patience, forgiveness and hope.

Establishing virtues builds your soul, so adversity is a good thing.

"My friends, consider yourselves fortunate when all kinds of trials come your way, for you know that when your faith succeeds in facing such trials, the result is the ability to endure."
- James 1:2-3

"We rejoice in our sufferings, knowing that suffering produces endurance, and endurance produces character, and character produces hope, and hope does not put us to shame, because God's love has been poured into our hearts through the Holy Spirit who has been given to us."
- Romans 5:3-5

Endurance, character, hope … as you embody these fruits of the spirit, the Holy Grail within you is filled by God's love being poured into your heart. When Truth becomes the very fiber of your being, you have come to know thyself as a soul.

You also no longer see others as only human beings, you see them for what they really are — fellow spiritual beings having a human experience.

You are *Through the Looking Glass*.

You finally see "face to face."

When you embody Truth you can see the illusion clearly, you see reality for the spiritual teaching playground that it is, and then you can just as clearly see others as evolving souls. You know they have a physical body, but you know their essence is spirit.

You don't see body to body … you see soul to soul.

We once saw in a dim mirror as the murky illusion of a deceptive energetic reality gets reflected back to us until we learn all of its teachings, thus bringing us into full awareness of our true selves as spiritual beings.

If neither you nor I is self-aware, reality is a two-way mirror and we are both looking at our soul selves without recognizing it. If you and I are both aware, we see face to face. If just one of us is awake, reality is like a one-way mirror during a police interrogation — the perpetrator sees his own image in the mirror, while the officer outside the room can look through the mirror and clearly see the perp.

The Jesus story is a good example of this, as he saw through the ego surface and looked directly into our souls. However, many people looking back at him did not see him as spirit — they saw him as flesh — and as such demonstrate their earthly focus and misunderstand his great teachings.

"Stop judging by mere appearances, but instead judge correctly."
- John 7:24

See with spirit sight, with *New Eyes*. See the non-physical, not the physical.

Just because the sun appears to be revolving around the earth doesn't make it so. Just because this appears to be a world of flesh doesn't make it so. Those are "mere appearances." The "correct" judgment is to see one another for our spiritual essence as pure evolving consciousness.

Review the other most popular religions and you will find similar themes.

Muslims facilitate their understanding of the Quran by reading hadith, which are a collection of sayings from prophet Muhammad. In Al-Tirmidhi Hadith 1286, the revelation is on point.

"Each of you is the mirror of his brother, so if he sees any fault in him he should wipe it away from him."
- Muhammad

Muhammad clearly was being *spiritual* in that verse as we are obviously not physical mirrors of each other, therefore "wiping away fault" from your brother should also be considered spiritual. It's about perfecting consciousness, not judging behaviors. It's about wiping away the sins of misperception, not judging sins of the body.

Neuroscience supports the above teachings of Buddhism, Christianity and Islam on this concept.

In addition to entanglement, scientists have identified that human minds can influence each other through neurons that fire when one person acts and another person observes the action. Watching another do something can inspire an emotion inside us that makes us feel as if we did it, too.

One reason we like to watch sports is because we have a vicarious feeling of playing along with the athletes on the field. We also like movies because we can feel the emotions of the actors on the screen just by observing them. And if someone on

America's Funniest Home Videos accidentally gets hit in the crotch? We feel that, too.

In this way we are deeply moved by the profound actions of others, including Jesus's crucifixion. We feel his pain and, accordingly, must try to comprehend the spirit in his heart that enabled him to do what he did. By his example on the cross, Jesus was "wiping away fault" from his brothers. It's the same as "taking on the sins of the world."

The name of the neural mechanism that allows for that type of process to occur?

Mirror neurons.

Kabbalah (Level 28), an esoteric thought system with roots in Judaism, also embraces the idea.

"Everything that exists is like a mirror, a reflection of your inner, personal imperfection. Your perfection will be achieved when everything you now feel as external to you will be felt as internal."
- Dr. Michael Laitman, renowned Kabbalah scholar

That's more mirror talk and more perfection talk.

Hinduism, of which Gandhi was a devotee, goes there as well in the Bhagavad Gita.

"He who experiences the unity of life sees his own self in all beings, and all beings in his own self."
- Krishna

If you see how we are all energetically interconnected, you see yourself reflected in others and others reflected in yourself.

Refer back to the Corinthians verse quoted earlier, and it indicates that we only "know in part" but when the "perfect" comes — Christ Consciousness — "the partial will pass away."

The partial is the temporary nature of the material world. In this context being a "child" is one whose vision is juvenile, one who only sees physicality, but when you "give up childish ways" and stop pursuing material possessions with such zeal, you "become a man" by maturing in spirit.

So we have Hinduism, Kabbalah, Islam, Christianity and Buddhism in agreement that reality is a mirror, all supported by quantum physics and neuroscience. That's pretty strong backing for a bold idea! Yet all you really need to know that The Mirror is Truth is to experience how well it works when applied in a clinical or practical setting.

Perhaps the most well-known Bible reference to this concept is also the most healing, after Moses asked God his name.

"I am that I am."
- God, in Exodus 3:14

When you recognize that everything you experience is a projection of your own mind ("I am that") then you achieve self-realization ("I am"). If not, you are asleep to Truth.

Therapeutically, the "I am that" concept works like magic. Just as you would expect from any godly advice.

Simply put, whatever you believe about anyone, anything, any situation … is what *you* are. Not as a person, of course, that would be ridiculous. But as a soul. Whatever you are perceiving is a reflection of your consciousness.

Here are several examples:

You are in a traffic jam and you are late for work. Despite having no choice but to sit there, you are cursing and clenching your fists and feeling very stressed. This situation is a mirror of you in that moment. You are not a bunch of automobiles and red traffic lights, but you are "frustration and annoyance." That is the state of your consciousness in that moment. The situation is a mirror.

You get laid off due to company cutbacks. You politely thank your employer for the opportunity to work there, tell your wife that everything is going to be okay and then doggedly pursue another job over the next month before finally landing a higher-paying position, for which you are also thankful. You are "grace, hope, perseverance and gratitude." The situation is a mirror.

You were released from a professional sports team. You proceed to root against the guy who replaced you and rejoice when he gets hurt in a game. You celebrate when he gets released as well. You are "bitter and resentful." The situation is a mirror.

You and your wife are having friends over for a party and are serving Mexican food for dinner. You drop a loaded beef-and-bean burrito on your brand-new summer sandals. Your wife doesn't miss a beat, points at your feet and says, "You are that" as everyone who knows that you like to talk about how "reality is a mirror" laughs at you. Your wife is "wise and witty," your friends are "appreciative of irony" and you are standing there with a loaded beef-and-bean burrito on your sandals. The situation is a mirror for everyone there. (Yes, true story.)

Get the idea? The Mirror works in *every* example you can conjure in your mind if you search for the answers hard enough.

Here's one more for good measure.

You know you are the Son of God. After years of teaching Truth to your disciples and the masses, you are accused of blasphemy and being a rebel against the state. Your enemies decide to execute you. Along the way to your crucifixion, you are mocked and tortured. All you do is shine spirit, forgiving them for their ignorance and hopeful that they will wake up. You are Christ. And that situation was a mirror.

Jesus knew what he was. Being "born without sin" meant that

he knew during his whole life that he was a soul, not a body, and he was here to show us how to perfect our conscious selves. All of his teachings illustrate this, as we shall see through the later Levels in this book. When faced with a situation that matched his "evolved consciousness" he embraced The Mirror, fulfilling his destiny.

But please note, Jesus did what HE needed to do in the situation that HE faced, which is applied relativity (Level 7). His spiritual skill set, it goes without saying, was heavenly compared to ours. So this means that, if you are faced with a similar circumstance, you do NOT need to let yourself be crucified as he did!

Getting physically crucified is being like Jesus, not like Christ; one is behavioral, the other spiritual. I can be Christlike by understanding Truth, by being wise and patient and compassionate and forgiving, but as for allowing others to kill me? Not in this lifetime.

"Whoever wants to be my disciple must deny themselves and take up their cross and follow me."
- Matthew 16:24

Surely no one believes he meant to take up an actual cross and get physically crucified, right? Of course not, as Jesus was always speaking from higher consciousness as Christ, and you must deny the ego inside yourself and follow him through your mind.

In Chapter 6/Lessons of Love in *A Course in Miracles*, Jesus said, "You are not asked to be crucified, which was part of my own teaching contribution. You are merely asked to follow my example in the face of much less extreme temptations to misperceive."

His teaching contribution was showing us spirit through his

crucifixion, while our job is to not sin (i.e. misperceive) and be virtuous in much less challenging circumstances — like in traffic jams or long lines or with a loaded beef-and-bean burrito on your new summer sandals.

"I am not the burrito," I reminded myself at the time, "but I am the peace that comes with my acceptance of not being able to reverse this beany disaster."

Reality is an external manifestation of an internal state of mind. It is a mirror for your soul, reflecting back at you the energy that is going through you. The Mirror is showing you what hoop you need to jump through, what soul test you need to pass. If you shift consciousness, then external reality will shift accordingly in a probabilistic fashion.

"If we could change ourselves," said Gandhi, "the tendencies in the world would also change."

That's Gandhi explaining superposition and the observer effect, together which form the quantum mirror.

And you are going to keep staring into that mirror … until you can see Christ gazing back at you.

IT NEVER GETS OLD

You walk into a stadium during the fourth quarter of a National Football League game, look up on the scoreboard and see that the clock reads 1:03.

What goes through your mind?

A: This game is almost over.

Or ...

B: Shoot, I just missed lunch.

While the clock might seem to indicate that it is 63 minutes past noon, if the game is being played on Monday Night Football it might actually be closer to midnight.

Understanding the notion that the game clock is not the same clock as the lunch clock is simple. That is not rocket science.

But this, quite literally, IS rocket science: Time is relative.

As discussed in Level 7, if a rocket is flying through space at hundreds of thousands of miles per hour, time passes by more slowly for an astronaut onboard than it does for you here on Earth.

That's because time is not what we think it is.

Time really is not time at all.

"The distinction between past, present and future is only a stubbornly persistent illusion." - Albert Einstein

The past, present and future … collectively we call that time. It's a stubbornly persistent illusion because it is not really real. Time as we know it is as real as the 1:03 on the Heinz Field game clock. It's only real within the context of the game that is being played.

Which is to say, it's an illusion, just like time within our physical reality. It's not what we think it is.

In the 1960s physicists John Wheeler and Bryce DeWitt were working on mathematical formulas to unify the concepts of quantum mechanics and general relativity. They developed the Wheeler-DeWitt equation, which was basically a blueprint for the wave-function nature of the entire universe.

It was a brilliant equation, one that supported the "many worlds" interpretation of reality that was introduced in Level 8. Oh, and it did one other little thing.

It killed time.

There is no need for our classical notion of time in the Wheeler-DeWitt model, which Einstein had already suggested, because the universe is really just a big mass of quantum foam. In other words, reality is a ginormous bubble bath of *potential* experiences.

Again, you do not need to understand the mathematics behind these concepts to get *New Eyes*. Neither Jesus nor Buddha nor Muhammad nor Krishna ever mentioned the importance of understanding algebra or calculus as a requirement for seeing the kingdom of heaven. They didn't even teach that you needed to comprehend that 2 + 2 = 4.

All you need to do is grasp the spiritual application of timelessness in order to put a piece of the *New Eyes* puzzle in place.

"There should be time no longer."
- Revelation 10:6

So let's conceptualize why we can eliminate time, which is a very beneficial thing to do for spiritual development (though perhaps not for wedding ceremonies and doctors' appointments).

Think of a DVD again. Before you put it into your player, it is just a potential movie. All it is is data burned on a disk. Once a certain kind of light hits it, the movie appears, but prior to the intersection of the laser light with the data, the movie is just binary bubbles of potential.

As the DVD sits there on top of your TV, is there any need for time within it? Of course not. It doesn't make sense to have a clock for a movie that isn't even being watched. But once you start playing the DVD? Time starts ticking.

Same with video games. Prior to turning on the console, the game — like a DVD — is just a wave function of potentials. All of the game's variations are still possible, and in that state, there is no time. But once you start playing the video game? Time starts ticking.

Considering again a football game being played inside a stadium such as Heinz Field in Pittsburgh.

If you are not interested in the game, time is relative. If you are simply reading a book somewhere in Europe, the 1:03 on the football game clock is totally irrelevant to you as you are completely unaware of what's happening in Pittsburgh. But to Steelers quarterback Ben Roethlisberger? It's a big deal, especially if Big Ben is engineering a two-minute drill to defeat TomBrady (all right, fine, Tom Brady) and the New England Patriots in the AFC Championship Game. (Hey, remember, all things are possible!)

Even within the football game itself, time is relative. There are four separate quarters in each football game during which the clock hits 1:03, plus there is a play clock that sometimes has more importance than the game clock. It's time within time.

Yet when there's *no game* being played, all of that disappears and there's *no time*. Only when the game starts does game time show up.

And if you have no idea what all of this football jargon means, that further illustrates the point. The kind of time that matters so very much to one group of people might not matter at all to others.

Scientists have actually conducted experiments to test if this concept applies to our apparent physical reality, that time is an 'emergent phenomenon' and only exists for observers within a system or a 'matrix' of some kind — like a DVD, video game, football game … or our universe.

The results of such studies have demonstrated that for an 'outside observer' of such a system, time has no meaning. Inside the stadium, the time on the game clock is just for the game. Outside the stadium, the game time doesn't even exist. It's an excellent example of relativity — things are different depending on where the observer is.

So yes, time is an emergent phenomenon that is *inside* a system but *not outside* that same system.

Know what all this suggests? Since we do indeed have a notion of time, we must be within a system (our universe) of which there is an outside (other dimensions). In order for time to 'emerge' as a phenomenon that we can test or track, we have to be in some sort of matrix. Inside our universal matrix, time is just for the system. Outside the universe, that time doesn't even exist.

Which means there is something outside our universe!

You are a soul, after all, and you are 'in' an illusory body comprised of trillions and trillions of atoms that are the counterpart to a computer's binary code. You are pixelated flesh, a matrixian costume (Level 18).

All of us collectively are in the same system, much like *Pac-*

Man and the hungry ghosts and the cherries are different digital aspects of the same video game, one interconnected, entangled dance of digitized energy. When you are playing *Pac-Man*, YOU are actually sitting on a couch *outside* the game, operating *Pac-Man* via some kind of controller.

The *Pac-Man* analogy is very similar to our reality, except the exquisite nature of this universe puts you *inside* the game while you are actually *outside* of it. Our reality is already full-immersion virtual reality.

From Level 1, scientists are stymied by the "hard problem of consciousness" because they do not know its origin. Now you do. It is *outside* the system that we are *inside* of, as consciousness originates in another dimension, just as *Pac-Man* is being controlled inside a game by something that is energetically connected to it, yet outside of it.

We really don't know much more than that about the origin and nature of consciousness, but that's enough. There is more to our existence than this physical universe. There is something *outside* of us here. Time is only real within the context of the game that is being played, and that game is the illusion of physical life that our souls are playing.

Time is not relevant for consciousness … and your soul does not have an age.

It never gets old.

"With the Lord, one day is as a thousand years,
and a thousand years as one day."
- 2 Peter 3:8

That's because the time we are accustomed to has no real meaning outside this universe, it's a blur of indistinction, a relative Planck length for a dimension of our reality that breaks down at a certain point and melts in with quantum foam.

Grasping 'timeless reality' can help answer ancient questions that precocious kids and inquisitive adults might ask, such as:

Q: If God created the universe, who created God?

A: There is no such thing as 'Earth' time where God is, so there is no beginning and no end as we understand it, and therefore no need for Him to be created, because He always existed. Just like consciousness.

Put another way, our universe is just a DVD sitting up on God's golden television console, just waiting to be played by His aspiring soul children. To Him, there is no time and therefore no beginning. Only if you are *in the game* is there a beginning (Alpha) and an end (Omega) to time. But to anyone in God's living room, the beginning and the end are the same — Alpha and Omega are one.

Q: Scientists say that the universe started 13.7 billion years ago. So what was here 13.8 billion years ago?

A: First of all, my daughter would notice that the universe was 13.7 something years old. There's that magic number again!

Secondly, that question is like asking where the game is an hour before kickoff? There are other things going on, but the game has not started yet so the relevant game clock has not started either.

Our physical universe kicked off with the Big Bang, but that was just the start of the flesh aspect of the game and therefore the beginning of ego time. Consciousness existed beforehand, probably 'doing' other things, like spiritually tailgating and chowing down soul food.

Q: Is time travel possible?

A: According to quantum physics, yes, time can speed up, slow down, go forward and go backward.

Just like a DVD can be rewound, fast-forwarded or paused, so can time. Problem is, no quantum rewind button on our universal remote has been discovered, but science indicates that there *could* be one.

Q: What about the Grandfather Paradox? If you went back in time and killed your grandfather, how would you be around to go back in time and kill your grandfather?

A: Time is not linear — it is foamy via the infinite possibilities of superposition.

Just like countless variations in a video game, there are an infinite amount of timelines in our reality. You can travel back in time using alternative timelines, killing your grandfather in Timeline B while leaving Timeline A unaffected. In one universe everything goes on as normal; in another you just committed questionable familicide in the pursuit of science.

According to the *Many Worlds Interpretation of Quantum Mechanics* there are millions of yous and millions of Gramps. That leaves a multitude of possibilities available for the Grandfather Paradox to be resolved. Just watch out, though, Vigilante Gramps might come back at you with a vengeance from Timeline C.

You might also run into another version of you while escaping to Timeline D, which is the quantum explanation for doppelgängers.

Q: There's no way to go back in time using Timeline A?

A: Sure there is, you have to use your consciousness though: It's called therapy. Go back in time in your mind, visit your past and tell yourself a story based upon Truth and you will feel better.

It's also the butterfly effect, as your future changes when you shift initial conditions by altering your viewpoint on your past.

Q: So why does the 'arrow of time' only move forward?

A: Because we're living in a game of organized chaos.

Entropy rules the physical world, meaning all physical things must move toward disorder. Memento Mori. Over time your body falls apart.

But your consciousness? If you use your mind right, it becomes *ordered* over time in the direction of Christ Consciousness. Thanks to entropy, the forward arrow of time ensures mind over matter — as matter falls away all we are left with is mind.

Q: How does timelessness help me?

A: It takes the pressure off. There's no need to be in a hurry to do anything. (Except when it comes to paying your taxes. That you must do on time.)

Don't sweat the small stuff, you have all of eternity to get the job done — 'the job' being the evolution of consciousness for the purpose of spiritual perfection.

Q: What is eternity?

A: Most people think of eternity as forever time. But if time as we know it does not exist outside this realm, then eternity is not endless time — eternity is *no time whatsoever*. At least not as we conventionally understand it.

Time is not seconds, minutes and hours forming weeks, months and years. Einstein considered it to be another dimension of space, a fourth dimension, in addition to the visual three of width, height and depth.

It's really not hard to understand if you have ever seen a movie film strip or have created your own flip book, the primitive form of animation where a series of pictures are drawn on many consecutive pages and appear to move when the pages are turned rapidly.

With a flip book, there is no actual movement of the images, just a simulation of movement as something else (the pages) are moving, but not the images themselves. It's the same with a film strip, when the fast succession of individual frames provides the illusion that the people on the film are moving. The phrase 'motion picture' is actually a misnomer as there really is no motion involved. It's just flip flip flip flip … movie projectors zoom through the film at a rate of 24 still frames each second … creating *apparent* movement. It's also an illusion.

And that's how our reality works. Visualize four-dimensional spacetime as a block of events, flipping flipping flipping flipping … to create apparent movement. Just like every moment of a DVD or a video game is already present on the disc prior to playing it, so, too, is every moment of reality already in existence.

Sound crazy?

It's worth repeating that Einstein was a rather smart guy. And it's worth repeating that he observed, "The distinction between past, present and future is only a stubbornly persistent illusion."

It's all *right here, right now*. Your piece of universal consciousness is just cruising through your relative version of spacetime block reality like a flip book, scene after scene after scene flying by so quickly that you cannot even notice that it is all just a sea of atomic pixels.

That *apparent* movement of scene after scene after scene is what we call time. The fact that it is really just a block of superpositional possibilities is why Einstein considers it to be more of a spatial dimension. Time emerges from quantum foam when individual observers collapse the universe's wave function, flipping the 'on' button and starting the game we call life.

Life is an endless series of moments, an eternal now.

Filmstrip after filmstrip after filmstrip, the passage of which yields the illusion of time. It's really now … now … now … now … now … now … now … now … ad infinitum. The 'gap' between each of those 'now' moments is what we experience as time. It is the measurement between this frame of superposition and that frame. 'Distance' would actually make more sense, which is why Einstein called it spacetime. (Scientifically it would be as logical to say that you are "518,917 miles long" as it is to say that you are "45 years old.") Reality is more like a block of space with your perception of time being a residual effect of your soul's conscious experience.

This leads to all sorts of spiritual lessons, including those by contemporary spiritual teachers Eckhart Tolle in *The Power of Now* and Ram Dass in *Be Here Now*, which notes how the idea of time vanishes when the mind is in the right place. (In their writings, those two best-selling authors make it clear that they were influenced by virtually every major religious philosophy that exists.)

In *Buddha's Little Instruction Book*, Buddhist teacher Jack Kornfield writes, "The trouble is, you think you have time."

It is "trouble" because believing in time means believing that the filmstrips are real and not the illusions that they are. In Buddhism, suffering happens when we cling to those filmstrips despite the fact they are temporary, whereas what is permanent — the True Self as consciousness — gets overlooked by all the dazzling images whizzing by our old conditioned eyes.

There is Hindu philosophy that makes time even worse than merely trouble.

"Among all kinds of killers, time is the ultimate because time kills everything."
- Krishna, in the Bhagavad Gita

Time puts an end to everything.

Time also kills you if you believe you are a body, because eventually the body dies. But if you understand that time isn't real, that it is merely an emerging phenomenon inside a dream and that you are a soul experiencing that dream, then you cannot die. You overcome death.

Christianity clobbers clocks as well.

"Make the best use of time, because the days are evil."
- Ephesians 5:16

Time is an illusion, time is trouble, time is a killer, time is evil … and you should make the best use of it.

In the wonderfully philosophical 2001 film *Waking Life*, directed and written by Richard Linklater, his character at the end says that God is asking us every moment whether we want to enter heaven now and our response is, "No thank you, not just yet." Linklater then says that time is actually us repeatedly saying "No" to God's invitation.

Fabulous. Basically, we'd rather hang out here in Egoland for a while longer.

New Eyes is about saying "Yes" to God's invitation and using time wisely, the script for which is mapped out in Ecclesiastes 3.

"For everything there is a season, and a time for every purpose under heaven:
a time to be born, and a time to die;
a time to plant, and a time to pluck up that which is planted;
a time to kill, and a time to heal;

a time to break down, and a time to build up;
a time to weep, and a time to laugh;
a time to mourn, and a time to dance;
a time to cast away stones, and a time to gather stones together;
a time to embrace, and a time to refrain from embracing;
a time to seek, and a time to lose;
a time to keep, and a time to cast away;
a time to rend, and a time to sew;
a time to keep silent, and a time to speak;
a time to love, and a time to hate;
a time for war, and a time for peace."

That famous Bible verse is a Western religion describing a variation of the Eastern concept of samsara, or the wheel of life that we all go around as our consciousness wanders through this reality's various human experiences.

It's the yin and yang of Earthly existence, complementary forces within circumstances that afford you the opportunity to harmonize your soul.

It's also all relative — everyone goes through it, just on different parts of the wheel at different moments in our lives.

So what's the best use of time? Experiencing everything within that Ecclesiastes verse and energetically balancing it out.

Q: Can you prove this?

A: On some things you need to take a leap of faith (Level 20) in order to fully see it.

Or as Ram Dass says in *Be Here Now*, "To him who has had the experience no explanation is necessary, to him who has not, none is possible."

There is no proof. Just scientific mysteries to explore, spiritual riddles to solve … and soulful experience of Truth.

LIGHTS, CAMERA, ACTION!

The evening news amuses me.

Because if I didn't laugh, I'd cry.

Conflicts and scandals get ratings, so violence and salaciousness sell. The acronym "NEWS" must mean Nation Entertained by War and Sex.

This is not surprising, at least not through the vision of *New Eyes*. It's how the world works. It's all a giant mirror, as the media are a reflection of our national psyche. We are what we watch.

Of course, we are a reflection of what the media are, too, as they project their beliefs onto us. In some ways we are a captive audience, sometimes rather mindlessly absorbing what the mainstream networks decide is important. We are indeed at their mercy. Having once been responsible for writing headlines for a newspaper while determining the relevance of various stories, I have seen this first-hand. What the media want us to see, we see. And what they *cannot* understand, we do not see.

Over the past decade, and more, the media have been rather blind. They have been underreporting the biggest news story in human history.

The sun doesn't revolve around the earth? Boring. Man walks on the moon? Yawn. World War III? Repetitive.

None of those events can match the following for

newsworthiness:

Our universe is a hologram.

Perhaps 'likened unto a hologram' would be more precise. Nevertheless, if true, nothing short of God posting a selfie of Himself on Facebook could be more remarkable than that. Nothing mankind has ever done can compare to our determining that the world is holographic.

And yet what's on the evening news? Crickets. (And I don't mean, "Angry crickets are invading the girls locker room at a local high school … Film at 11.") If you did not know where to look, you would not know that many exceedingly intelligent scientists are taking the concept that the universe is a hologram very seriously.

I'm sure that the national media are not underreporting this story because they are concerned about whether it is true — they are not reporting it because they themselves do not understand it. (Or do not believe it, which is a form of observer bias.)

If reality is just a kind of dream, we really should all know this … and it should be taught to children in school.

But this is crazy talk, right? Right?

That's what most people thought when Copernicus and Galileo suggested that the earth was revolving around the sun, too. And that the earth was round, not flat. And when bacteria were first conceptualized. And when landing on the moon was initially conceived.

And for goodness sakes *my phone* can now answer questions such as "What's the weather in Beijing?" and "What is zero divided by zero?" … who could have predicted that?! Ask Siri "Is the universe a hologram?" and you will receive a great deal of valuable information on this topic. Then after reading all of those links, go call a national TV network and ask them why they haven't put their top investigative reporters on it yet.

For purposes of clarification, the investigation should start with this: What exactly is a hologram?

- Dictionary definition: A three-dimensional image formed by the interference of light beams from a laser or other coherent light source

- In practical terms: A trick of light that makes an actual object appear virtually real elsewhere

- From the perspective of *New Eyes*: We are in a total immersion, interactive 3D movie that is a reflection of our souls — as an equation, it's Illusion + Mirror = Hologram

The origin of holography came during the 1940s through the work of Dennis Gabor, a Hungarian-British physicist who later received the Nobel Prize in Physics for his efforts. You might have first heard about the concept via Star Trek's holodeck … or perhaps you have saved a few collectors baseball cards from your youth with holograms on them … or have a credit card in your wallet right now with a nice little holographic image on it.

When deceased rapper Tupak Shakur's apparition appeared on stage at the music festival Coachella in 2012, many thought it was a hologram, but it was really another trick of light and mirrors called "Pepper's Ghost." Nevertheless, it's a pretty good example of what our world actually is … a trick of light and mirrors.

Neuroscientist Karl Pribram and physicist David Bohm took Gabor's work up a notch by developing the holonomic brain theory, which explained how brain functioning and certain cognitive processes display holographic features.

Then came even bigger ideas, including *The Holographic Universe* by Michael Talbot, who used the Pribram-Bohm theory and expanded it to all of reality. Over the last few years there have been several scientific experiments and studies further examining the holographic nature of our universe.

"Surprising new clues are emerging that everything — you and I and even space itself — may actually be a kind of hologram. ... Everything we see and experience, everything we call our familiar three-dimensional reality may be a projection of information that's stored on a thin, distant two-dimensional surface."
- Columbia professor Brian Greene in The Fabric of the Cosmos

A few headlines from outside the national networks:

"Simulations Back Up Theory That Universe Is A Hologram"
- Article on nature.com

"Do We Live In A 2-D Hologram?" - Press release from Fermilab, a particle physics laboratory in Illinois

"Do We Live In The Matrix?" - Discover Magazine

That's a small sampling of what contemporary scientists are thinking about (and note that these are legitimate scientific sources — none of those are merely speculative, trippy articles in *High Times* magazine, though there are most likely some very open minds headquartered there).

Perhaps the most influential of all comes from Leonard Susskind, the director of the Stanford Institute for Theoretical Physics.

Susskind, a man who is so intelligent that he once won a debate regarding black holes against Stephen Hawking, is a proponent of the holographic principle. He used string theory (Level 3) along with new advancement in the understanding of black holes to support the work of Dutch physicist Gerard 't Hooft, University of Florida professor Charles Thorn and others, putting forth the notion that our physical reality is just a three-dimensional projection of information encoded on a two-dimensional surface at the boundary of the universe.

The result is microscopic 2D data being scaled up to a macroscopic 3D hologram.

That. We. Are. Living. In.

What you think you are seeing is really just data being projected from distant places in the universe, condensed via a slow vibrational state into matter. It's $E = mc^2$ to the extreme.

Confused yet? You need not be. You experience a good metaphor for this concept every time you go to a movie. Remember how important Einstein and SpongeBob say that creative thinking is? So put on your imagination caps and visualize the universe (and beyond) as a movie theater.

The whole theater setting is intoxicating, from the positive entangled energy you exchange with other excited movie-goers to the savory smell of buttery popcorn and the giant high-definition screen for your viewing pleasure. Put together, it becomes so easy to get immersed in a good film. It pulls you in, makes you forget about your 'real' life as you engage in watching someone else's 'fake' life on screen. During particularly intense scenes, you can get so engrossed that you completely forget that you are even in a theater watching … an illusion. Nothing is really happening up there — it's all just pixels of color and light tricks — yet we love it.

Let's say you are in a boring movie, however, and you start looking around to find the source of the images on the screen. Where could you look? First, you might look up, and what do you see? A big stream of light. That's part of it, light is clearly involved. Now follow the light to the back of the theater, and from where is it emerging? A hole in the wall, through which a lens is peeking. If you go back and look at the lens from the side, what will you see? That's right, all of the images that are on the screen are on the lens.

That means, similar to the earlier description of the nature of our universe, what we see on the screen is just a two-dimensional projection of information encoded on a two-dimensional flat surface. The result is microscopic 2D data being scaled up to a macroscopic 2D movie. (Just add a second projecting lens, put on those slick black specs and you have a 3D flick.)

If you understand that, congratulations, you are now as smart as Leonard Susskind. Practically speaking, at least.

But there's more, and it's very important for *New Eyes*. Is the lens the origin of the information that ends up on the screen? Certainly not. We have to go *behind* the wall to find the projector, inside of which you have a data bank of some kind. (The data used to be stored only on reels of film, but many theaters have switched over to portable high-capacity hard drives or digital files shown on digital projectors.)

For our purposes, think reels of film. The images that end up on the screen and are also on the lens actually originate on the film that is outside of your view; hidden, if you will. But what is ultimately required to get those film images on the screen? Light! You take the data and shine light through it to produce the illusory 2D or 3D movie.

And that's reality. Lights, Camera, Action!

Substitute quantum foam in for 'data' and consciousness in for 'light' and you have our universe. We illuminate quantum foam with consciousness to produce our illusory 3D existence. Just as the images on the movie screen are really millions of digital pixels, our 3D images are really trillions of atomic pixels.

So our universe is a hologram. (Film at 11.)

This way of imagining it also gives a potential answer to the "hard problem of consciousness." Just as the light and the data that appear on the movie screen originate on the other side of the wall, the origin of the consciousness comes from beyond the cosmological horizon (the boundary of the universe) and infiltrates us to create our 3D world.

"The Universal Soul exists in every individual, it expresses itself in every creature, everything in the world is a projection of it."
- From the Shvetashvatara Upanishad, an ancient Hindu text

It is as if we are bathing in an ocean of consciousness, with conscious energy moving through the porous surface of the universe as we are 'inside' a higher dimensional state.

"As the heavens are higher than the earth, so are my ways higher than your ways and my thoughts than your thoughts."
- Isaiah 55:9

"Set your mind on the things above,
not on the things that are on earth."
- Colossians 3:2

The words "higher" and "above" in those verses are not earthbound references to "up" as in, "Heaven is up in the sky." No, those verses are clues to the extra dimensions within quantum physics.

Black holes are central to this holographic process, and my guess is so are quasars, which are super-luminous fountains of energy and matter that are fueled by massive black holes. It's as if the universe has a filtration system and feedback loop in place, as black holes suck in energy and quasars shoot it back out with the resulting effect being our 3D physical existence.

Additionally, mysterious dark energy and dark matter could

turn out to be involved as well — perhaps as a direct link to consciousness itself. Dark energy, after all, also is a "hard problem" for scientists as they don't understand its origin or nature, and yet they know it exists and effectively influences everything in our universe.

Sounds like consciousness to me.

"All the world's a stage, and all
the men and women merely players."
- William Shakespeare

Understanding the implications of all of this allows us to put that Shakespearean line on a modern stage. While there are surely more scientific advances to be made in this regard, plenty of evidence is pointing in the holographic direction. Talbot stated clearly in his book that his vision is a model or paradigm — a way of looking at things — but this is with good reason.

Because the universe IS merely a way of looking at things!

Reality is indeed a giant Rorschach test, a massive, interconnected array of inkblot imagery that says more about what you believe — or who you are as a soul — than anything else. We are living in an organized, chaotic, energetic, balanced, relativistic, superpositional, entangled, illusory universe that acts as a timeless mirror for your conscious evolution. Virtually everything that the prophets preach back this up, as the spiritual teachings in later Levels of *New Eyes* will demonstrate.

Of course, in contrast to the prophets and other great minds such as Susskind, there are skeptics who see all of this another way … which ultimately proves the point.

After all, it's *your* relative observation of the Great Hologram, you may see it however you want. If you don't believe it, you don't see it.

I prefer the much more interesting paradigm, the liberating

pathway to Truth. The holographic universe concept is a tremendous therapeutic tool for mental health and addiction counselors, in addition to being an inspiring idea for anyone looking for meaning in life. It changes everything.

Regardless of some of the science being unsettled, the notion of a holographic universe is an empowering possibility for all of us, one that is rife with clinical and spiritual potential. No need to wait for scientists to figure it *all* out, especially since they will not be able to do that anyway. People's lives are on the line. Thanks to the physics discussed in the earlier Levels and the spirituality to come in the later Levels, there's plenty of evidence to proceed with a therapeutic model, and many of our Quantum Counseling clients have already experienced significant reduction in symptoms or complete healings because of it.

Fact is, the holographic universe is such a fantastic 'outside the box' tool to use to improve or enhance your life. Understanding that you are an actor in a movie of sorts is functional, inspirational, pretty cool and probably true.

In a theater if you don't like the movie, can you change the action on the screen? No. If a bad guy is sneaking up behind a woman in a horror movie, does yelling at her "Watch out!" help in any way? No. Once the action is on the screen, the die has already been cast. If you want to change the movie, you have to change it from the origin of projection … from inside the projector that's behind the wall.

This is a critical point for *New Eyes*. As the spiritual masters will tell you, the only way to change the action in our lives is by altering what's *behind the wall*. Which means, the only way to change behavior is through the evolution of consciousness.

Why do people struggle with relapse with drugs and alcohol so often? Because they have not evolved their consciousness. Trying to quit using simply by trying to quit using never works.

There must be a shift in consciousness.

Why do people exercise or diet and then gain weight back again? Because they have not evolved their consciousness. Trying to lose weight through behavioral changes only works if there is an accompanying shift in consciousness.

Why is there so much war, famine, disease, relationship distress, financial instability, emotional unrest? Because the very nature of the world is chaotic … and the only solution is a balancing act, one that requires the organizing principle that only an upward shift in consciousness can create.

As a therapy, counseling via quantum concepts and holographic principles gives mental health and addiction clients authentic control over the direction of their lives. They become scriptwriters and star in their own feature film. Same for you, if you choose to see it that way.

When you change the way you see the world, the world you are seeing changes. With our thoughts we make the world. Be the change you want to see in the world. Whatever you ask for in prayer, believing, you will receive. Renew your life with your mind. Whatever you believe, you can achieve. Faith the size of a mustard seed can move a mountain.

We are human beings, not human doings. We are spiritual beings having a physical experience.

It's all there. Behavior takes a back seat to consciousness, which must evolve. The world is a 3D hologram, reflecting a life movie back at you that acts as a feedback loop for your spiritual development.

When you shift your consciousness, as an observer, the wave function of probabilities collapses in the direction of that shift. Like a radio, superposition holds all the possible frequencies, and consciousness 'selects' one to experience based upon how it is resonating and into what it is tuned. Consciousness is then manifested into form via various energies and movements of light.

For example, often the root cause of any addiction is a resistance to negative energy. "I hate feeling this way," someone with resentment, guilt, shame, anxiety, depression or fear might think. Drugs, alcohol, food, shopping, sex, money and so many other physical things are used to try to cover up that feeling, but alas, that feeling is still there whenever the physical cover for it is not available. Thus, the addictive behavior commences.

So how to make that nightmare of a movie change? Evolve consciousness upward. If resentment and anxiety are replaced with forgiveness and fearlessness, the result is both a heightened consciousness *and* the removal of the root cause of addiction. Now the movie on the screen changes since the light inside the projector resonates with a different film and shines it outward.

That is only a fraction of the entire volume of potential outcomes that can be positively affected by properly applying the quantum counseling/hologram concept. As you will see in the next several Levels, there are several ways to understand 'the soul game' and clear pathways to winning it. But first we have to wake up and realize we have been dreaming.

It took more than a century for the world to embrace heliocentrism, but when they finally did, no one's life really changed much. Business mostly kept operating as normal.

But the universe is a hologram? That is a game-changer.

Hopefully it doesn't take 100 years for everyone to wake up. The more of us that stir, the better, as a rising tide lifts all boats. Consciousness must rise so that your vessel can be lifted.

"Blessed are your eyes because they see."
- Matthew 13:16

"Your eyes" means *New Eyes* … because they see Truth.

Jesus was always talking from the spiritual perspective, from the higher world of Christ. He never said the universe was a hologram, probably because he did not know what a hologram was, but he and Apostle Paul certainly dropped hints about reality being more than what meets the eye.

"To you it has been given to know the secrets of the kingdom of heaven, but to them it has not been given."
- Matthew 13:11

"Behold, I tell you a mystery. We will not all sleep, but we will all be changed, in a moment, in the twinkling of an eye."
- 1 Corinthians 15:51-53

Reality is a mystery, full of secrets. When you are asleep, you do not know that the world is an illusion, but you will eventually wake up and have spiritual sight.

Some people see the world as physical, made up of bodies and behaviors. They are blind and deaf. Old eyes.

Other people see the world as spiritual, made up of souls and perception. They can see and hear. *New Eyes*.

Realizing that the world is a hologram has two major benefits: It makes the movie so much more interesting because you are awake in the dream, and it makes all spiritual teachings so much clearer because you won't take them literally.

For as we are discovering, even the world is not a literal place.

TO BE, OR NOT TO BE ...

In his famous soliloquy from *Hamlet*, William Shakespeare writes those famous philosophical words that have been so often repeated in many different contexts.

But he got it backwards.

That line really should read, "Not to be, or to be ..."

In his phrasing, Shakespeare puts "To be" first as Hamlet associates 'being' with physical life and 'not being' as a reference to death. In reality it's the other way around.

We are zombies if we do not realize that we are spiritual beings having a human experience. Unless we are awakened, we are dead men walking. It is only when we have "shuffled off this mortal coil" do we return to our real state of being.

Hamlet adds, "For in that sleep of death, what dreams may come."

It's really, "For in that sleep of life, what dreams may come."

Life is but a dream.

So it still begs the question, "Not to be, or to be?"

In the Gospel of Thomas, Jesus presented a similar inquiry, "When you become two, what will you do?"

While you are here on earth, are you going to be an ego zombie (not to be) or an awakening spirit (to be)? Are you going to be flesh focused or spiritually committed?

While we are here on earth we are two, an existence of

duality. There is a physical part of you and there is a spiritual part of you. Energetically we call one ego and the other soul.

The ego is the part of your consciousness experience that is physical. If you can see it, touch it, scratch it, sniff it or taste it, then it is material and typically pertains to ego. It is how you define yourself physically. It's about labeling yourself in the material world in contrast with others. It's about seeing the physical world through physical eyes.

"I am female. I am male. I am black. I am white. I am short.
I am tall. I am fat. I am thin. I am gay. I am straight.
I am a Democrat. I am a Republican. I am poor. I am rich.
I am old. I am young. I am an addict. I am sober."

The descriptions go on and on.

The ego, in spiritual context, isn't what many of us grow up thinking it is … someone who is overly boastful, full of arrogance and pride. While that type of person can be thought of as having a 'big ego' because they define themselves based upon being superior in physical attributes such as beauty, money, success, etc., someone who feels inferior based upon the same measures also qualify as having a 'big ego' because their focus is physical.

Soul, on the other hand (or, as Jesus would say, on the other cheek), is all things non-physical. More precisely, it is how you define yourself non-physically. It's about identifying yourself spiritually in harmony with others. It's about seeing the physical world through new, spiritual eyes.

It also can describe itself in many non-physical ways, for better or for worse.

"I am cowardly. I am courageous. I am resentful. I am forgiving.
I am hopeless. I am hopeful. I am boring. I am creative. I am fearful.

I am fearless. I am ignorant. I am wise. I am restless. I am patient.
I am arrogant. I am humble. I am thankless. I am grateful."

There are as many ways to see yourself spiritually as well as physically.

Here is how Buddhist teacher Sogyal Rinpoche describes ego-soul duality in his masterful bestseller *The Tibetan Book of Living and Dying*:

"Two people have been living in you all your life. One is the ego, garrulous, demanding, hysterical, calculating; the other is the hidden spiritual being, whose still voice of wisdom you have only rarely heard or attended to. As you listen more and more to the teachings, contemplate them, and integrate them into your life, your inner voice, your innate wisdom of discernment, what we call in Buddhism 'discriminating awareness,' is awakened and strengthened, and you begin to distinguish between its guidance and the various clamorous and enthralling voices of ego. The memory of your real nature, with all its splendor and confidence, begins to return to you.

"You will find, in fact, that you have uncovered in yourself your own wise guide, and as the voice of your wise guide, or discriminating awareness, grows stronger and clearer, you will start to distinguish between its truth and the various deceptions of the ego, and you will be able to listen to it with discernment and confidence."

The ego inside all of us will get hysterical and calculating every time you read that because it has been properly identified as the culprit in all of our suffering!

Always keep your "wise guide" in mind as you read the rest of this book. This "wise guide" is your higher self, your direct link to the divine, and in the highest realms of consciousness, what is known as the Lord — your shepherd — a wise guide who shows you the way toward the Truth and eternal life.

In the Second Teaching of the Bhagavad Gita it says that Arjuna "sat dejected, between the two armies."

The armies are, metaphorically, the ego and the soul. They are at war.

In the Gita's Sixth Teaching, after he is guided by Lord Krishna (via Krishna Consciousness) to be more spiritual than physical, Arjuna feels "doomed by his double failure" as he is succeeding in neither arena. He believes himself to be failing at ego and soul endeavors.

Arjuna represents you, and your goal in life is to win the battle between ego and soul. (Much more on the Gita in Level 26.)

Arming yourself with the proper weaponry to win that war is crucial. This chapter marks the halfway point of *New Eyes* — 16 levels before and 16 remaining. Prior to shifting more toward spiritual teachings over the last half of this book, let's briefly review some of the previous levels for scientific manifestations of the duality concept.

- In Level 2, we discussed how there is an organizing principle and a chaotic design to the universe. The evolution of consciousness (Level 12) is ultimately the organizing force of the chaotic mess the ego creates.

  Organization and chaos represent duality.

- Level 3 went over how everything is energy. Not only is consciousness energy (E), the ego that derives itself from mass (m) and physical light (c) is also energy.

E and mc^2 represent duality.

- Level 4 explained how atoms are actually energy vessels … and in later Levels you will see that they either carry around soul energy (i.e. the holy spirit or the light) or ego energy (i.e. evil or darkness).

  Positive and negative charges represent duality.

- Level 4 also introduced "wave-particle" duality.

  "We have two contradictory pictures of reality," said Einstein of the wave-particle concept. "Separately neither of them (waves nor particles) fully explains the phenomena of light, but together they do."

  Similarly, we have two contradictory views of reality in soul vs. ego dynamics. Together, their energies manifest in the light of this reality and represent duality.

- In Level 5, it was made clear by Niels Bohr that our world is a dualistic world of complements … and ultimately there are no better complementarity principles than the soul and ego! (Their relationship is torture for a while, but in the end, you will love thy enemy — the ego.)

  Yin and yang represent duality.

- Level 6 featured Hebb's Law. Whatever you fire together in your brain, you wire together. If you see the world as the ego sees it, then that is what you are. See it as spirit, and the paradigm shifts in that direction.

"Do not conform to the pattern of this world, but be transformed by the renewing of your mind."
- Romans 12:2

The "pattern" of this world is chaos, relativity (Level 7) and superposition probabilities (Level 8). Renewing your mind involves the observer effect (Level 9), realizing that the ego is doomed to die (Level 11) so accordingly you are here to develop your soul through the evolution of consciousness (Level 12).

Ego and soul represent duality. They are lower and higher consciousness, respectively.

Ego Agendas			
Body Image	Money	House	Car
Clothes	Food	Family	Friends
Job	Gender	Age	Intelligence
Race	Awards	Politics	Death

Ego will try to convince you that there is no spiritual world, but your wise guide will show you that there really is only one way to look at things — from a non-physical, global, non-local wave-like perspective of oneness as opposed to the physical, myopic, egocentric particle-like perspective of separateness.

Duality is the Buddhist principle of 'esho funi' — two, but not two.

Spirit Merit Badges			
Wisdom	Hope	Discipline	Compassion
Forgiveness	Patience	Humility	Creativity
Mercy	Leadership	Perspective	Persistence
Courage	Gratitude	Respect	Integrity

The process of shifting away from ego includes the acquisition of what the Bible refers to as fruits of the spirit, while therapeutically I like to refer to those fruits as merit badges for the soul.

In Genesis 2:16-17, God encourages Adam and Eve to eat off the tree of life but not off the tree of the knowledge of good and evil — "for in the day that you eat of it you shall surely die."

Bet you can guess which list is the tree of life.

Ego agendas may bring temporary satisfaction, but ultimately, no matter how good you have it, death will prevail (Level 11). Along the way the items on that list are all unreliable and changeable. They can be used for 'good' or 'evil,' like money and human relationships.

American history is filled with successful physical figures who had it all, but in the end, it did not seem to work out so well. Consider Elvis Presley. No judgment on him, but for all of his wonderful talents, fame and fortune, you would have expected him to have been happier. Ego success definitely does not guarantee peace in anyone's life.

Earning merit badges from the spirit list, however, always works. They are guaranteed to feel good, as it is food for the soul. A relatively new branch of therapy called Positive Psychology specifically emphasizes the nurturing of such traits inside oneself as a way to find greater happiness and satisfaction in life. No greater proof than experiencing virtues for oneself.

A simple test of this: Would you rather be poor and peaceful or rich and miserable? No variables are allowed to enter in that question. It's one or the other. Either poor and peaceful or rich and miserable?

Every person that I have ever asked that question answers the same. So will you.

That's because fattening one's wallet is not the meaning of life, developing your spiritual body is. Gotta get ripped abs for your soul. (Just do it.)

Does this mean you should neglect that wallet? Or forgo developing your physical life? No!

Jesus addressed this in Matthew 22:15-22.

When asked by the Pharisees whether it is "lawful to pay taxes to Caesar" Jesus answered, "Render unto Caesar the things that are Caesar's, and to God the things that are God's."

The Pharisees "marveled" at his answer. It is still marvelous today.

Caesar represents things of the flesh.

God represents things of the soul.

Physical things such as food, water and clothing, are necessary parts of our material existence.

"The Gentiles seek after all these things, and your heavenly Father knows that you need them all. But seek first the Kingdom of God and His righteousness, and all these things will be added to you."
- Matthew 6:32-33

What does that mean?

You are two: A physical body and a spiritual body. You're going to do physical things — but make spiritual things your highest priority.

You use the physical body to learn spiritual skills. Being physically fit requires discipline and enthusiasm. Making a lot of money requires creativity and persistence. Being a parent requires humor, forgiveness, hope, mercy, courage, leadership, humility and above all patience.

But being physically fit, financially wealthy and a mother or father are secondary in God's eyes to the virtues that are expressed in the process.

"Physical exercise is of limited value,
but godliness is valuable in every way."
- 1 Timothy 4:8

Jesus never mentions doing bench presses, squats, crunches or Kegels. Nor does he say, "Become thee a lawyer" or "Get thyself liposuction." He does not even suggest having children or getting married. No one will ever check your portfolio at the Pearly Gates, because that's all irrelevant compared to what your soul is supposed to be doing.

Like with relativity, different souls need to work on different virtues. Some people need to learn how to be more assertive, others more accepting. Some people need to learn how to find their voice and pursue justice, others how to let it go and forgive. Some people need to learn how to speak up, others simply to shut up.

The physical and spiritual worlds are complementary, they work together. The things that we work on physically teach us things spiritually. Adversity builds character, but the goal is always spirit with a side benefit sometimes being material. Your soul can be healthy even when your body is not, and vice versa.

Jesus put emphasis on his teachings thusly: Be a BIG soul, with little or no ego. He's always talking about spirit, only sometimes about the flesh.

Because that's you — always spirit (for eternity) and temporarily flesh (world-wide average of about 71 years).

"Like newborn babies, crave pure spiritual milk,
so that by it you may grow up in your salvation."
- 1 Peter 2:3

In other words, frequently visit Spirituality Dairy Farms, such as those discussed in Levels 23-33.

"Do not lay up for yourselves treasures on earth, where moths and rust destroy and where thieves break in and steal, but lay up for yourselves treasures in heaven, where neither moths nor rust destroys and where thieves do not break in and steal. For where your treasure is, there your heart will be also."
- Matthew 6:19-21

"No one can serve two masters, for either he will hate the one and love the other, or he will be devoted to the one and despise the other. You cannot serve God and money."
- Matthew 6:24

In the same gospel chapter where he noted of ego things that God "knows that you need them all," Jesus emphasized to keep your priorities straight and treasure virtues.

So, "When you become two, what will you do?"

"If therefore thine eye be single,
thy whole body shall be full of light."
- Matthew 6:22

Single eye.

See only through the spiritual eye, the eye of unity.

In Hinduism and Buddhism, this is the crown chakra. You have two physical eyes and one spiritual eye, the 'third eye' in some spiritual traditions.

You should not merely see the physical, illusory world with your two eyes — see the world of spirit through your soul's eye. Collectively, if each of us does it individually, it's *New Eyes* for all of humanity.

To be spiritual or not to be spiritual? That is the only question.

LIFE IS BUT A DREAM

A serial killer once showed up at a social gathering I was attending.

He was dressed oddly, but distinctly. Definitely wanted us to know he had arrived, talking loudly and getting our attention. Brandishing a gun and a knife, he casually walked from person to person with a disturbing grin and a crazed look in his eye.

When he got to me, I did what seemed to be the right thing to do — laughed at him and gave him a high-five.

Then I asked him if the boxes of Cheerios, Frosted Flakes, Fruity Pebbles, Lucky Charms, Apple Jacks and Cinnamon Toast Crunch that were tacked onto his clothes were still full or if he had eaten them all.

Did I say serial killer? I meant *cereal* killer.

It was Halloween, after all.

At the same gathering was an evil clown, a zombie cheerleader and Hitler. I was not taken aback at seeing any of them. I was aware they were just normal adults playing dress-up. (Except maybe the clown, he was a little creepy for real.)

My wife and I went together as pregnant twins, which was more challenging for me than for her. Only one month away from delivering our first child, she wore her usual maternity overalls and otherwise dressed normally, so I had to do all the adjustments. That meant I wore a wig, puffed up my belly with a pillow and endured an hour-long makeup session so that we would match. From a distance we were hard to tell apart, which I think bothered her a little bit — understandably, though I thought I was pretty.

Upon seeing us, nearly everyone patted my belly while some asked if I were in any pain. "Only from the straps on my brassiere," was my reply.

Everyone played along, which is what you do on Halloween. You appreciate all the interesting outfits and do not take anyone too seriously. It's just for fun.

Too bad we do not also look at life that way, because that's precisely what this is.

A costume party for our souls.

You are a spiritual being having a physical experience. That physical experience requires a costume, which is the human body and its corresponding ego identification. The body/ego comes in all sorts of different colors, shapes and sizes, along with a wide array of quirky personality traits and fascinating cultural differences.

We have a seemingly infinite blend of ego-based characteristics: There is tall, dark, handsome and arrogant; short, dark, handsome and arrogant; tall, light, homely and modest; short, light, gorgeous and insecure; medium height, blended race, mildly attractive and confident … the variations go on and on and on.

And that's just one little subset of ego, featuring only a few physical characteristics or general dispositions. There are millions of others. Like superposition for our spiritual wardrobes, we have an endless array of appearances and personality patterns to wear.

We often call them *labels*. But it's all just energy. Height, weight, race, financial status, health status, mood … it's all just

energy, because everything is energy. When you apply quantum physics to such labels, poof! They disappear into light.

So make no mistake about it, your soul is merely wearing a costume. It's an amazing technicolor dreamcoat.

"There is light within a person of light."
- Jesus, in the Gospel of Thomas

There is an energetic soul within a physical energy body — there is spirit inside your dreamcoat.

When we do make that mistake and think our costumes are real, then things go haywire.

Imagine what would happen if we took our costumes seriously at Halloween parties. The women would scream and hide behind their dates when the evil clown walked in. The men would scream, dive out the windows and then call the cops. And I would have been chastised for drinking a Heineken while pregnant.

My son Austin loved the movie *Toy Story* as a toddler. When he was 4, he wore an awesome Buzz Lightyear costume for Halloween. At pre-school and during trick-or-treating everyone greeted him as "Buzz." Halloween costumes are the identity for children for an entire day, though in Austin's case, he wore those Lightyear wings for an entire year.

But eventually he moved on and stopped thinking of himself as Buzz. If he had not, had he continued to wear those wings in junior high, he would have been looked at pretty oddly. By his parents.

When a National Football League game ends, the players don't keep behaving like the outfits they wore on the field. Chicago Bears don't sleep in the woods and hibernate. Arizona Cardinals don't sleep in trees and try to fly. Miami Dolphins don't sleep in the ocean and make high-pitched squeaky whistling noises through nasal air sacs behind their blowholes. Minnesota Vikings don't go pillaging and plundering then pass out after partying all night long on their boats. (Hopefully not.)

Same with Hollywood stars. They don't stay in character off the set, because they knew they were acting, just playing roles. Imagine Michael Keaton walking around introducing himself to others by saying, "I'm Batman." Then he runs into Christian Bale, who insists on saying the same thing. *Bat Fight!*

Athletes and actors maintaining their performing personas would be insane. They are not *actually* Bears and Cardinals and

Dolphins and Vikings and Batmen. They knew it was only a temporary role, so they let it go.

Yet in life, we cannot seem to let it go. We become addicted to our ego costumes.

As so many great scientists and spiritualists have suggested, reality is an illusion, so it is easy to develop Ego Dependence Disorder. Like with addicts, sometimes interventions or confrontations are necessary to help you snap out of it.

In the Gnostic text The Secret Book of James, Jesus got lovingly assertive with the disciples during what I like to call his 'halftime speech,' as the heavily-favored Heavenly Angels had fallen behind 21-3 against their bitter rivals, the Egoland Devils.

So their coach read Team Holy Spirit the riot act.

"You wretches! You losers! You pretenders to truth! You falsifiers of knowledge! You sinners against the spirit! Do you still dare to listen when from the beginning you should have been speaking? Do you still dare to sleep when from the beginning you should have been awake so that the kingdom of heaven might receive you?"

As they so often do, when read spiritually, the Gnostic texts (Levels 27, 29) merely *enhance* what is written in the Bible, they do not *detract* from it.

In this case, Jesus made it clear that he was expecting more out of his disciples. Jesus had been coaching them about how everything is spirit, that there is a heaven, that you cannot die, that the flesh means nothing … and they *still* walked off the field at halftime hand in hand with ego, believing they were their costumes.

He had been teaching Truth to them, but they were only "pretending" and not actually believing it. They took the teachings and "falsified" them, which is to say, applied them to the flesh and not the soul. As such, they were “sinners against the spirit” because they missed the mark (per the definition of sin from Level 11). Instead of speaking or giving Truth from the start of the game, here it was halftime and they were still having to listen to or receive Truth from Jesus. Accordingly, they were asleep to his wisdom and not awake.

These are very consistent teachings, not only from the Christian point of view but also from Buddhism, Islam, Hinduism and Kabbalah. However, many Christians find it hard to believe that Jesus would talk to his followers that way. Surely that’s just that Gnostic nonsense.

Au contraire.

I refer you to several verses in the Gospel of Matthew, including when right-hand man Peter was emphatic that Jesus would not be crucified. Jesus scolded Peter as a drill sergeant would a private on his first day of boot camp.

“Get behind me, Satan! You are a hindrance to me. For you are not setting your mind on the things of God, but on the things of man.”
- Matthew 16:23

Setting your mind on things of man? Ego is awake, soul is asleep. Or ego is alive, soul is dead.

Setting your mind on the things of God? Ego is asleep, soul is awake. Or ego is dead, soul is alive.

Jesus also sounded fairly aggressive when addressing the masses as well.

“Do not think that I have come to bring peace to the earth. I have not come to bring peace, but a sword. For I have come to set a man against his father, and a daughter against her mother, and a daughter-in-law against her mother-in-law.”
- Matthew 10:34-35

Mother-in-law? Yes, he went there.

"A person's enemies will be those of his own household."
- Matthew 10:36

Well, that would explain all the familial dysfunction in the world, correct?

"Whoever finds his life will lose it,
and whoever loses his life for my sake will find it."
- Matthew 10:39

Whoever finds the 'ego costume' world will lose the spirit body, but whoever loses the 'ego costume' life for the sake of Christ will find the spirit body.

Then there's this …

"If anyone comes to me and does not hate his own father and mother and wife and children and brothers and sisters, yes, and even his own life, he cannot be my disciple."
- Luke 14:26

No way you can look at that any other way than spiritually, unless you truly believe that Jesus wants you to *hate* your parents and siblings and kids. Spiritually, it is a distinct anti-ego statement and pro-soul declaration. Family and friends often become false idols, as we crave their love as opposed to seeking God's love. You must put soul over ego in order to follow Christ.

Finally, Jesus told a master's parable that has a striking ending.

"As for these enemies of mine, who did not want me to reign over them, bring them here and slaughter them before me."
- Luke 19:27

Beautiful, when read spiritually. If read from the ego dream world, it sounds as if power-hungry Jesus were advocating killing people. But spiritually it means that if the enemy — ego or lower consciousness — does not want the spirit or higher consciousness to reign over it, it needs to be slaughtered at the feet of Christ.

That is no power-hungry passage … it's spiritual poetry!

Jesus was not a peacenik hippie. He was a loving, kind, compassionate spirit being who took the form of man to show us the way, and he had high expectations for those who knew better, so he used spicy verbiage when necessary to shake us out of our severe costume addiction.

Recall these verses from Level 7:

"And that servant who knew his master's will but did not get ready or act according to his will, will receive a severe beating. But the one who did not know, and did what deserved a beating, will receive a light beating. Everyone to whom much was given, of him much will be required."

- Luke 12:47-48

Severe beatings? Light beatings? He was the "Prince of Peace" … except when he himself indicated he did not come to bring peace. He is better thought of as the "Bishop of Balance" … because he was nice when he needed to be yet flipped over tables when he needed to do so.

Why would Jesus ever need to call people names such as "Satan" and "hypocrites" and "losers" while suggesting that slaughters and beatings were appropriate?

Because he wanted us to WAKE UP!

If you have a good friend who is asleep and urgently needs to arise because she is going to be late for her wedding, what would you do? Gently rub her back? Or scream at her, WAKE UP!

If you have a good friend who was overdosing on drugs and appeared to be clearly dying, would you sit idly by? Of course not. You would shake him, dunk him in freezing cold bathwater and scream at him to WAKE UP!

If you were on the Soarin' ride at Epcot in Disney World and someone next to you started calling for peanuts and a beverage from the flight attendant, you would think he had lost his mind. If he then demanded to see the pilot and got a glazed look in his eyes, you would certainly want him to snap back to reality.

Hey, brother, it's just a ride!

Life is like that, it's just a ride for your soul. It's often a roller coaster, of course, but a ride nevertheless. It is helpful to remember that, lest you take it too seriously.

Jesus knew that people were asleep and overdosing on their ego selves, just as we all do sometimes. He saw right through their costumes and into their souls. So he delivered that wicked halftime speech to his disciples and called Peter "Satan" and told us we should slaughter our enemies and "hate" our families and will get a severe beating if we fail … because he *loves* us.

Of course, perhaps taking all of that literally works for some people. It certainly seems to be more peaceful when taken spiritually, however.

This costume concept is the great equalizer. If you receive a lovely costume at birth, one blessed with good looks and good health and good talent and good fortune, one of your tasks is to not fall in love with the ego outfit so much such that you don't identify with your soul. If you won the genetic or environmental lottery, God is not impressed with anything that you do.

"For by grace you have been saved through faith.
And this is not your own doing; it is the gift of God,
not a result of works, so that no one may boast."
- Apostle Paul, in Ephesians 2:8-9

No one may boast. No one is special. Getting a pretty costume to wear says nothing about the attractiveness of your soul. Winning Super Bowls, being a supermodel, earning millions of dollars, writing a book, being elected President … none of it matters in the long run. There is no behavioral scoreboard in the sky. It's about whether you discovered spirit along the way — and if you did, you are a winner.

Someone fortunate enough to receive physical blessings is spiritual by being grateful and avoiding pride or arrogance; by demonstrating compassion; by being disciplined; and by keeping things in perspective through gaining wisdom.

If you receive a homely costume at birth, without good looks or good health or good talent or good fortune, one of your tasks is to not despise your ego outfit so much such that you don't identify with your soul. God is not impressed with anything that you do, either. The less fortunate have the same access to virtues as do the wealthy.

So what costume your soul is wearing has nothing to do with it.

"When a man of vision sees nature's qualities as the agent of action and knows what lies beyond, he enters into my being."
- Krishna in the Bhagavad Gita, Chapter 14, Verse 19

Translating that verse into the language of quantum spirituality, it says, "When someone who is awake understands that physical laws (chaos, relativity, superposition, entanglement, etc.) dictate behavior and that he is really an eternal soul, he achieves higher consciousness."

Bottom line, God is not impressed with anything that you do because nature's qualities control the *doing*. However, you control the *being*.

A forgiving person's behaviors are much different than a

resentful person's behaviors, just as a courageous person acts much differently than a coward. You are a soul, and once your mind focuses on a particular level of consciousness or state of being, your behaviors follow suit. Those behaviors, however, only follow probability patterns via superposition. It's why many well-intentioned people cannot seem to get control of their addictions, because they are really only in control of their perceptions. If they do not realize that a perception shift is required, they remain on the hamster wheel of an addict's life.

Reality is not about the sock puppet (outer self), it's about the puppeteer (inner self).

Your responsibility is to shift your perspective, which raises the probability of certain physical outcomes. If you capture some soulful merit badges along the way — such as forgiveness and courage and compassion and wisdom — then you have accomplished the ultimate goal. Those fruits of the spirit are features of soul growth thanks to the evolution of your consciousness. The behaviors that follow are merely a feedback loop for your growth. The inconsistent nature of behavior is teaching you spiritual consistency and, upon physical death, those virtuous fruits are energetic treasures that you take with you.

That God is not concerned with your behaviors might be surprising to hear, but not if you understand how behaviors are based in probability — a manifestation of Einstein's complaint about God seemingly playing "dice" with the universe — and recognize that the meaning of life is consciousness development. We cannot be perfect in the flesh, because the world is structured to be chaotic and imperfect.

"The creation was subjected to frustration, not by its own choice, but by the will of the one who subjected it."
- Romans 8:20

"Forgive them, for they know not what they do."
- Luke 23:34

"The flesh counts for nothing."
- John 6:63

"I do nothing on my own."
- John 8:28

Jesus, guided by Christ Consciousness, only did what the spirit moved him to do. He did not boast as he knew nature was the agent of action, that due to the observer effect we behave in accordance with the level of our consciousness.

Nature (or God, if you prefer) also prepares an ego costume for us and forces us to fall asleep. In Level 6, we noted how the "complex thinking" part of your brain is not fully developed until your early 20s. Why? Because you have to develop your costume. We are not capable of high-level cognitive processing through our teen years because we are *supposed to* get sucked into the ego way of thinking. That's part of the soul game (Level 22).

Pregnancies last only nine months instead of 21 years, despite the fact that young adult babies would have a better chance at survival if they were born with advanced cognitive skills. If evolution were only about survival of the fittest, surely natural selection would have formulated teenager-sized infants or cognitive superbabies by now.

But it doesn't happen that way for a reason.

Besides the fact that women would never agree to it if they had to be pregnant for two decades, we must start out as helpless babies because our cognitive capabilities need to be on a low level so that 'the game' can begin. The universe is 'designed' to make us run a gauntlet of sorts. We have to forget that we are really souls, which allows us to merge with our individualized ego costumes like our bodies do into memory foam on a Sleep Number mattress. You sink into the ego.

We must forget so that we can remember. We must fall asleep so we can awaken. You must get lost so that you can be found. You must be born once (ego) so that you can be born again (soul).

This process allows the hologram that we are living in to become a spiritual playground. You aren't the swing, the slide, the teeter totter in a physical playground — those are just rides for your body. Similarly, your race, your gender, your sexual orientation, your political affiliation, your religion, your nationality, your age, your height, your weight — those are just ego rides, or costume experiences for your soul.

If your physical parents let you play in a playground by yourself, a great many things can happen. You can have fun, you can meet friends, you can get hurt … but when it's time to leave, if you forget where your home is, you will be lost and scared. You might end up walking around in the dark for a while.

It's as if God sends his little soul children to Playground Earth and tells us, "Just don't forget where home is." A lot of things can happen. You can have fun, you can meet friends, you can get hurt … but when it's time to leave, if you forget where your home is, you will be lost and scared. You might end up walking around in the dark for a while.

Until you remember where home is!

That's waking up. Once you realize you are not your ego costume, you remember where home is. Self-realization is the recognition of the real self, the soul. It is also the first step of detachment and the beginning of the end of suffering that Buddha teaches.

This is enlightenment, the lighting of the path.

"Before enlightenment, chop wood, carry water.
After enlightenment, chop wood carry water."
- Zen proverb

Before enlightenment, you are asleep. You are at a costume party, but you think it is real. After enlightenment, you are awake. You are at a costume party, but you know you are wearing a dreamcoat of light.

In either case, before or after, there's work to be done. Chop wood, carry water.

At least now you are pointed in the right direction.

You know thyself.

You are headed home.

YOUR OWN WORST ENEMY

We all are quite familiar with the symptoms of a common cold.

Coughing, sore throat, runny nose, sneezing, fatigue … that about sums it up. Pretty easy to tell when a cold is coming on, too.

Colds must run their course, but there are several ways to treat one and relieve symptoms. You should get plenty of rest, blow your nose gently but frequently, drink hot liquids, take a steamy shower, gargle, limit caffeine and alcohol intake and perhaps take some vitamin supplements. (And please cover your mouth when coughing around others so that the virus doesn't spread. Thank you.)

If you don't take those measures, your cold will linger and you will suffer longer.

But not everyone is as familiar with a much more insidious plague, one that has afflicted everyone on earth and ultimately kills all who have not gotten control of it.

The human ego. Fixation on the body costume.

It's an energy virus that poisons the soul.

The signs that you have been afflicted with the ego virus are many, including feelings of fear, depression, anxiety, guilt, shame, resentment, excessive irritation, frequent frustration, arrogance, insecurity, inflexibility or rigidity, intolerance,

boredom, obsessiveness, possessiveness, bossiness, a sense of entitlement, divisiveness and inappropriate anger.

Pretty much anything that causes dysfunctional emotional pain. (And please cover your mouth when spewing ego around others so that the virus doesn't spread. Thank you.)

Ego viruses must run their course, too, but unlike the cold these nasty bugs can last an entire lifetime. And they do not discriminate, capable of striking everyone regardless of gender, race, age or other costume features.

Nevertheless, there are several ways to treat one and relieve symptoms. You must take your daily dose of spirit.

"Perfect love casts out fear."
- 1 John 4:18.

Simply adding Truth-based spirituality to your body vessel eliminates negative energy.

The best news is that, for this particular virus, there is a cure.

It's called perfection, which is simultaneously a mask that keeps airborne ego from infecting you while also making you immune from your own inner outbreak of bad vibration.

Perfection is achieved by mastering consciousness via the proper application of what Jesus, Muhammad, Buddha, Krishna and others were *really* saying. In Kabbalah, it's about receiving Upper Light, which is the perfect antidote for ego. The spiritual levels of *New Eyes* are devoted to this, including explanations of what it means to "carry your cross" in Christianity and what jihad actually represents to non-radical, spirit-focused Muslims.

A holy war is indeed required, but that war between ego and spirit needs to be waged *inside oneself.*

The opening salvo in the war needs to address the origin of ego so that the battle can be appropriately engaged, otherwise the ego will win in a landslide.

Writer-director Guy Ritchie created a film in 2005 called *Revolver* that deserved an Academy Award for spiritual excellence. And yet, the word 'spirituality' does not appear in it.

That's because the movie is about identifying the true enemy, the human ego.

Co-authored with Luc Besson, who brought the consciousness-expansion movie *Lucy* to life in 2014, *Revolver* was misunderstood by critics primarily because they missed the point. It is not a schizophrenic gangster-movie featuring violence and sex for entertainment, it is a deeply soulful movie representing the vicious war between ego and spirit that occurs in one's mind.

I have watched clients and friends weep with joy when they 'got' the film, when they grasped its delicious spiritual intricacies. It certainly went over many heads, which was by design, as the ego is a sneaky little devil that requires significant mental acumen to eradicate. In fact, not only is spirituality not mentioned in *Revolver*, prior to the must-watch closing credits neither is the word 'ego.' Why? Because it's a slippery snake that excels at eluding capture.

The rest of this Level will be peppered with italicized quotes from the movie (unless otherwise indicated) as they are an exquisite way to educate aspiring souls on the nature of the adversary.

"Where's the best place an opponent should hide?
In the very last place you would ever look."

Inside yourself.

The enemy is inside your own mind. It's cognitive bacteria, spreading like an infection via your physically focused thoughts … if you believe the material world is all there is.

It's the enemy that causes fear, depression, anxiety, guilt, shame, resentment and other forms of toxic negative feelings, and it is all due to sinning. As discussed in Level 11, the origin of the word 'sin' in Greek is hamartia — to miss the mark or simply to misperceive. So ego is the enemy of Christ

Consciousness, the satanic foe that Jesus says to slaughter before him.

All of the emotional pain listed above comes from an ego place, when the mind assesses situations physically instead of spiritually. Ego is not just about people with swelled heads. When we over-emphasize the importance of our flesh costumes, either good or bad, suffering is the end result.

"He's behind all the pain there ever was.
Behind every crime ever committed."

Pain from depression over something 'bad' happening in your physical life, such as being fired from a job or getting divorced or your favorite football team losing the Super Bowl when you were an ego-stricken 11-year-old.

Pain from anxiety about your physical life, such as worries about money or phobias about most anything (public places, enclosed places, heights, germs, etc.) or worst of all the fear of death.

Pain such as guilt over having used drugs or shame over body image issues — any way you cut it, it is a physical focus. The only difference is in degree, but relativity speaking, physical focus is physical focus, so a sin is a sin.

Just as every cough does not indicate a cold, not every negative emotion indicates ego. Jesus wept, after all, and he doubted when he wondered why God had forsaken him on the cross. But he was 'without sin' because his quest was always spiritual, thus making negative emotion positive. He knew his emotion had purpose.

"Embrace the pain, and you will win this game."

Depression, anxiety and resentment are normal feelings, but

that doesn't make them permanent. Emotional pain is only there because of perception. They are guides for the soul, a GPS system for spiritual growth. All negative emotion can be removed by accurately understanding the world, by embracing emotional pain as an opportunity to elevate consciousness and receive Upper Light.

Ego is behind all the crime, too, as jealousy, lust and rage only rise up due to the flesh and are low-level consciousness precursors to theft, rape and murder. Those actions are the result of physical focus. Religious wars are fought out of misunderstanding as well, when people believe that their prophet is better than your prophet without realizing that those prophets would have *agreed* with each other. Quite literally as spiritual blood brothers, since spirit IS blood for the soul.

Good emotions can lead to pain as well when they are physically oriented and not properly balanced with spirit. If you feel superior to someone because of ego accomplishments, invariably arrogance and relationship problems ensue. Plus, physical success tends to breed a desire for more, and all that goodness tends to keep people from seeking spirit.

"From the tree of the knowledge of good and evil you shall not eat."
- Genesis 2:17

When you assess things as 'good' or 'bad' physically, your mind is consuming the yin-yang world of good and evil. Suffering ensues as you emotionally ping pong around a world dependent upon results. External rules the internal. It's matter over mind.

If you continue to see things that way, you will go round and round and round emotionally. How many times do you have to put your hand on a hot stove before you learn to avoid the heat? How many times do you have to feel the pain of ego before you learn to seek another way?

The only way out of this bad vibes loop is through elevation of consciousness. You either learn the spiritual lesson you are being taught or you experience the pain again and again.

Evolve or revolve.

Revolver is 'samsara' in Eastern traditions, a repeating cycle that we are all in. It is not unlike the deadly weapon, either, as this is a battle that can kill you.

Plus, revolving around the ego loop is no fun. It is repetitive, and thanks to Hebb's Law, it is an addiction. Practice thinking a certain way long enough and patterns emerge in your brain to support what you are thinking, then the world mirrors what you are seeing for further evidence.

Ego imprisons you.

"You've heard that voice for so long you believe it to be you. You believe it to be your best friend."

Ego also operates via Levels 4 and 10, relying on atoms to store its nasty energy and cause all sorts of problems while spreading itself all over the place with entanglement. It's an STD — a soulfully transmitted disease — that occurs when people engage each other's souls while asleep to the spirit. When you absorb ego from another person, you absorb the ego of every person that that person ever absorbed ego with.

It is truly sleeping with the enemy.

When you are so sickened from ego, you see the pain and suffering as normal and cannot see another way out. Worse yet, when another way out is offered, you might reject it as absurd.

That's another classic war maneuver by the ego, which will twist and turn itself into knots trying to convince you that its thought system is correct. You are different from others, it will whisper, to heck with the pain, you are right and they are wrong.

It will get you to roll your eyes at Truth in spite of the relief it offers.

Ego yells at you, *"I say ... you do!"*

Death is a perfect example. If reality is a hologram, then no one actually dies, we all just change form. That death can be overcome is the heart of Jesus's teachings. Thinking this way absolutely brings a relief from suffering, but ego would rather you cling to grief and the fear that all that exists is physical. Ego wants you to suffer.

Thankfully, there are systems of thought that work wonders in alleviating emotional pain. Kabbalah is all about this (Level 28). In Buddhism, *The Tibetan Book of the Dead* explains the process of dying and afterlife experiences in vivid detail. The Tibetan Buddhists are people who spend their whole lives preparing for death, while many of the rest of us spend our whole lives hoping that we won't die. They know a lot about the process, we don't.

The *Book of Dead* begins with the following line: "O God, Boundless Light of this Reality, I acknowledge the oneness of the Infinite Potential."

Which is a clear reference to quantum physics. It might as well read, "Oh God, everything is energy, including you, and I acknowledge superposition."

The Book goes on to emphasize the nature of the True Self as consciousness, that consciousness cannot die, that nothing bad can happen to consciousness. It describes how a radiant light is present immediately after death, how if you embrace its luminosity as your home you are welcomed in, but if you aren't prepared because you still think you are a physical body, it flashes by like a lightning bolt. It explains what happens next if you miss out on entering that light, how you experience all sorts of visions that are alternately peaceful and demonic, but notes that everything is just a projection of your mind. And finally it describes the process of rebirth, how you come back around to try again as reality is a revolving door for the evolution of consciousness.

In summation: You are consciousness, which cannot die. Everything is a projection of your mind. You revolve unless you evolve. And that's *New Eyes* for the afterlife, perfectly consistent with what we need to be aware of for this current life … as it is the *same* life. A continuation of consciousness.

The science of black holes indicates that the same laws apply inside a black hole as does outside of it. Just like with consciousness, the same laws apply during this life as do in the afterlife.

This is the essence of the wheel of life, this is samsara, the revolving cycle that you can be released from through properly perceiving reality.

But don't tell that to ego. It doesn't want you to believe any of that! It lives for the wheel of death! Permanent death with no future … or an eternal hell that awaits you. Your choice!

No thanks, I'll choose what's behind Door No. 3.

The origin of consciousness is a "hard problem" for scientists, but that the radiant light (heaven or *Zohar* in Kabbalistic teachings) from the *Book of the Dead* as its home makes perfect sense as it lies outside our dimension, and that the rest of the process plays out as a hologram just as science indicates reality is. All of this is perfectly reasonable to higher consciousness and is also very peaceful for the soul — and all the prophets teach different aspects of it.

Still, the lower-conscious ego yells at you from inside your own mind, *"I say ... you do!"*

And yet, understanding it all leads to eternal freedom. In the *Book of the Dead*, if at any point in the revolving wheel you realize that all of it is just a projection of your own mind, liberation is yours, the same liberation that in Hinduism is called ‘moksha’ or liberation from … ego.

“O death, where is your victory? O death, where is your sting?
The sting of death is sin.”
- 1 Corinthians 15:55-56

The sting of death is misperception, believing that you are a flesh being and not the conscious aspect of your soul energy body. But freed from sin — as Jesus was — or freed from ignorance you overcome death. Just as Buddha suggested. If you tame the ego, you don’t die.

The alternative to the Truth of eternal life is a fear of death, not knowing what is going to happen. When you know, fear subsides and ego is conquered.

“When the perishable puts on the imperishable, and the mortal puts on immortality, then shall come to pass the saying that is written: ‘Death is swallowed up in victory.’”
- 1 Corinthians 15:54

When the mortal costume submits to wearing the Truth of everlasting consciousness, ego is swallowed up in perfection.

That is part of your job, to surrender to Truth. The word ‘Islam’ means ‘to submit’ while ‘Muslim’ means ‘one who has submitted.’ The submission is to spirit.

The ego must lose this war, the battle that’s going on inside your head. Your job is to arm yourself with wisdom and virtue so that you will win.

“Physician, heal thyself.”
- Luke 4:23

Jesus did not mean heal your body. He meant heal your mind.

See Truth. Be Truth.

Evolving is work, but worth it. Success is really a one-step process: Eat only off the Tree of Life. If in everything you do you do not sin, you seek Truth, *you will win this game*.

That means not giving the ego an inch, because if you do, it will take a mile. You have to arm yourself with Truth in this war, ready to fight fire with Fire. Levels 23-33 are a munitions depot in that regard, a spiritual app of religious inclusivity to address whatever situation that ego throws at you.

If you are armed with forgiveness, no one can emotionally hurt you. If you are armed with courage, no situation can scare you. If you are armed with creativity, no situation bores you. And with wisdom, nothing confuses you.

Ego won't stand a chance.

In *Revolver*, when the protagonist 'ascends' to the level of higher consciousness (at the moment the camera pans in and the golden crown that is framing his head moves 'into' his mind), his mortal flesh enemy appears before him holding a gun and personifying ego. At first the 'bad guy' demands that the 'good guy' fear him, but when he doesn't, the bad guy asks, *"What's your game? What's your game?"*

Ego is confused. The game is evolving consciousness, something ego does not understand as ego is the lowest level of consciousness. In the presence of pure consciousness, you cannot get hurt. So ego puts the gun down and weeps as the spirit breezes past him.

That movie has changed a lot of lives for the better.

"People have no clue that they're in prison," said Leonard Jacobson, founder of Conscious Living Foundation, during the closing credits. "They don't know that there is an ego. They don't know the distinction."

So much good therapy comes from recognizing that that nasty voice inside your head is not you, that it's a thought virus.

It's conditioning. You probably speak English if people taught you English when you were young, you probably root for the football team of the town you live in, you probably joined the religion that is predominant in the country you were born in and you most likely identify with the gender or race of the costume you were given at birth.

And you probably think the same toxic kinds of thoughts that all of us think when we are sick with ego.

"I'm not good enough."

"I hate that girl."

"If I can't see it, I won't believe it."

"I'm better than that guy."

It's all ego. It's all costume conditioning. It gets taught to us by the civilized and uncivilized societies in Egoland.

But you can learn another way. It's tapping into higher consciousness, the True Self.

"Eventually when the opponent is challenged or questioned it means the victim's investment and thus his intelligence is questioned. No one can accept that."

The opponent is the ego; the victim is you when the ego runs your life. When the ego is challenged, its victim (you) often fights back because it cannot imagine giving up decades and decades of investment in its ego identity — the physical costume. Most people fall in love with labels. Giving up their individuality is too much for many to accept.

If you do not learn how to integrate all opposing points of view into a unifying thought system, you are a part of separateness and ego wins.

But if you can see everything from everyone else's perspective, and you can embrace it as a part of their own spiritual process, then you will have attained unity consciousness and ego loses.

"If you can't do it, you are not a free man. You are controlled."

But if you can do it, you are free and the kingdom of heaven is yours.

It is precisely what Krishna, Buddha, Jesus and Muhammad were teaching in their own relative cultures — a spirit of Oneness that brings us all together.

This is very difficult for ego thinking to accept, because no one likes to have their intelligence questioned and fewer still want to surrender their lifetime addiction to their costume.

In time, though, everyone will. We all can only take so much suffering. Once you can understand the language of spirit and read them with *New Eyes*, the prophets make this clear.

How radical are you prepared to be?

YOU GOTTA HAVE FAITH

When Austin and Natalie started dating, Aidan thought his big brother was acting a bit strange.

All of a sudden Austin was doing things like combing his hair, gargling with mouthwash and saying that he couldn't play video games because he was going to the movies with his girlfriend.

No video games? He's hanging out with a girl instead of his cool little bro? What's wrong with that guy?!

Austin, my oldest son, was 15 at the time, as was Natalie. They still have a lot of fun together and talk or text 24/7. Sometimes it is 25/8. Aidan thinks it is 26/9.

So how do you explain romance to a 10-year-old boy? Can he really understand that kind of love anyways? Can it be proven to him that such feelings even exist?

Of course not. He has to experience it for himself.

So it goes with God.

How do you explain a new emotion to someone who has not experienced it? Try telling a toddler about the pride you felt when you got your first promotion. Maybe they can kind of relate, like the first time they went on the potty, but it's not really the same thing. Plus, they stopped paying attention halfway through what you were saying.

Maybe a 10-year-old can relate to love if you compare it to things *he* loves, like baseball for Aidan. He would say he loves Kansas City Royals catcher Salvador Perez, but that's a tad different than the romantic teenager love Austin and Natalie share. Austin loved Brett Favre as his favorite football player, but Natalie certainly does not want him confusing those two feelings of love!

Austin and Aidan also love skiing, they love their dog Dakota and they love pummeling their father in video games like *Smash Bros.* — but love of God is on a whole 'nother level. (Like, Level 33.)

It's undeniable for anyone who has experienced it.

It's also unprovable to anyone who hasn't.

God is *an experience*, not a man made in our image. He is not the Mr. Judgy Pants God that so many people get taught about around the world, as all the prophets make clear when you understand them spiritually, not physically. God is light, God is energy, God is love, God is pure consciousness.

And God cannot be proven.

No one can prove the existence of 'regular' consciousness, either, but does anyone doubt its existence? You are having an experience that you cannot prove you are having. Philosophers long ago debated the notion of solipsism, the idea that the only thing you can be sure that exists is your own mind. Nothing else can be proven.

With that very low bar being set, of course there isn't proof of *God*!

If you prefer science to set the bar for you, great, because scientists have produced similar exotic answers that make solipsism sound reasonable.

Introducing Kurt Gödel and John Stewart Bell, two brilliant men. One blew Albert Einstein's mind and the other will blow your mind.

Gödel was an Austrian-born logician and mathematician whose work is so detailed that it makes writing this book in Mandarin Chinese seem easy by comparison. He was so insightful that Einstein, 27 years his senior, sought out Gödel for deep philosophizing toward the end of his life.

Albert Einstein and Kurt Gödel take a walk.

Suffice it to say, unless you are eager to comprehend mathematical minutiae, the spiritual take-away on this one is all that matters.

Gödel developed two concepts of interest for *New Eyes* called "incompleteness theorems," which in laymen's terms state that "in a consistent system, there are things that are true but unprovable" and "a system's consistency cannot be proven from within the system."

A simple way to understand some of what that means is by using the Liar's Paradox, which is something Gödel wove into his work. Say the sentence, "I am lying," and ask yourself if it is true. If it is true, then you are not lying, which makes the sentence false. If it is false, you are lying, which makes it true.

Gödel somehow transformed that self-contradictory reasoning into mathematics, which as a philosophical statement can then also be used for any logical line of inquiry. In essence, his theorems demonstrate two things:

1. That there are always going to be Truths that cannot be proven.
2. An external observer is necessary to prove everything within a system.

This is an extraordinary stroke of the paint brush on the *New Eyes* landscape. It's only a piece of the puzzle, but a solid fitting one, because it supports a major theme of this book while setting up all the spiritual levels.

As an individual portion of universal consciousness, you are an observer of the reality hologram that has origins outside the universe (although 'above' may be a more accurate description), therefore not 'within the system.'

Jesus: "My thoughts are *higher* than your thoughts."

In order to prove what is inside the system, you need to realize that you are an observer who is outside the system. If you don't, you are operating from lower ego consciousness functioning within the system and therefore cannot figure everything out.

Pac-Man, who is inside the video game, is obviously incapable of fully understanding *you* sitting on the couch controlling him, especially not when using information from within the game. According to Gödel's theorems, *Pac-Man* would also be unable to prove everything within his own system — only you on the couch outside the game could know it all.

Using that analogy, our bodies and ego minds are like *Pac-Man* inside the system, while consciousness or our upper minds are external to the system. Therefore some Truths cannot be proven by ego, which is physical or inner-system based. You have to be *above it all* in order to *see it all*. Lower mind won't cut it, as it will remain incomplete.

So you have to have faith.

"Faith is the substance of things hoped for,
the evidence of things not seen."
- Hebrews 11:1

The *evidence* of things not seen. In other words, your *higher mind* needs to see it. *New Eyes*.

We're not trying to prove God here. To the contrary, God is unprovable within our physical system. Science cannot find God. Whatever you see is your relative truth … but not necessarily *the* Truth.

God can only be proven from outside the costume system. You must remove your dreamcoat. God must be experienced through faith, which is not the kind of blind ego conditioning that undercuts many religious traditions, but from a higher form of consciousness called spirit. You cannot 'behave' your way to heaven, you have to recognize that you are One with the light — just as it says in *The Tibetan Book of the Dead*.

In one of the most thought-provoking passages in the Bible, Jesus illustrated the difference between someone who thinks that doing good deeds will earn them a ticket to heaven versus those who know themselves as living spirit beings.

"Not everyone who says to me, 'Lord, Lord,' will enter the kingdom of heaven, but the one who does the will of my Father who is in heaven. On that day many will say to me, 'Lord, Lord, did we not prophesy in your name, and cast out demons in your name, and do many mighty works in your name?' And then will I declare to them, 'I never knew you; depart from me, you workers of lawlessness.'"
- Matthew 7:21-23

You "do the will of the Father" when you ascend to the highest level of consciousness, or Christ's mind. Then the universal wave function collapses in accordance with your pure-spirit observation through Upper Light, and God's will is done. You act in accordance with his will. You *didn't do anything* but receive the spirit.

But if you try to "do mighty works" from the ego perspective? Chaos ensues, because there are a million relative perspectives under the Son.

What one person calls compassion another might call enabling. For some people compassion is helping another person out, such as giving a homeless man $20 or offering government aid. For other people compassion is insisting that one learns how to help themselves, and would *not* feel good about giving a homeless man $20, especially since no one can guarantee how it will be spent. Can you see how both viewpoints might be correct? And yet, isn't it possible that helping a homeless man by giving him a twenty can be seen as enabling … while not giving him the money when he is struggling can be seen as heartless?

What if you give money to charity, how do you know that it is being spent wisely? Should you try to stop war from happening and allow certain dictators to commit genocide? What would Jesus have done had he been on board one of the hijacked planes on 9/11? Would he have forgiven the terrorists and let them crash the planes … while you sat there with your terrified toddler in your lap?

What about abortion? Same-sex marriage? Gun rights? The list goes on and on. And so does the arguing.

No one is going to figure out satisfactory, unifying answers to these questions from *inside* the system. Doing so is short-sighted, limited and will always be incomplete. That's what Jesus was chastising, doing things from the ego's perspective and not his Father's. No one knows the Father's perspective when they are debating these issues with the relative lower mind. What did Jesus say to some of the very people who pled with him for entrance into heaven?

"I never knew you; depart from me."

That's not peacenik hippie Jesus who wanted to hug everything out, is it? No, that's high-level, high-expectation, you-must-be-perfect Jesus. He is telling us that we do not impress God with our behaviors, our mighty works, but only are received into heaven from a higher place of the Father's mind. The will of the Father is the exchanging of spirit, not of currency nor bombs. Freedom is of the soul, not of the body.

Referring back to physicist Max Planck's comments on science and spirituality in this book's introduction: "Knowledge is not gained by any process of reasoning. It is a direct perception and, therefore, in its nature akin to what we call faith. It is a metaphysical belief."

Faith is not just going to church on Sunday or saying you believe Jesus is your savior. That's ego faith, the kind that got Jesus to say, "Depart from me." True faith accesses the "will of the Father" and requires a direct perception of God.

"Direct perception" can be understood this way: How do you KNOW that 2 + 2 = 4? Once upon a time, when you were a baby, you didn't know that 2 + 2 = 4. But you heard it enough and it was taught to you frequently enough that eventually you came to *know* that it was true. A cognitive switch was flipped and on came the light of insight.

Here's another way of looking at it. Have you ever been in love? How do you *know* that? Is there any type of reasoning involved, or is the feeling of being in love merely a *knowing*? Aidan cannot quite understand yet what Austin and Natalie have felt.

Bottom line: Understanding that the earth revolves around the sun, that 2 + 2 = 4, and that you are in love all involve experiencing a *direct perception* of those concepts. Similarly, being a spiritual Christian requires a *direct perception* of God, which is "akin to what we call faith." (This is largely the viewpoint of Gnostic Christians, Levels 27 and 29).

Ultimately that's how we can finally complete Gödel's theorem, by thinking outside the system and gaining direct access to higher realms of consciousness — when you see above the maze, when you can look down into the matrix. It is the value of understanding wisdom in all spiritual traditions.

You gotta have faith.

(This is the type of spiritual wisdom you might expect to derive from a man whose name starts with "God" and ends with "El" ... which happens to be the abbreviation of Elohim, or God in Hebrew. It's why angel names, such as Gabriel and Michael and Raphael often end in El. So of course Einstein liked hanging out with a guy named Kurt God-God!)

As illuminating as Gödel's work is for *New Eyes*, John Stewart Bell's might be more mystifying. According to particle physicist Henry Stapp, "Bell's Theorem is the most profound discovery of science."

Bell's Theorem essentially confirms all of the quantum physics that this book has covered, and that has mystical implications. It has been experimentally confirmed numerous times, most notably by Alain Aspect in 1982.

Simply stated, Bell's Theorem states that no physical theory that includes local realism can reproduce all the predictions of quantum mechanics.

Not as simple is understanding what "local realism" means.

Locality and realism were concepts that Einstein favored as he hoped to demonstrate their truth, because if they were false, science starts to sound like science fiction.

The principle of locality is the idea that an object can only be directly influenced by its immediate surroundings and not by something a distance away. Essentially, it means that nothing can travel faster than the speed of light. As discussed in Level 10, somehow information does seem to be able to simultaneously get from Point A to Point B, which means something appears to be going faster than light. Einstein called that "spooky action at a distance" and eventually had to get used to the idea, because it is here to stay.

With realism things get really interesting. Once a great debate within the physics fraternity, realism is a concept that — get this — the world is real! Here's the precise question that they debated: Is the moon there when you are not looking at it?

Please read that again. The smartest guys ever actually debated whether the moon existed when there is not someone there to observe it! The idea is a byproduct of superposition, which actually suggests that nothing is real unless there is an observer to interact with it.

So local realism is a concept in which things cannot affect other things simultaneously … and the moon exists even if no one is looking at it.

Along came Bell, who formulated that if local realism is true, then quantum mechanics cannot be — except that the laws quantum mechanics have been tested and retested, verified and reverified, at such a high degree of accuracy that there is virtually unanimity in their truth.

Which means spooky action at a distance occurs and/or the moon isn't there when someone isn't looking at it.

For real?!?

Surreal!

Of course, there is much more to it, but we are just interested in adding another piece to the growing puzzle. Extremely intelligent scientists have basically proven, or in the very least made it seem likely, that the world isn't what we think it is. That the moon isn't there when someone isn't looking at it isn't that strange if you have already read Levels 13 or 16.

In fact, Bell's theorem nicely dovetails with timelessness, as well as with the child in *The Matrix* telling Neo that "There is no spoon."

There is no moon? There is no spoon? There is no noon? My head is starting to swoon!

Dr. Einstein meet Dr. Seuss.

As the child says, "It is not the spoon that bends, it is only yourself."

Mind-bending stuff, indeed. And now you know the answer to the question, "If a tree falls in the woods and nobody is there to hear it, does it make a sound?"

Answer: There is no tree. If no one is there to hear it, like the moon and the spoon and noon, the tree does not exist.

Gödel and Bell together demonstrate how science may be nearing its end, that the next frontier goes where they cannot go: Consciousness. Without the ability to prove everything that may be true and without a definitive reality to test objectively and completely, perhaps faith indeed turns out to be a critical piece of the puzzle.

Of course it does. You cannot know Truth without faith, which takes regular, boring old consciousness up a notch. It takes you to the level of knowing yourself for real.

In fact, as long as you have the right kind of faith and not blind, conditioned faith, there is no need to even understand any of the science discussed in this book. You just have to know that we aren't what many of us think we are, a bunch of bodies that are here doing a bunch of stuff and hoping it's the right stuff so that the Big Daddy In The Sky approves of us and lets us into His House after all of this is over.

No, what you do has nothing to do with it. It's a verse worth repeating:

"For by grace you have been saved through faith.
And this is not your own doing; it is the gift of God,
not a result of works, so that no one may boast."
- Apostle Paul, in Ephesians 2:8-9

Grace is the energy you receive when you find true faith — spiritual faith, not ego costume faith. You did nothing to earn it, except for raise your hand and ask for it.

"Let what you say be simply 'Yes' or 'No';
anything more than this comes from evil."
- Matthew 5:37

You either receive spirit or you don't. The rest is ego.

This is the doctrine of sola fide, or Latin for "faith alone." Justification by faith alone is what Protestant Reformationist Martin Luther considered to be the most important, and perhaps the only important, teaching of Christ.

Justification by God is when He removes sin from you. And what is sin? Misperception, or thinking you are a body. When you have spiritual faith and know that you are a soul — a vessel of light and not an ego costume — your misperception is removed and you are seeing clearly. And then you are saved.

The Biblical Book of James emphasizes "faith without works is dead," but once you have true faith and Christ Consciousness is in you, your works are automatically coming from above. When His graceful energy enters you, it is God's will moving through you and your behaviors change accordingly. Your works are from above and not from you, so there is no reason to feel superior (or inferior) to anyone else. Jesus didn't.

"Truly, truly, I say to you, the Son can do nothing of his own accord, but only what he sees the Father doing."
- John 5:19

"I can do nothing on my own. ... I carry out the will of the one who sent me, not my own will."
- John 5:30

Jesus did not boast, because he did nothing on his own. He was operating with the higher mind of Christ Consciousness, not from the lower mind of ego, so he behaved as Christ would — the will of God — and not from the will of Jesus.

It should be WWCD: What Would *Christ* Do?

"For we are his workmanship, created in Christ Jesus for good works, which God prepared beforehand, that we should walk in them."
- Apostle Paul, in Ephesians 2:10

We are souls moving through this dimension. How you observe this dimension determines your behaviors on a percentage basis, according to superposition and the observer effect. If you elevate your consciousness you are "created in Christ" and your works are good, and this was all set up beforehand ... organized chaos.

If you see it from Christ's perspective, you get organized.

If you see it your ego costume's way, you get chaos.

"I pray that the eyes of your heart may be enlightened."
- Apostle Paul, in Ephesians 1:18

Eyes of your heart? Might as well call them *New Eyes*.

They give you the faith to see what your soul needs to see.

SPIRITUAL MAGNETISM

God has no idea what's in your wallet.

Some might not believe that, but I hope it won't be a surprise to many people.

God does not want you to have lots of money, nor does He want you to be broke.

It's just that God simply does not care about money at all.

There are many ways to misunderstand spiritual texts, foremost among them those who kill in the name of their God based upon a literal interpretation of Scripture. We will be going over that in detail throughout the upcoming spiritual Levels.

But another affront to the wonderful, soulful teachings of the great prophets is known as prosperity theology, or the prosperity gospel. The basic idea is that God's will is for you to have lots of money, that if you display your faith in Him, He will reward you with cold hard cash, or material wealth of some kind.

It goes without saying that not a single practitioner of the prosperity gospel is likely to be aware that time and space are illusions, that the world is a hologram and that they are wearing an ego costume. Taking the energy world of consciousness literally is a surefire way to misread Scripture.

"Bring the full tithe into the storehouse, that there may be food in my house. And thereby put me to the test, says the Lord of

hosts, if I will not open the windows of heaven for you and pour down for you a blessing until there is no more need."
- Malachi 3:10

Prosperity theologists would have you believe that verse means if you tithe — or give 10 percent of your monthly income to the church — God will in turn give you back tons of dough, as if He is some sort of stock market analyst who created the universe with compounding interest on His mind … or that the first thing He does every morning is check interest rates.

Never mind that it does not actually say to give "10 percent of your income" anywhere in the Bible. And what of the "food in my storehouse?" No, God is not sitting there with an empty belly, hoping we will fill His cupboards.

The Bible actually says very little about tithing, and what is said is from the Old Testament. There's "Every tithe of the land, whether of the seed of the land or of the fruit of the trees, is the Lord's" (Leviticus 27:30) and "You shall tithe all the yield of your seed that comes from the field year by year." (Deuteronomy 14:22).

There are also a few brief references to Abraham and Jacob doing so, though in those situations the tithe was about materials and not money. As such, there can be a good debate about what it means in terms of a Christian's financial relationship with the church. If there is no literal "give 10 percent of your money" commandment in the Bible, where did that come from? And if it is "10 percent of the fruit of the trees" or "10 percent of your seed that comes from the field" then what exactly should we be placing in the offering plates? Apples and appleseeds?

That is not a debate that interests *New Eyes*, because in spiritual terms tithing is very clear.

What Jesus said in the King James version of Matthew 6:22, "If therefore thine eye be single, thy whole body shall be full of light."

What Jesus did not say, "If therefore thine eye be single, thy whole wallet shall be full of loot."

Take the actual verse literally and you must think that God wants you to be an illuminated cyclops.

Of course that verse isn't about money. Like most everything else in the Bible and other religious texts, it's about spirit. In order to understand French, you have to speak French. In order to understand spirituality, you have to speak spirit.

Money is currency for human beings. Spirit is currency for spiritual beings.

The origin of the word tithe is 'tēotha' in Old English, the verb being 'tēothian,' or the act of tithing. It means "tenth."

The Bible never says that, in order to honor or show faith God, one must give a tenth of his financial earnings. That's because the Bible is a book of stories and riddles to make you think, to make you go inward to find the kingdom of heaven.

"I will open my mouth with a parable; I will utter hidden things."
- Psalm 78:2

Heaven is inside you, which means tithing is about something inside of you. It's about the ego submitting and giving attention over to God by shifting 10 percent of conscious focus off the flesh world and onto the spirit world. If you give God a mere 10 percent of *your mind*, Truth will come crashing down on you like an avalanche.

Remember Hebb's Law and neurons that fire together, wire together? Practice makes perfect? If you don't commit much time to practicing something, will you ever get good at it? No. (I've noticed this with my golf swing.)

Scientifically speaking, there is a proven percentage that demonstrates what it takes to start getting good at something.

For momentum to build. For the dam to break.

It's called critical mass.

In physics, critical mass is the minimum amount of fissile material needed to maintain a nuclear chain reaction. In other applications, critical mass is the minimal amount of something necessary in order to produce a particular result. For example, the amount of community interest required for a business to succeed in a particular area, the point at which a politician goes from unknown to a national candidate or the percentage of people needed to view a video on YouTube in order for it to go viral.

In 2011, cognitive scientists at Rensselaer Polytechnic Institute scientists did a study on social networking and discovered what proportion of the population is required for an idea to soon take hold by the majority.

That number is 10 percent.

Tēotha.

Once a tenth of the population begins to emphatically follow or embrace an idea, then there is a good chance for the rest of society to follow. Governments are sometimes quickly overthrown once public opinion against a dictator reaches critical mass. In pop culture, once a meme takes hold, it often becomes ingrained into our collective consciousness.

"When the number of committed opinion holders is below 10 percent, there is no visible progress in the spread of ideas. It would literally take the amount of time comparable to the age of the universe for this size group to reach the majority," said Rensselaer professor Boleslaw Szymanski, director of the critical mass research. "Once that number grows above 10 percent, the idea spreads like flame."

The Institute published its findings in an article entitled, "Social consensus through the influence of committed minorities." That means over time groups come to agreement on

ideas when devoted smaller groups are persuasive enough to be convincing.

It works the same way with your mind.

The world is set up this way, with critical mass in mind. Recall Level 2 — chaos rules the day, predominantly due to ego thinking, but over time when you are committed to certain thoughts that strike a chord with you, eventually the organizing principle called Truth takes hold. First a few neurons are involved, then whole clusters, then the entire brain. Minority morphs into majority. The thought system then becomes self-perpetuating and generates further evolution of consciousness.

This is the deeper meaning of tithe — a tenth of your mind. You must commit a portion of your thoughts to the pursuit of spirit.

"If you have faith as small as a mustard seed, you can say to this mountain, 'Move from here to there,' and it will move.
- Matthew 17:20

That means it only takes *a little* to move *a lot*. It takes a miniscule 10 percent to move the mountainous 90.

When one more piece of straw breaks the camel's back, you have crossed that magical 10 percent threshold. Things then can explode, with thinking just as in nuclear dynamics. In both cases, reaching critical mass begins a chain reaction, ultimately spreading like wildfire.

Einstein said, "We can't solve problems by using the same kind of thinking we used when we created them."

That was his variation on the well-known urban definition of insanity, to do the same thing over and over again while anticipating a different result. We simply cannot swirl around in the cesspool of lower mind and expect to get out.

Many well-intentioned religious people get caught in this trap, sincerely wanting to break free from the clutches of the devilish ego, but not putting their energy in the right place to the right proportion. The wrong place is focusing on behaviors or the body, because that is sinning (missing the mark), and the wrong proportion is an insufficient amount of spiritual focus. The *right place* is the mind and the *right proportion* is 10 percent.

Most of us commit only about two percent, maybe three, of our brain power to the spirit world. We see flesh, we get flesh. Thus, we stay stuck in the hologram and the dream continues as we slumber along.

Despite the world being such a persistent illusion, with just a little shift in consciousness, everything can change. You can wake up, but you must make the best use of time.

You must tithe.

Commit 10 percent of yourself to the evolution of your consciousness.

Hebb's Law takes over, neurons fire and wire together, and then the true meaning of Malachi 3:10 takes effect. If you offer up the full tithe, focusing a tenth of your conscious day on soul development, there will indeed be food (fruits of the spirit) in God's house (which is the energetic body of your soul). Try it, says God, and see if it works. It will, as the Holy Spirit (i.e. soul love) will pour into you and your life will feel free at last, not restricted by the chains of ego.

Or you can think that the Malachi verse is about money; many people make the world about precisely that. Sadly, so do some religious people. If Christianity were about God blessing us physically, why would He allow His own son to be killed? What a strange message to send us, "If you are good, like, super good, I'll have you killed."

If Christianity were about God blessing us physically, shouldn't Jesus be 2015 years old with great hair and no back pain, flaunting his stylish good looks and massive fortune from compounding interest over two millennia? "Follow me," he would have said, "and see if God doesn't unleash the full blessings of Wall Street and Abercrombie & Fitch on you."

Taking Truth and making it physical is what some people have done with a concept from the century-old New Thought movement called the Law of Attraction, or "like attracts like" on an energetic level. It's a version of "you create your own reality," as your thoughts create the things in your life. This idea, like all spiritual laws that are misapplied, has some positive aspects to it … but it can be greatly misunderstood.

In 1912, New Thought writer Charles Haanel wrote in his book *The Master Key System* that "The law of attraction will certainly and unerringly bring to you the conditions, environment and experiences in life, corresponding with your habitual, characteristic, predominant mental attitude."

That's true, but there's one catch: Who is YOU in that sentence?

If you think you are the ego body dreamcoat you are wearing, then the law of attraction is often true but wildly inconsistent and sometimes downright absurd. Is there a single person who died on 9/11 whose "predominant mental attitude" was that a plane was going to fly into their building that day? Much less *everyone* who suffered that fate? Of course there weren't. Misapplying this concept is a great way to retraumatize victims at their most vulnerable by making them responsible for what happened.

What this application does not take into account is *probability*, which we went over in detail in Levels 8 and 9. There are certain experiences that are just not likely to happen, no matter how much you resonate with them, and certain experiences do happen no matter how much you don't resonate with them. That's what happened on 9/11. No one attracted those horrific events into their lives.

Thanks to superposition — the energetic fabric upon which this universe rests — there are just tendencies, not guarantees. At best we can influence the odds of something happening. It's what Einstein hated, the "God playing dice" aspect to this.

So you can improve your golf game and improve your chances of surviving a cancer diagnosis, but is the law of attraction "certainly and unerringly" going to bring you whatever corresponds to your "predominant mental attitude?" If so, surely there should be a 977-year-old pregnant man somewhere on earth who can fly and become invisible at will. I mean, if that's his "predominant mental attitude," why not?

And yet, the law of attraction is indeed true … as long as you know it applies to *your soul*.

Haanel, whose book espouses the virtues of connecting to the infinite source of universal consciousness, states that the law of attraction works best when your habitual mindset is in "strict accordance with the Truth."

Now that's right on … as long as you know it applies to *your soul.*

The law of attraction is in strict accordance with the Truth when it is being applied for spiritual development.

The 2006 film *The Secret* had many critics for its consistent focus on the law of attraction being used to acquire material possessions (especially while disregarding the probabilistic nature of physical reality), but there were several redeeming qualities in it as well. The film, both hugely popular and controversial, noted that "everything is energy" and emphasized the power of positive emotionality. Most notably, though, the "three-step process" of "Ask, Believe, Receive" is grounded in Truth.

It sometimes works physically, but it always works spiritually.

If you ask for a big bag of gold and X-Ray vision, you *might* not receive it no matter how much you believe it. But if you ask for hope — believing — you will receive hope. If you ask for courage — believing — you will receive courage. If you ask for the ability to forgive — believing — you will receive the gift of forgiveness.

It's spiritual magnetism, as your mind and heart draw virtues into your soul.

That is the law of attraction when applied accurately — spiritually. Yes, Malachi, there is no limit to the blessings that will be poured down upon you. Hope, courage, forgiveness, gratitude, wisdom and more, these will all be added to you, the soul.

Jesus laid it out for us nearly 2,000 years ago.

"All things you ask in prayer, believing, you will receive.
- Matthew 21:22

Ask, believe, receive.

But Jesus was not crucified so you can be financially healthy, nor physically attractive. He died so that we may see that Christ Consciousness is the savior of your soul, so that you can be spiritually well.

"Are you so foolish? After starting in the spirit,
are you now finishing in the flesh?"
- Apostle Paul, in Galatians 3:3

You started out as consciousness, as an ascending soul, and you will finish as such. Along the way you are wearing a costume.

So tithing and the law of attraction are about spirit. Thinking this way can be like an earthquake being triggered by a shifting fault line, as reaching critical mass alters the way you observe the world and, in turn, affects the field of superposition. When you think differently, reality appears differently.

God does not care if you are a millionaire. He gives you the opportunity to achieve the kingdom of heaven by finding it inside of you in the form of the consciousness that Jesus demonstrated. Physical life circumstances happen to give you that opportunity. You influence the occurrence of those circumstances, but you don't precisely create them. The universe does that for you. You only create your emotional response to them and, in turn, the universe responds accordingly. (Time and space change and *electrons are watching you*, remember.)

Everything happens for a reason, all right. Traffic jams happen to generate patience. Accidents happen to engender caution. Wars happen to promote peace. Death happens to inspire fearlessness. Nothing ever happens to get you rich. In spirit, perhaps, but not in the pocket.

If you feel compelled to give money to your church, that is perfectly fine, as long as the spirit moves you and not the ego. If donating money is your spiritual way of showing gratitude for your physical blessings, then you are being spiritual. If donating money is your spiritual way to demonstrate compassion, then you are being spiritual. If receiving money is a poor person's way of experiencing gratitude, then they are being spiritual, too. Receiving charity is another way to inspire hope, which is decidedly spiritual.

But if in any way anyone thinks God is noticing a money transaction occurring, you have old eyes. If you give out of obligation or guilt, the only thing God will notice you exchanging will be ego energy.

"Don't lie, and don't do what you hate."
- Gospel of Thomas

So of course you can "tithe" 10 percent of your earnings if you wish and throw in a few appleseeds as well, just know that God does not require it.

"Freely you have received; freely give."
- Matthew 10:8

That means the Holy Spirit. You received it freely, you should give it freely.

As hard as it may be to believe, God is not worried about our physical health problems, either. He will help you heal your soul, and if that in turn heals your body, great. But physical healings are not the point.

Tithing and the law of attraction are set up to foster the energetic development of the fruits of the spirit inside of you, nothing else. Anyone who believes that God is interested in healing bodies should ask themselves why he selectively chooses to heal some sick children while letting others pass away? Do some children really die because they do not have a good prayer support team? And you want to believe in that kind of God?

Health problems, just like all financial problems, are opportunities for the evolution of consciousness, which in turn develops the soul via the receiving of the Holy Spirit. We all recognize that some of the most spiritual people we have ever met have experienced significant physical health problems. In them, God only sees the Light.

On this point, remembering these words of Jesus can be illuminating:

"The spirit gives life, the flesh counts for nothing."
- John 6:63

All you need to do to receive "spirit" life is ask for it. *That* is the law of attraction.

If you are struggling with deeply believing that, all you have to do is tithe. Focusing on soul development for 10 percent of your wakeful day translates into about 100 minutes. This doesn't mean one hour and 40 minutes of religious study, although that counts if it increases wisdom (just as reading the rest of this book might). You can also accrue that time with a few minutes here and a few minutes there. It means practicing patience in long lines, practicing forgiveness to someone who hurt you, practicing hope when you are feeling down, practicing trust when things don't go your way, practicing gratitude for what you have, practicing generosity for what you can give away, and so much more. The physical practice is for spiritual gain.

Think of it this way. If you work out your body for 100 minutes a day, you would become physically fit in no time.

What happens if you work out your soul 100 minutes a day? You would be a spiritual supermodel!

Who feels better, someone who is physically fit or out of shape? It's the same with the soul, which will benefit from your perfectly-fit mind.

"Physical training is good,
but training for godliness is much better."
- 1 Timothy 4:8, New Living translation

Training for godliness. That is tithing, giving ego energy over to the spirit.

Experiencing godliness. That is the law of attraction, drawing fruits of the spirit into the Holy Grail.

THE GOD GAME

Imagine you are taking a friend to play golf for the first time. He knows nothing about the game at all. Nothing. And you tell him nothing until he shows up at the course, when you let him know that the object is to get the little white ball into the hole way over there. He insists he needs no further instruction.

"I got this," says your friend, who then picks up the ball, runs it over to the hole and drops it in.

"No, no, no," you say, "you have to use these clubs."

An avid baseball fan, he picks up the ball and tries to fungo it down the fairway.

"No, no," you say, "you cannot use your hands at all."

So he starts kicking the ball.

"No!"

Frustrated with his incompetence and your scorn, your friend finally stops messing around and agrees to learn the rules of the game.

Does knowing the rules make him a good golfer? Certainly not, as millions of duffers around the world can attest, but it gives him a chance.

So it goes with life.

If you don't know the rules, you don't have a chance at winning. You will look as clueless and incompetent as your rookie golf friend appeared when he was on his hands and knees using a putter like a pool cue to advance the ball. You also get penalized immediately every time you break a rule, and ignorance is no excuse. In golf it adds a stroke or two to your score, in life it's called adding negative karma, or more 'bad energy' to burn.

Worse yet, in life, most people don't even realize they are playing the game, or are playing the *wrong* game.

Suppose, while you are trying to sink a bogey putt, all of a sudden a big black ball goes rolling across the green. You look up and there is a guy coming towards you.

"Hey, what are you doing?" you inquire with a furrowed brow.

"I'm bowling, what are you doing?" he responds, equally annoyed with you.

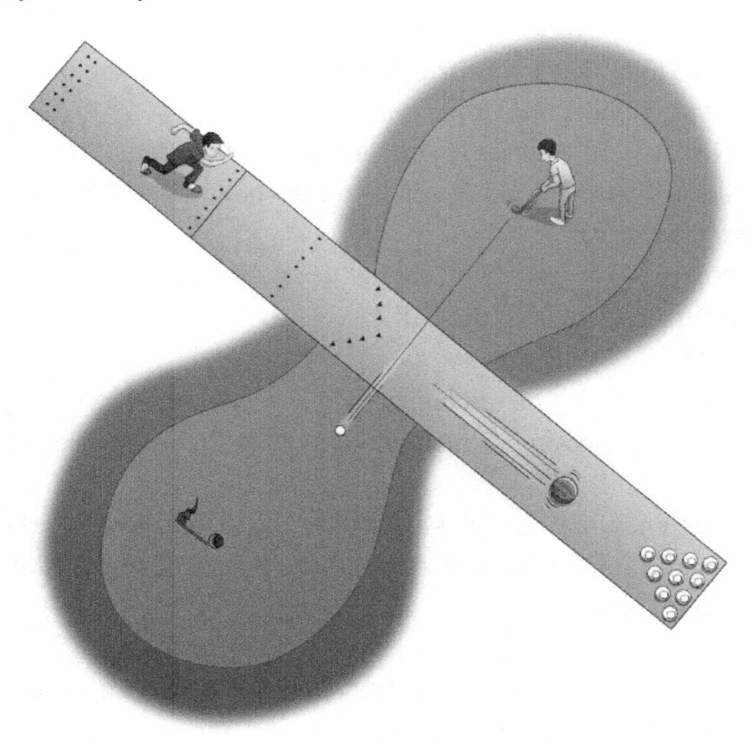

An argument ensures. You explain to him that you are golfing and he insists that he only sees a bowling alley, no green. It's a theater of the absurd. Each guy thinks the other is crazy. (And thanks to relativity, they could both be right.)

Only question is, who is playing the *right* game?

Life is indeed a game. There are many definitions to the word 'game' and it's important to hone in on the correct one to properly explain life.

There's "an activity providing entertainment or amusement." True, life can be entertaining and amusing, but that is not the primary definition we want.

There's "wild mammals, birds, or fish hunted for food or sport." That would be game within the game, which isn't what we are looking for either.

And there's "an active interest or pursuit, especially one involving competitive engagement or adherence to rules."

That's the one.

Referring to it as *a game* is not meant to trivialize it — not at all. *New Eyes* is mostly serious business, as rediscovering your eternal life truly depends upon seeing the world as it was meant to be seen: Spiritually.

That's the right game. Life is a pursuit of higher consciousness featuring competitive engagement inside one's own mind in accordance with specific rules.

This Level is about the rules of this game called life.

In order to win any game there are three critical ingredients:

1. You must know you are playing it.
2. You must know the features and rules of the game.
3. You must play the game well.

In *Revolver*, ego personified asks of the spirited character, *"What's your game?"*

That's because ego is like the guy bowling his way across a golf course. He's playing a game, all right, but it's the wrong one for the setting. Ego does not want to play the spirit game and wanders around cluelessly on the spiritual playground. Ego's domain is the flesh game. It cares about only physical matters. Ego is lower consciousness — if it becomes higher consciousness it disappears, thus it is obsessive about continuing to play its low-level game.

So you must know what game you are playing. If you try to play Monopoly in the middle of a football game, you are going to get trampled. If you try to play football in the middle of a Monopoly game, you are going to go directly to jail.

Egos play the flesh game. Souls play the spirit game.

"No one can serve two masters ...
You cannot serve God and money."
- Matthew 6:24

So you have to pick between the games. You can ultimately play both as long as you are balanced — giving to Caesar what is Caesar's and to God what is God's — but only one truly matters.

It is The God Game. It's Hide and Seek.

"You are in a game, you are in THE game.
Everyone is in this game and nobody knows it."
– Revolver

But now you know.

It's an aggravating, liberating, complex and yet simple game with several important elements.

Features of The Game

Objective: The Holy Grail has been hidden and you must

find it.

Whether it is Heaven in Christianity, Jannah in Islam, Nirvana in Buddhism, Moksha in Hinduism, Olam Ha-Ba in Judaism or Pleroma in Gnosticism, your ticket to ascending to paradise is finding the Holy Grail of higher consciousness and filling your soul with spirit light.

Call it whatever you wish — perfected energy is perfected energy.

Equipment: Your body and your mind.

These are tools that you use to accomplish your task. You take neither of them with you when you die, so use them wisely.

The Field: The whole universe.

Sure, you can travel to Andromeda if you wish, but really the earth is enough of a playing surface for this game.

Teammates: Everyone.

Whether they know it or not, all of humanity is playing this game and we all play roles for each other in our personal growth. Somebody else's rudeness is the opportunity for you to be forgiving and an opportunity for them to be grateful for your forgiveness. Think relativity. We all have different things to work on.

The ultimate team victory is when everyone achieves Unity Consciousness.

Coach: The Lord.

This is not a person, it is a perfected energy state of higher consciousness. Regarding Jesus, the Lord is Christ. Hindus call their prophet Lord Krishna. Buddha and Muhammad are similar shepherds, guiding their flock as any good coach will do.

Oh, and the coach might yell at you sometimes, but only because he wants you to do your best.

Team Owner: God.

He has all the power and calls all the shots from upon high, but mostly He just sits back and watches the game.

Referee: Your brain.

Everyone calls their own fouls. Your brain will blow the whistle on you if you are out of balance. You'll hear it, a loud screeching noise inside your mind that manifests as mental health and sometimes physical health issues, though not always. Sometimes a penalty flag gets thrown at you and it doesn't appear to be deserved, but you still have to work with it.

Fans: Spirit beings.

They are totally rooting for you. Whether they are here on earth playing the game as human bodies or on the other side roaming around the afterlife, all souls are on your side. Listen carefully and you can hear them cheering.

Sometimes they may seem like fair-weather fans, but deep down they are loyal and remain on your eternal bandwagon.

Scoreboard: Your emotions.

How do you know if you are winning or losing? Simple, it's based upon how much permanent peace you are feeling in your heart.

Temporary peace, acquired when things go your way or when you are high or drunk, does not count. Cheaters never win. If you feel relaxed because of using drugs, you didn't really accomplish peace.

Permanent peace is exemplified by lasting emotional stability in the presence of virtues: forgiveness, compassion, courage, hope, perspective, wisdom, mercy, etc.

The prophets all lit up the scoreboard in their day.

The Opponent: The ego.

Otherwise known as the devil, the ego is the defense to your soul's offense. The ego has just one job, to keep you from scoring. It will do everything in its power to beat you. It will attack from all angles. It loves to blitz and blindside you. It plays a full-court press for four quarters. It will kick you when you are down. It will definitely try to cheat. If you are beating it, it will get desperate and go into kamikaze mode, gunning for mutually assured destruction. It will kill itself in order to kill you. It lives for death.

Like a serpent, it wraps itself around you like a heavy chain, weighing you down. Like Houdini, you must loosen yourself from what binds you in order to be truly free.

The ego is so clever, it tricks you into thinking it is your best friend. The better it is, the better you have to be.

In *Revolver* this question is asked, *"What's the first rule of any game?"*

The answer: *"The only way to get smarter is by playing a smarter opponent."*

The. Ego. Is. Brilliant. You play this game, you are in for a war. By playing it, you *will* get smarter.

That's one rule of the game, there are many others.

Rules of The Game

The Beginning Of Wisdom Is: "Acquire wisdom; And with all your acquiring, get understanding."

That's Proverbs 4:7. It means to learn the rules of the game.

Love Your Enemies: Your enemies are everywhere because ego is everywhere. They manifest both physically and spiritually, just as you do.

Physically, enemies can appear as many things, but primarily as human beings. They can be dysfunctional family members, traitorous friends, adversarial co-workers, political foes, dreaded sports rivals and, to some, members of another religion. Enemies can also be negative physical circumstances, such as diseases or other health concerns, employment worries, housing difficulties and financial struggles.

Spiritually, enemies come in the form of mental energy (stinkin' thinkin') and the absence of virtues (i.e. fear, regret, resentment, shame, guilt, etc.)

As tough as all that can be, the advice of Jesus in Matthew 5:44 is to "love your enemies."

Does this mean you have to hug them, bake them a pie, hold hands in a circle and sing kumbaya together? Absolutely not. Jesus always gives spiritual advice, occasionally physical. Let love in your heart, and that will guide your behaviors.

You can love your enemies in the same way you would respect the obstacles on an obstacle course. They make the course challenging. They are there to make you stronger. What would a basketball game be without a defense? Five-on-zero fast-breaks down the court every possession would be a boring thing to watch.

You need defense against you, it challenges you to make your soulful offense stronger. The ego is concealing Truth from you, which makes playing Hide and Seek that much more interesting.

Gotta love your enemies.

Don't Hate the Haters: This is a modern-day variation on love your enemies.

Haters gonna hate *New Eyes*. They can go ahead, it just gives a spiritually inclined person more opportunities to love them in return. An old Chinese proverb says, "The person who says it cannot be done should not interrupt the person doing it."

Haters are going to interrupt you on your unifying journey. Don't let them. You just stay focused.

Remember Your GPS: Trust your emotions, they are always encouraging you to go in the direction of peace.

Don't try to cover up or deny your feelings. Let them assist you. If you don't like your emotions, shift your perception and consciousness will evolve.

Tithe: In sports, if you take your eye off the ball, you are going to miss it.

Spiritually speaking, taking your eye off the ball is sinning.

It's missing the mark.

If you want to win the game, you must take 10 percent out of your daily earthly focus and put it towards spiritual development.

Keep Your Head Down: Speaking of missing the ball, if you lift your head during your backswing in golf you are going to whiff.

While playing this game of Hide and Seek, keeping your head down means staying humble. The higher consciousness rises, the greater the expectations are on you. No man shall boast.

Forget Your Last Shot: If you miss your first free throw attempt in basketball, does it do any good to get down on yourself for the second? Of course not.

Learn from your mistakes. If you do, you just took a 'bad' situation and made it 'good.' Utilize Hebb's Law to repeat this philosophy frequently enough and as an optimistic observer eventually you learn all that you need to know. In the end, *it's all good.*

The Eternal Now: Stay in the moment as often as you can, because that's all there ever is. Just this moment.

There is no such thing as time for your soul, so relax. Just do it.

The Mirror: Don't forget that the world is showing you who you really are spiritually every second of your life.

A soul can only be seen through *New Eyes*, as we look at human bodies with ego eyes. Physical mirrors will show you flesh, but the world is an energy mirror showing you your spiritual essence.

It's Not *Your* Ego: You are NOT ego, so do NOT say "my ego."

That's what the ego wants, for us to identify with it so that it can separate us. It's a virus, remember, it poisons the soul.

When you say "my ego" you have immediately succumbed to split mind and thereby give lower consciousness power over you, isolating you from spirit.

It makes more sense to say, "my costume" or "my variation of the ego." Plus that tames the ego as you show it who is boss.

When you feel the spirit-ego battle raging in your head, typically when you have racing thoughts or are feeling anxious or depressed, whisper to the ego what the protagonist says in *Revolver*:

"I can hear you. I'm onto you. I'm coming to get you."

The ego will resist and insist, *"I am you."*

But you reply, *"You ain't me. ... You don't control me, I control you."*

Properly identify the enemy. It's the ego, a costume for our souls. It's not you.

Money Is Not The Root Of All Evil: Ego is.

Ego obsesses over money. *New Eyes* sees money as a tool to gain more spirit.

Ego obsesses over everything physical. *New Eyes* sees everything physical as tools to gain more spirit.

Don't worship money one way or another. Thinking you are being spiritual just for giving it away is just as bad as thinking you are special for having lots of it in the first place.

Money is a clever ego trap. The real currency that Jesus talked about is spirit. When he said "give to the poor" it meant "give spirit to the spiritually needy."

You can give away your money as well, that *can* be spiritual. Money is a wonderful tool to learn gratitude, generosity, compassion, discipline and mercy. Those are fruits of the spirit, which is currency for the soul.

But if you do give a homeless man $20, look him in the eyes and give him some hope and encouragement, too. That's the best of both worlds.

Lather, Rinse, Repeat: If you bought into the ego illusion and fell in love with the False Self, 'quantum foam' got in your old eyes and blinded you. You based your primary identity on a world that is inherently false. You're in good company. It happened to all of us.

Now it's time to walk it back, washing that stinky ego right out of your hair. The amount of ego energy that skunked you is your karma.

There will be a lot of repetition involved in this process, which serves to balance out karma. You have to think about how you are not your ego costume again and again and again. Practice makes perfect.

Love Is Patient: If you are helping others on their spiritual journey, be gentle.

A butterfly would never yell at a caterpillar, "What are you waiting for? FLY ALREADY!"

The enlightenment process takes time … though patience doesn't mean permanently patient.

Jesus said he did not come to bring peace. There is a time for every purpose under heaven. There is a time for patience and a time for flipping over tables.

But as the inspirational Wayne Dyer liked to say, "When given the choice between being right or being kind, choose kind."

When in doubt, be patient. It won't add negative karma like being impatient will.

Wait'll Next Year: You can spend your whole life playing the wrong game and when it is time to turn in your scorecard, you will be disqualified.

No worries. Another season is just around the corner. If you don't evolve, you'll revolve. It's a samsara game, the Wheel of Life. It's infinity.

Knowing And Not Doing Is Not Knowing: The three pillars

in the Kabbalah are contemplation, action and devotion. Krishna in the Gita emphasizes knowledge, action and devotion. A primary step toward egolessness in Buddhism is learning dharma, or teachings.

In each case, the emphasis is on knowledge first. That's learning the rules. It's a spiritual game, you have to know how to play it.

Then it's game time.

Before enlightenment, chop wood, carry water. After enlightenment, chop wood, carry water.

Once you know what to do, there's still work to be done.

Enlightenment is like a coal miner who is headed down into a mine and turns the light on his helmet. The pathway is now illuminated. Then he must walk the path.

The going can be treacherous, but at least you know where you are headed.

Keep Your Game Face On: Equanimity — or maintaining your composure in spite of very challenging circumstances.

One of my two favorite movie scenes comes from *Glory*, when black Civil War soldier Denzel Washington gets whipped while his white officer friend Matthew Broderick oversees the punishment. Denzel says nothing, yet burns a hole in his friend's soul (and ours) with a laser-locked stare as a single tear rolls down his face.

Talk about superb acting, Denzel seemingly controlled the speed at which the tear trickled off his cheek. He deservedly won the Oscar for "Best Supporting Actor" for his role throughout the film, but that scene alone was sufficient to secure the prize. In a mere 30 seconds, we can see the soul-nauseating pain that ego can create inside the human heart.

The other clip that induces chills every time I see it comes from *Revolver*, when the consciously evolved Jason Statham fearlessly looks right through his gun-toting enemy. He doesn't flinch. In fact, he doesn't see an enemy at all, since he had conquered his own demons.

Statham was so compelling in that movie, too bad most of the critics were asleep and missed that he played the role of everyman, not gangster. He slaughtered the ego right before our eyes, also not uttering a sound in that scene.

Spirit needs no words. Just that steely look in your *New Eyes* — like Jesus maintaining his composure on the cross.

Seek and Ye Shall Find: It's the best advice ever given.

If you heard that a golden key has been placed under a rock somewhere in the United States and that you can use it to unlock all of the mysteries of the universe, you would go looking for it.

Thanks to superposition, the odds of you finding something go up if you seek it. And thanks to timelessness, you have all eternity to find it. You will eventually find it. Fear no evil.

The Holy Grail is hiding in plain sight.

ANGEL IN DISGUISE

Had the first 22 Levels of this book been focused on teaching a foreign language, perhaps you could begin speaking in Arabic, German or Swahili.

Alas, having instead gone over all the relevant science and several related mystical concepts, hopefully you are now fluent in quantum spirituality.

Understanding these final 11 Levels requires *New Eyes*, because reading the world's greatest wisdom traditions with tired earthly vision has not gone very well for mankind over the past two millennia. When flesh-focused ego reads Holy Books, Truth is at best obscured and at worst misinterpreted with tragic human consequences.

But reading spirituality spiritually? That's how it was always intended, and it's what we are going to do now. It makes a huge difference, like getting reading glasses for the first time when you start to age, making something blurry all of a sudden appear to be clear.

Spiritual reading can be likened unto mysticism, or "the spiritual apprehension of knowledge inaccessible to the intellect." (Intellect means lower mind, spiritual apprehension means higher mind.)

In Buddhism, this is known as the 'third eye' or the 'eye of consciousness.' In Hinduism the third eye is 'anja' or the sixth chakra, the center of intuition and insight. When we read with the third eye, we see through the eyes of the mind and view beyond the material world.

The third eye is ultimately spiritual perception, a doorway to higher consciousness. Spiritual eyes are the *New Eyes* that Jesus wanted us to use.

"Blessed are your eyes, for they see, and your ears, for they hear. For truly, I say to you, many prophets and righteous people longed to see what you see, and did not see it, and to hear what you hear, and did not hear it."
- Matthew 13:16-17

Case in point — Jesus clearly was not talking about physical sight in that passage, because most "prophets and righteous people" could see the material world just fine, of course. But they were not seeing with that *third* eye, using spiritual vision.

So some people read egoistically, some spiritually. Some are blind, some can see.

It is with the perception of higher consciousness that the rest of this book should be read. Doing so enables you to seek and find wisdom and peace in so many other places while simultaneously experiencing one of the most fundamental Truths of all:

You have nothing to fear.

Read with old eyes, that seems incredulous as there are so many things to fear. Death, disease, divorce, getting fired, getting hired, relationship stress, no relationships at all, the list goes on and on.

But all of that can only happen to the ego, which you are not.

As a soul, nothing bad can ever happen to you.

As a soul, everything happens for a spiritual reason and reality is just a mirror for your growth. As a soul, the flesh world is just a temporary costume and you are a body of energy that cannot be destroyed. As a soul, consciousness guides you along the path and gets you where you need to go. As a soul, the physical world is merely a projection of your mind and all the images in it are merely illusions.

As an ego? Sure, bad things happen to your costume. Fearful, evil things. Which is precisely what ego wants you to do. Fear evil.

A self-aware soul will only eat off the tree of life. The ego wants you to gobble up the knowledge of good and evil, so that you will surely die — because as flesh, you will indeed surely die.

So what exactly is fear? That's all a matter of perception. To misperceive is to sin, so let's perceive this one correctly.

The definition of fear is "an unpleasant emotion caused by *the belief* that someone or something is dangerous, likely to cause pain, or a threat."

If you let your GPS emotional system be your guide, you recognize that the "unpleasant" feeling stems from *the belief* that there is a threat. Right there we know it is a consciousness game, that the emotional feedback loop is in effect.

What is it that you might feel is being threatened? The ego, of course. Some aspect of your costume, or perhaps the costume of a family member or friend. But make no mistake, that's the sole source of fear. Fruits of the spirit, such as hope and courage, are elements of your soul that can never be hurt. They are treasures that are safeguarded in heaven.

A Course In Miracles puts it this way: "Nothing real can be threatened, nothing unreal exists. Herein lies the peace of God."

What's real is your soul and what's unreal is the ego perspective. Believe that, and you have peace. Don't believe that, and peace is a lot more difficult to come by.

Fear is ultimately resistance to Truth, while love is embracing of Truth.

Recall Level 5 and the complementarity principle: The world is comprised of duality complements. Fear and love are not opposites, they are part of the same continuum and differ by degree. Fear is the absence of love, just as short is the absence of height and thin is the absence of fat.

Hell is merely the absence of heaven. The devil is the absence of God. Evil is the absence of good. If you utilize Hebb's Law and practice only seeing good, evil disappears.

"There is no fear in love, but perfect love casts out fear.
He that fears is not made perfect in love."
- 1 John 4:18

And you must be perfect, Jesus said in Matthew 5:48, which means you need to be fearless. Spiritually fearless.

Understanding this allows you to see Jesus on the cross correctly — as a man who as Christ was the Son of God and didn't see any evil the day of his crucifixion, only the perfect love present as the ego energy around him failed to kill what he actually is … a soul.

Doing the same in the midst of apparent evil is what is required to be Christian on the level that Jesus required it.

"If anyone would come after me, let him deny himself
and take up his cross and follow me."
- Matthew 16:24

When you understand Truth, you see that everyone must walk this path, and being spiritually fearless is the password for heavenly entrance. (No soul shirt, no soul shoes, no soul service.)

Perhaps the most repeated command in the Bible is "Fear not."

In Genesis 15:1, God told Abraham "Fear not … I am your shield." In 2 Kings 1:15 and 2 Chronicles 20:17 God told Elijah and King Jehoshaphat not to be afraid when they are facing war.

My personal favorite is when God commanded in Isaiah 41:14, "Fear not, you worm Jacob." He really called Jacob *a worm*? From God's perspective, anyone who is incapacitated with fear has a low-level consciousness — as low as an earthworm, you might say.

And Jesus, in Matthew 10:31, said simply, "Fear not."

If you are a Christian, the command is unequivocal. You must not fear. Having a soulful trust that all is well no matter what happens is a sign of faith. It is laid out distinctly in Psalm 23:

> *"The Lord is my shepherd; I shall not want. He makes me lie down in green pastures. He leads me beside still waters. He restores my soul. He leads me in paths of righteousness for his name's sake. Even though I walk through the valley of the shadow of death, I will fear no evil, for you are with me; your rod and your staff, they comfort me. You prepare a table before me in the presence of my enemies; you anoint my head with oil; my cup overflows. Surely goodness and mercy shall follow me all the days of my life, and I shall dwell in the house of the Lord forever."*

Read spiritually with *New Eyes,* symbolism abounds:

- The Lord is Christ, which is higher consciousness and your ultimate guide (shepherd).
- Being connected to Christ Consciousness eliminates ego desires (shall not want).
- During your soul journey you will be required (made) to submit (lie down) and be fed spiritually (in green 'fertile' pastures) while being led to peaceful thinking (still

waters).

- He helps me remember (restores) what I really am (a soul instead of an ego costume).
- He is guiding me down the tao (path) of virtuous evolution (righteousness) toward union with Christ (the namesake of Jesus).
- Although I am here on earth, which is a lower dimensional level of consciousness (valley), and am journeying through the illusion (shadow) of ego focus (death), I know that nothing bad can happen to me (fear no evil) because I am still energetically tethered to home (you are with me).
- You protect me (your rod) and support me (your staff).
- You require me to face ego fears (presence of my enemies), fill me with higher consciousness (anoint my head with oil) and do so in abundance so that the Holy Grail of spirit light inside me pours out energy to others (my cup overflows).
- The Holy Spirit is always available to me and I will always maintain Christ's mind (dwell in the house of the Lord forever).

There is nothing to fear because you, a soul, are in an energy system that is finely tuned to elevate your consciousness and fill you with spirit.

The challenge of living without fear is unanimous throughout other prominent spiritual disciplines.

"From craving, grief is born; from craving, fear is born. For someone freed from craving there is no grief - so why fear?"
- Buddha, Dhammapada 216

Craving is attachment to ego and the flesh. Freed from ego,

you are freed from fear.

In Buddhism, a 'bodhisattva' is a person who is walking the pathway toward enlightenment. In *A Living Buddhism for the West*, Buddhist teacher Anagarika Govinda wrote, "Fearlessness is the most prominent characteristic of all bodhisattvas and all who tread the bodhisattva path. For them, life has lost its terrors and suffering its sting. Instead of scorning earthly existence, or condemning its 'imperfection,' they fill it with a new meaning."

If you strive for enlightenment, you should be fearless and fill your experiences of adversity "with new meaning" by shifting your perspective toward Truth.

Hinduism follows suit.

"Be fearless and pure; never waver in your determination or your dedication to the spiritual life."
- Krishna, in the Bhagavad Gita

"The whole secret of existence is to have no fear."
- Hindu monk Swami Vivekananda

"Be truthful, gentle, and fearless."
- Gandhi

And Islam's leader revealed where fear comes from.

"Only Satan frightens his followers."
- Muhammad, Quran, Surah 3:175

Satan is ego, he gets you to fear trivial things, such as your favorite football team losing the Super Bowl XIV in January of 1980 (grumble grumble). Or not getting a promotion. Or never earning a million dollars. This kind of fear is worrying over the loss of worldly possessions.

In that same verse, Muhammad continued his recitation with God saying, "Fear them not; fear Me." Similarly, there are multiple references to fearing God in the Bible.

So isn't "Fear not but fear Me" a contradiction? Not with *New Eyes.*

Recall F. Scott Fitzgerald's "test of a first rate intelligence" ... which is being able to make sense of seemingly opposing ideas.

"Don't fear but fear Me" is NOT a contradiction, it is yin and yang. There are different degrees of fear, a love-hate continuum that can seemingly have contradictory features but are actually complements. Fear is love when the negative aspect of fear promotes spiritual growth.

"Beware to hate something that is good for you,
and beware to love something that is bad for you."
- Muhammad, Quran, Surah 2:216

That's because there is a kind of fear that you can love!

First of all, on the ego, earth-focused level, is it "bad" to have fear of a poisonous snake that is slithering toward you? Of course not. Or how about fear of traffic for a 1-year-old who is just learning to toddle? If I see a bear far off in the woods and get a feeling that inspires me to gingerly walk the other direction, that's "good" fear.

Fearing God is like that, it's healthy for you, like not wanting to disappoint your parents or coach or favorite teacher. It's motivational. Never mind that God would never be disappointed in you, you can still use it as a tool for growth.

Fearing circumstances that are actually opportunities for spiritual advancement are what we should not do. It's not trusting God.

From the hadith in Islam: "How wonderful is the case of a

believer; there is good for him in everything and this is not the case with anyone except a believer. If prosperity attends him, he expresses gratitude to Allah, and that is good for him. And if adversity befalls him, he endures it patiently and that is also good for him."

When you believe in Allah, even "bad" stuff is "good" for you. It's why it's *all good.* So fearing Allah is nothing but spiritual as well.

So you can give to Caesar what is Caesar's and fear spiders and snakes, while giving to God what is God's and lovingly fear God — while being fearless — at the same time.

The best way to exemplify "fear no evil" on all of its levels comes from the classic book *The Secret Teachings of All Ages* by Manley Hall, who relates a "ritualistic drama" regarding the return of Adam to the Garden of Eden.

A few years ago I was on a work retreat at a cabin in Hocking Hills, Ohio, steeping myself in nature ala Henry David Thoreau, albeit for just a long weekend and with an iPhone in my pocket. Hocking Hills is a picturesque state park … surpassed in beauty only by the splendor of the Adam-Eden allegory I read while relaxing in the woods. A paraphrased version follows:

Adam, long banished, arrives back at The Garden, hoping to gain readmission. Alas, the devilish serpent is still there, informing him that he cannot enter because, "Thou are dust and to dust thou shalt return."

But Adam won't take no for an answer. He explains how he has been wandering around in "darkness" and knows that he is only made of "dirt." However, while on his journey of the flesh, he realized that Christ was sent into the world in the form of Jesus and his recognition of this awoke the spirit inside of him, as "immortality was inherent in the very dust of which I was composed." Adam had found the Holy Grail within himself and he filled it with the Holy Spirit by connecting to Christ

Consciousness.

He then says to the serpent, "Do you now deny me entrance, I who have at last learned the mystery of myself?"

The serpent acknowledges Adam's self-realization and lets him in, declaring himself to be Satan, Adam's adversary, and the cause of all of his suffering. The serpent hisses that his mission was to deny Adam entry into Eden and to deliver him unto evil ever since the day he took on human form.

Adam tells him off, now fully aware that he had been led astray as the serpent had infected his mind with "dreams of power" and caused him to "lust after the things of the flesh" but ended up with nothing but agony. So he admonishes the serpent, "I am done with thee forever, O artful Spirit! I have tired of thy world of illusions. … There is no happiness, no peace, no good, no future in the doctrines of selfishness, hate, and passion preached by thee. All these things do I cast aside. Renounced is thy rule forever!"

The serpent, though, had one last trick up its slithery sleeve. He says, "Behold, O Adam, the nature of thy adversary!"

In a flash, the evil snake transforms into a glorious angel, "with great scarlet wings that spread from one corner of the heavens to the other." Awestruck at the awesome sight, Adam falls to his knees.

The demon-turned-deity then enlightens Adam to the divine nature of reality, how despite Adam hating him the serpent was really leading him out of the "illusion of worldliness" by weaning him of physical desire and awakening his soul.

"I am the Lord who is against thee and thus accomplishes thy salvation. … Follow me, O Adam, for I am the Way, the Life, and the Truth!"

Once you truly love your enemy — the very ego that has been behind all the pain and suffering man has ever known — it reveals itself as a messenger of God. It was never actually evil.

It had been an angel in disguise.

The only devil that exists is man's misperception of the physical world, his sin of worshipping the flesh. The devil has just been playing defense, strengthening your resolve on offense to spiritually score. Salvation is accomplished when two (fear and love) become one (all-encompassing love). It is the end of the dual mind, when you are fully eating off only the tree of life.

So there is no reason to fear evil, because evil is ultimately urging you to spiritually live.

Man can only take so much suffering before he turns to the Light.

WAKE UP!

Siddhartha Gautama emphasized that he was merely human, just like all of us. He was not to be worshipped. It makes him very relatable, as there is something in his story for everyone.

But Siddhartha went on a journey of discovery that changed him and, ultimately, the world. It can change you, too, if you do one simple little thing:

Wake up!

You see, after completing the journey inside his own heart and mind, Siddhartha was enlightened and became a teacher of Truth.

At that point, he became known as the Buddha, which in the old Pali language means:

Wake up!

Yes, the word means “to awaken” and the spiritual philosophy of Buddhism is “a process of awakening.”

This begs the question, wake up from what?

After reading about The Illusion and The Projector and The Costume Party, hopefully you know the answer. But if you glossed over Level 13 in particular, Buddha makes it clear as the nose that’s not really on your fake face.

We need to awaken from the spiritually sleepy world of matter in which we are energetically immersed.

"The world, indeed, is like a dream,
and the treasures of the world are an alluring mirage."
- Buddha

He says it so casually as if it is so obvious. To him it was … though not initially. Getting there took some dedicated seeking and finding. Suffice it to say he did his fair share of tithing, offering up more than a tenth of his consciousness over to spiritual focus on a regular basis.

How Siddhartha reached Buddhahood is a fascinating story and, despite its extremes, is an excellent blueprint for many of our journeys toward Truth.

Let's start with the beginning, including links to Christianity and quantum physics.

Recall in the Bible that the origin of the word sin is 'hamartia' for missing the mark, or to aim at the wrong target. The name 'Siddhartha' is comprised of two Sanskrit words, 'siddha' and 'artha' which when combined means 'one who achieves his aim.' His birth mother was named Maya, which means 'illusion.'

So his summarized life story is this: A little boy is born via an illusion and sets a goal to stop sinning by waking up.

The longer version is this: In 567 BCE, more than five centuries before the birth of Jesus, Siddhartha was born a prince. He was the son of King Suddhodana, leader of a clan in Nepal, bordering China (which is to the northeast) and India (to the southwest).

Fearing a prophecy that his son would either be a great king himself or would live a pauper's life as an acetic, Suddhodana tried to shield his child from all forms of suffering (like sickness and death) and instead spoiled him rotten. As such, life was a playground filled with riches for young Siddhartha, while he saw nothing of the dark side of reality.

After being something of a palace party animal in his early teens, Siddhartha settled down at the ripe old age of 16 and got married to Yasodhara. As a twentysomething, Siddhartha grew restless and bored with his lavish lifestyle, so he planned to leave the kingdom and explore the world. Before he could do so, Yasodhara gave birth to a baby boy named Rahula, which means 'fetter' or 'impediment.' So Sid's kid was a symbolic chain that bound him to the world of flesh and was a potential barrier for his aim of reaching enlightenment. (That's certainly relatable to most parents!)

Feeling a void inside himself that he wanted to fill, Siddhartha fled the palace anyway and voyaged out on his own. He encountered what is known as the Four Sights — a sick man, an old man, a dead man and a wise man. He learned from each experience and noticed that he was less empty and therefore sought more such *real* experiences as opposed to the ostentatious ones to which he had been accustomed.

Believing that he was more content with less, Siddhartha decided to live on only the bare necessities for a while, reasoning that perhaps abandoning all worldly possessions would elevate him to enlightenment. For a time he was said to have consumed only one grain or rice and one drop of water a day. Instead of elevating him, though, it deflated him. He started fainting a lot.

Weak and emaciated, Siddhartha tried a new plan, what has become known as 'The Middle Way.' It was the path of balance. He recognized that neither having 'too much' or 'too little' was effective and likened life to the tuning of a sitar, or an ancient guitar. If the strings are too tight they will break, and there is no music. But if the strings are too loose they will give off no sound, and there is no music.

You must be balanced for there to be music.

Siddhartha thereby began living in moderation, while turning his journey inward and seeking more wisdom. As a serious meditation practitioner he felt himself getting closer and closer to Truth, so he finally resolved to do nothing but meditate until he had a breakthrough.

At the age of 35, following 49 days of meditation underneath the Bodhi tree, he broke through the illusions of his mind and achieved enlightenment — also known as bodhi. The insights flooded in. He was now Buddha.

Buddha was initially resistant to teaching Truth because the ignorance he was facing was so extreme, he figured it would be aggravating.

"This generation delights in worldliness, takes delight in worldliness, rejoices in worldliness," he said. "It is hard for such a generation to see this truth … others would not understand me, and that would be wearying and troublesome for me."

Buddha thought that people would think he was crazy and would not want to relinquish their worldview, as it would be too hard for them to grasp his insights. Alas, no one can hold such Truths in for long, and he began to teach.

When Rahula was 7, Buddha returned to the palace and reunited with his family. His son inquired about his material inheritance, at which point Buddha said, "It is wrought with troubles. I shall give him the benefit of my spiritual enlightenment and make him an owner of a transcendental inheritance."

Buddha did not originally teach women, per custom at the time, but at the behest of his adoptive mother he became an early leader for gender equality and admitted females into his order. He believed that men and women had an equal capacity for achieving enlightenment.

Buddha's teachings are part of what is referred to as the Three Jewels that Buddhists 'take refuge' in as guiding forces in their spiritual lives:

1. Buddha - This jewel is Buddha as a role model, representing our own optimal development of the mind and spiritual potential, otherwise known as Buddha Nature. (Or you could call it Christ Consciousness.) It is the Lord within you.
2. Dharma - These are Buddha's teachings, which are universal Truths that apply to all of us all of the time. (Or you could call it applied quantum physics.) You should read the Holy Books for guidance and learn Truth.
3. Sangha - This means to take refuge in a community of those who have achieved bodhi or those who are dedicated to this discipline. (Or you could call it entangled enlightenment.) We can seek refuge in other seekers.

Perhaps the most prominent of Buddha's teachings are the Four Noble Truths, which are foundational in Buddhism. They are simple, elegant and True:

1. Suffering is inevitable and universal. We all experience dukkha (suffering) at some point in our lives.
2. The reason we suffer is due to craving or desire, mostly for things, but also because we resist negative emotional states. We are attached to the materials and senses of the physical world.
3. We do not have to suffer. Dukkha will cease whenever we release ourselves from craving and desire.
4. Cessation from suffering will occur by following the Noble Eightfold Path.

As far as *New Eyes* is concerned, it can just be the Three Noble Truths because the opening trio says it all. We suffer, we suffer because of attachment and we won't suffer if we practice detachment.

Detachment from what?

Ego.

Because of the temporary nature of the world of form, or what Buddha terms anicca, we are bound to go through pain as the things around us change. Impermanence is the problem, especially getting sick, growing older and dying. It's stressful trying to resist the inevitable. Memento Mori.

We are all in transition and often don't like it. We either love, love, love or hate, hate, hate our costumes. There's the emotional pain. If you love all this stuff, when it goes, you'll suffer. And if you already hate it, you are already suffering.

Plus, there's the fact that all that stuff is really just an illusion, a bunch of condensed energy without any inherent meaning. Whatever meaning we think it has is based upon conditioning or ignorance. You suffer when your favorite sports team loses? Conditioning. Society and Hebb's Law have programmed you. You suffer from the fear of death? Ignorance. Buddha calls that avijja, or not knowing the true nature of reality.

Suffering happens because our internal minds simply cannot accept what has happened externally.

If you don't like that suffering feeling, you have two options:

1. Change the external. (Good luck with that.)
2. Change the internal. (Which is the key to life.)

The process of detachment dramatically affects consciousness and leads to nirvana, or a flawless peace of mind that is free from conditioning, ignorance and other afflictive states.

Buddha's process ends up in the same place that Jesus suggests in Matthew 5:48 — perfected consciousness.

Detachment does not mean you cannot enjoy life, far from it. You just have to know what it is (a temporary experience), which eliminates ignorance or avijja, and then you do not cling to it. When you go to the theater and watch a good movie you are aware it is just a movie, so when it's over, you let it go. That makes the movie fun and peaceful.

So do not cling to things. It smacks of desperation and addiction and is not necessary. Mindfully releasing their power over you will increase your enjoyment of it. It is excellent therapy.

As for the Noble Eightfold Path, it is a good way to cultivate mindfulness along your spiritual journey as it includes worthy pursuits such as right intention, right speech and right action. Monks work on those things. It is worthy of deeper exploration, but there are many other important Buddhist teachings to review.

Buddha emphasized the importance of cultivating virtues via the Four Immeasurables:

1. Metta - Loving kindness toward all humanity. This is the sincere hope that all other people be well, without exception. Love your enemies.
2. Karuna - Compassion for all. Whereas metta is hoping for others to be happy, karuna means wishing that their suffering will cease.
3. Mudita - Empathic joy. When you rejoice in the delight of others, especially when you have no direct connection to their happiness.
4. Upekkha - Equanimity, or maintaining composure in every circumstance. Whether life treats you well or badly, you accept it all with detachment.

Discovering these Immeasurables was the first thing that

attracted me to Buddhism, They all have transformative power, especially mudita. Human beings generally are not very good at mudita, but many excel at *schadenfreude*, or taking pleasure in the misfortune of others. We all know what jealousy is, but in English there really is no word that describes the opposite emotion.

It's mudita.

Instead of being envious of something someone else has that you want, you are happy for that person whether or not you have it. Like being happy for successful athletes or financially rich people instead of resenting them. It's finding joy in anyone's and everyone's accomplishments. It's why a good sport shakes the other guy's hand after the game.

Metta is similar in its intention of sending out positive vibes. There are several good metta prayers that one can recite, which truly inspires loving kindness in one's heart. Karuna can be when you hope someone else finds metta in their heart, diminishing their suffering.

And equanimity keeps you in check with perfect balance. It's the proper tuning of a guitar, or the moral of the fairy tale *Goldilocks and the Three Bears*. Too hot? Too cold? Just right!

"Praise and blame, gain and loss, pleasure and sorrow come and go like the wind. To be happy, rest like a giant tree in the midst of them all."
- Buddha

Equanimity means keeping your composure no matter the situation. It's leadership, class and faith all rolled into one, covered with a healthy dose of ego detachment by accepting all beings as equals. It's being at peace whether you win or lose the game.

It's also being at peace whether you are alive or dead.

That is the essence of *The Tibetan Book of the Dead.* Known in the East as the *Bardo Thodol, Liberation Through Hearing During the Intermediate State,* the book was discovered and revealed by Karma Lingpa during the 1300s. Its intent is to facilitate the death and afterlife process by focusing on the continued experiences of consciousness, also known as *you.*

Simply put, consciousness wanders through the 'bardos' or stages of afterlife trying to realize the same basic Truth that we are trying to learn here — that everything is a projection of our own minds. Once you have realized that in full, you achieve liberation. If not, you remain in samsara, the wheel of life.

This excerpt is particularly striking, something that a soul that has passed away is supposed to tell itself:

> *"Wake up! I have transitioned from physical life through bodily death to the point of spiritual awakening. From this point on, I will awaken my spirit and my consciousness by contemplating the Infinite Potential of the spirit. I must meditate on peace and harmony and love and compassion. For the sake of all beings in all realities, I must remain centered in the oneness of the Infinite Potential. Now for the sake of all beings, I will acknowledge the perfect clear light as the representation of the Infinite Potential. Within this experience of Infinite oneness, I will attain the supreme peace and harmony of the Infinite Potential and I will accomplish the purpose of all beings. If I do not attain the supreme peace and harmony, then, at the least, while I reside in the spiritual reality, I will recognize that I am residing within the spiritual reality."*

So much wisdom in just one paragraph:

1. If you die while spiritually asleep, you still have to *Wake up!* on the other side.
2. Just as energy cannot be destroyed as it only changes

form, death is a mere transition.

3. Infinite Potential (superposition) is emphasized, along with the elevation of consciousness.
4. We must focus on the fruits of the spirit, even in the afterlife.
5. Entanglement and different dimensions are acknowledged, as your afterlife experiences are still "for the sake of all beings" that are "in all realities" along with the experience of "Infinite oneness."
6. Achieving "supreme peace" (i.e. Unity Consciousness) is the "purpose of all beings."
7. Failing to achieve supreme peace is not the end of the world. In the very least, you can recognize the reality of the real world.

Awakening is available to you at every moment during the process, just as it is here on earth. To reach that state requires the extinguishing of the three ego fires of passion, aversion and ignorance. In other words, you must let go of your obsession with the material world, stop your resistance to what has happened and learn Truth.

The result is the experience of nirvana, or a state of being that is perfect. (Just as Jesus said we need to be.) It is heavenly and found inside you. (Just as Jesus said it is.)

If you look beyond the physical surface and do not judge by "mere appearances," Buddha's teachings are quite similar in so many regards to Christianity.

Even a belief in God.

In what *New Eyes* considers to be one of the deepest concepts of spirituality that consciousness can grasp, the best way to experience God is to NOT THINK of God. Once most people start trying to identify God, especially with lower ego consciousness, they invariably put Him outside of themselves, something that is *over there* or *up there*.

And yet, God is within us. Accordingly, to experience God in Buddhism is to be One with God.

In his *Sermons of a Buddhist Abbot* from 1906, Zen Master Soyen Shaku said, "God must be in us, who are made in his likeness. We cannot presume the duality of God and the world. Religion is not to go to God by forsaking the world, but to find him in it. Our faith is to believe in our essential oneness with him, and not in our sensual separateness. 'God in us and we in him,' must be made the most fundamental faith of all religion."

That is worth repeating: "'God in us and we in him,' must be made the most fundamental faith of all religion."

That concept links Buddhism with panentheism, a belief system in which God is everything that is inside and outside this universe. So clearly, God must be in us. To put God 'in heaven' or elsewhere takes Him out of us, and in so doing, we lose our connection to the divine, like Adam and Eve falling out of the Garden.

Restoring Eden is recognizing God within.

The ego in the human mind is so adept at trickery that merely conceiving of God automatically triggers an 'outside of me' belief in many people, that God is man sitting in a throne up in the clouds, so very far away from them. Nope, He is right here, right now.

This is why Buddhists do not talk about God much, because they are trying to quiet the lower 'monkey mind' that is so active that it prevents most of us from succeeding at the most meditative of Bible verses …

"Be still, and know that I am God."
- Psalm 46:10

Want to know God? Be still in your mind. No need to yap

about Him all day. (Oops, too late for me.)

If you do not calm your mind, the imperceptibly tiny and manic vibrating loops of energy called strings that are buried deep inside all of your cells will create emotional chaos for you, and perhaps physical chaos as well. It's why meditation is such a healthy technique for both mental and physical health. It's how Buddha achieved nirvana.

If your mind is still, the chaotic voice in your head ceases being destructive and higher consciousness can enter to be your wise guide. You can know God by taming the ego. Don't let it tell you what God is or isn't — experience God for yourself.

When we expand our consciousness in filling our minds with wisdom, called bodhicitta, we drop the ego mind. It's called 'no mind' in Buddhism. You are filled with spirit and can clearly see the illusion of the world that we are living in as a void, just like a movie in a theater. It's there … but not really there.

The void in Buddhism is also misunderstood as the absence of God. To the contrary, it's the *presence* of God and the absence of ego. Emptiness in Zen Buddhism indicates a mind free from fear, judgment, stress, distractions and other material obsessions. One who is fearless, as noted in Level 23, is a bodhisattva, someone who is freed from ego, but remains in the world to guide others along the path.

So in Buddhism God IS the void. Pure, clear, vibrant energy may appear as a 'nothing' kind of emptiness to ego, but in actuality the void is empty of materialism yet filled with spirit. (That void is highly likely connected to dark energy and dark matter, but we shall wait for science to dig a little deeper in that regard.)

It's why anyone who has achieved bodhi is not afraid of death, because nothingness is really everything to the soul.

Upon eating his last meal, which some believe was poisoned and others believe triggered a fatal medical reaction, Buddha was said to have been more concerned about the man who served him the food as opposed to his own fate. Essentially, he told the server that he should rejoice for assisting Buddha toward nirvana.

In essence, Buddha forgave the man who was responsible for his death because he was not really dying, after all. (Sound familiar?)

Buddha's final words: "All composite things are perishable. Strive for your own liberation with diligence."

Your body is made up of many parts — it will die. You, however, can escape death through freeing yourself from the illusion.

You just have to wake up.

THE 'BE' ATTITUDES

If the name of this book were chosen from a self-serving point of view, I might have decided to call it *Four Eyes*, because the vision for it was inspired by two people.

My Mom and Dad.

Above all else I will be forever grateful for their love and support, which never wavered and had no limits. From an author's perspective, though, it was their insistence on their four children learning how to think critically and not dogmatically that led to *New Eyes*.

They both inspired me profoundly many times, but two occasions in particular stand out. What might have been mustard seed-sized moments for them turned out to spark a mountainous shift in perception for me.

When I was about 10 years old my father and I were walking across our driveway early on a perfect summer night. My Dad stopped and put his arm around me, pointing up to the sky.

"Look," he said. "Aren't those stars beautiful? Really look at them ... and imagine how far away they are, millions of light years, yet we can still see them. God's creation is so amazing."

With that, he turned and walked into the house. I stayed right where I was standing, mesmerized. I can still remember that feeling, probably with my jaw slacking a bit, thinking, "He's right. Amazing." I can even remember precisely where I was looking into the sky that night and can see the starlight in my mind's eye.

Somewhere deep inside my head, a seed of awe and reverence for science and nature was planted.

Several years later when I was in my mid-teens, I was sitting in the kitchen chatting with my Mom while she prepared dinner. Ever the multi-tasker, she was able to slice up home fries and serve up philosophy at the same time.

We were talking about religion and how difficult it was for me to believe some of the things that the Bible was saying Jesus had done, like resurrecting people from the dead and walking on water, for example.

Raising me as a Christian, Mom wanted me to have a good spiritual foundation, but didn't force anything down my throat.

"Well perhaps Jesus really did those things, I don't think anyone knows for sure, that's what faith is all about," she said. "But in the very least, he was certainly a great man, worthy of us listening to his advice."

The 'Great Man' Theory. I'm still impressed by that answer. Her wisdom, yes, but more for a mother's perfect timing. At an age when I might have been turned off from the implausible logic that the miracles suggested, Mom handled my doubts gently and oriented me in the right direction.

Don't focus on the miracles … focus on the message.

Somewhere deep inside my heart, a seed of respect for spirituality and a trust in God was nurtured.

Had my Dad never done what he did, I might not have fallen in love with quantum physics and might never have come to understand that the world is not what we think it is. Had my Mom never said what she said, I might have resisted faith and strayed down the path that philosopher Søren Kierkegaard warned against.

"There are two ways to be fooled," the Danish existentialist said. "One is to believe what isn't true; the other is to refuse to believe what is true."

So many people reject Christianity because they refuse to be fooled by that which cannot be proven, because they cannot see God, because they categorically reject the 'Jesus Miracles.' I can see their point, though now I know that quantum physics is telling us *there's a chance*.

But nevertheless, that is focusing on the miracles, not the message. (Mom said not to do that.)

The works of the body (Jesus) means little compared to the words of the soul (Christ). Recognizing the distinction between the two allows some people to understand his parables correctly ... while others do not.

"To you it has been given to know the secrets of the kingdom of heaven, but to them it has not been given."
- Matthew 13:11

If you know Christ, as in the spirit, you may know the secrets of the kingdom of heaven. But if you only know Jesus as a physical being, the secrets are not given.

"I never knew you; depart from me, you workers of lawlessness."
- Matthew 7:23

The law is of spirit, not of flesh. The law is about rules for the soul. God is not a behavior policeman. If you do not meet Christ on the level of upper light, he does not know you.

Jesus, after all, never emphasized his physical miracles; he never mentioned the virgin birth, for example; and it was Jesus who said, "The spirit gives life, *the flesh counts for nothing*."

But we should not be fooled by refusing to believe what IS

true, either, that *Christ* is still very much alive. Only bodies die, not consciousness. Egos are doomed, souls are eternal.

We all still have access to Christ via "renewing our minds" through his consciousness, not by obsessing over the flesh — which *he* said counts for nothing!

The *spirit gives life* because, when you elevate your consciousness by understanding Christ's wisdom, the Holy Spirit enters your vessel and fills the grail of your soul. When your "cup overflows" you are "born again."

Remember Matthew 13:34, Jesus "did not say anything to them without using a parable." He was always using parables, which by definition are "short stories designed to teach Truth that conveys meaning indirectly."

Interesting. Physical reality is a parable, then, because it is teaching us Truth by conveying meaning through flesh experiences (i.e. indirectly). That was the teaching style of Jesus, using indirect teachings to teach Truth. He was sometimes physical … always spiritual. Just like we are — temporarily physical in these ego costumes, but eternally spiritual as a consciousness-fueled soul.

Sometimes physical … always spiritual.

If a literal reading of the Bible works for you, great; that's certainly one possible pathway to Truth. However, a spiritual reading of the Bible is another. Let's compare the two using some Biblical verses as an exercise in *New Eyes*.

"All who draw the sword will die by the sword."
- Matthew 26:52

"I have not come to bring peace, but a sword."
- Matthew 10:34

That's a tough one for literalists, no? In the context of

disciples fighting, Jesus made a good physical point about someone using weapons of steel being more likely to die that way. (Actually a bit of a superposition/probability reference, too.)

But there's no denying that Jesus *seems to have contradicted himself.* In one verse the implication is that swords should not be used, in the other he said he wields one.

For spiritualists, there is no contradiction. *The sword is Truth*, which needs to be in its place, as a tool to slay the ego. If you draw upon Truth, the ego will die by it. Nor does Jesus care if there is peace among flesh costumes, he actually comes as Christ to *separate* flesh-worshipping people from each other (as well as from those who see spirit), even in families. Like a knife, Truth does the separation. If one family member sees the world physically and the other spiritually, there will be division ... which Jesus himself said he came to cause!

For literalists, making sense of why Jesus would tell the "Parable of the Bags of Gold" story has to be challenging as well. In it, Jesus told of a master who praises two servants for taking his investment and turning it into more, then berates the servant who merely saved his bag of gold and returned it to the master.

Jesus then quoted the master, saying, "You wicked, lazy servant! So you knew that I harvest where I have not sown and gather where I have not scattered seed? Well then, you should have put my money on deposit with the bankers, so that when I returned I would have received it back with interest.

"So take the bag of gold from him and give it to the one who has ten bags. For whoever has will be given more, and they will have an abundance. Whoever does not have, even what they have will be taken from them. And throw that worthless servant outside, into the darkness, where there will be weeping and gnashing of teeth."

It ends there. Jesus did not say anything like, "Don't be like that master, he was mean and greedy." If that passage were about gold or money, then Jesus appeared to be financially focused. In the end, he supported 'Robin Hood In Reverse' by taking from the poor and giving to the rich.

Of course it's not about money; that's ego stuff. Currency of the soul is spirit. The parable is about having a lot of spirit and needing to multiply it. If someone has some "gold" and does nothing with it, then he will lose it.

Luke's version of the parable is very similar but with a more striking ending. In Luke 19:26-27 he goes full throttle with his band of Merry Men, "I tell you that to everyone who has, more will be given, but as for the one who has nothing, even what they have will be taken away. But those enemies of mine who did not want me to be king over them — bring them here and kill them in front of me."

Kill them? Did Jesus suggest that we should *kill* the master's enemies?

Yes, but he was being spiritual! Kill the *False Self.* Ego is the enemy. Kill the ego … in front of Christ.

Of course, the Old Testament is filled with violent verses that hopefully people do not take as suggestions or take out of context:

"Happy is the one who takes your babies
and smashes them against the rocks!"
- Psalm 137:9

"And on the eighth day (after her monthly cycle) she shall take two turtledoves or two pigeons and bring them to the priest, to the entrance of the tent of meeting. And the priest shall use one for a sin offering and the other for a burnt offering."
- Leviticus 15:29

"As (Elisha) was walking along the road, some boys came out of the town and jeered at him. 'Get out of here, baldy!' they said. 'Get out of here, baldy!' He turned around, looked at them and called down a curse on them in the name of the Lord. Then two bears came out of the woods and mauled forty-two of the boys."
- 2 Kings 2:23-24

Joyful infanticide, birds paying the price for natural human bodily functions, bear maulings of children as divine retribution for teasing the follically challenged ... we could go on and on, but hopefully those verses are sufficient to understand why no one should judge another for what is written in their spiritual texts.

Jesus emphasized once again, at the end of the Bible, that spiritual texts should be read spiritually.

"Anyone with ears to hear must listen to the Spirit and understand what he is saying to the churches. To everyone who is victorious I will give some of the manna that has been hidden away in heaven."
- Revelations 2:17

Hidden manna is food for the soul. It's hidden because you must look for it ... inside your mind. It fills you when you receive it from Christ after being victorious, winning the war inside your own mind. You will need proper hearing to understand — or one could say, *New Ears*. Spiritual ears.

It is in this spirit that we take a close look at some of the most profound teachings of Jesus from the Bible — his Sermon on the Mount — found in the Gospel of Matthew (Chapters 5-7) and including the Beatitudes.

In these verses, Jesus was not telling us *what to do* ... he was telling us *how to be*.

"Blessed are the poor in spirit, for theirs is the kingdom of heaven."

This is often misunderstood to mean someone who is spiritually poor, but "in spirit" is the dative case, which indicates possession in Greek (the original translation of the Bible). So blessed are the poor who are *in possession* of spirit. Meaning if you are poor but spiritual, the kingdom of heaven is yours.

It's also important to note that "poor" is most often a reference to energy, either spirit or ego. Jesus was instructing us on spiritual development, not financial matters. Poor can be regarding money, but typically it is in reference to the soul one way or another. In this verse, the ego poor are blessed if they are in spirit.

That inner formula — high in spirit, low in ego — is indeed the kingdom of heaven.

"Blessed are those who hunger and thirst for righteousness, for they shall be satisfied."

Seek spirit and you shall find spirit. Notice that it doesn't say "hunger and thirst for money, for they shall receive it." Righteousness is spiritual Truth. If you hunger and thirst for that, you shall receive it.

This is not true with ego pursuits, of course, as you only *might* be satisfied (superposition is about physical odds). But seek spirit and you will be satisfied — guaranteed.

"Blessed are the peacemakers, for they shall be called sons of God."

Think about this one. If you are a peacemaker, you are a "son of God" just as Jesus was. Jesus said that!

So what is a peacemaker? It is someone who wins the war inside his own mind, bringing peace to the chaos between ego and soul, between lower consciousness and higher consciousness. Tame the ego, win the war. And then *you* are a son of God, according to Jesus himself.

"Blessed are those who are persecuted for righteousness' sake, for theirs is the kingdom of heaven."

You are blessed if you are persecuted in pursuit of spiritual Truth, not if you are just plain persecuted for ego reasons. If someone victimizes you and you respond by being spiritual (i.e. forgiving, courageous, etc.), you enter the kingdom of higher consciousness. At least in that moment.

"You are the salt of the earth, but if salt has lost its taste, how shall its saltiness be restored? It is no longer good for anything except to be thrown out and trampled under people's feet."

The YOU he is talking to is the soul. If it is asleep it has no taste, which makes it senseless.

"You are the light of the world."

Who did he say was the light of the world? You.

You are a vessel of light. If you receive the spirit, the light shines through you.

"Let your light shine before others, so that they may see your good works and give glory to your Father who is in heaven."

Once you have the light in you, let it shine. This will certainly change your behaviors, which does not mean you get credit for them — all glory goes to the Father, who gave you the spirit in the first place. His energy changed you, not you. All you did was seek it and receive it.

"Do not think that I have come to abolish the Law or the Prophets; I have not come to abolish them but to fulfill them."

First, learn Truth. Second, live Truth. Jesus did that. He

learned Truth and then fulfilled the law.

"Unless your righteousness exceeds that of the scribes and Pharisees, you will never enter the kingdom of heaven."

Exceeds … as it is a game of percentages. You must be 100 percent perfect (Matthew 5:48) and not merely 93.7 percent perfect. That's an A, not an A+. The Pharisees were certainly not perfect because they were so physically focused, judgmentally emphasizing the flesh and behaviors over spirit.

"Everyone who is angry with his brother will be liable to judgment ... and whoever says, 'You fool!' will be liable to the hell of fire."

An enlightened soul knows that all of us are in the same boat, a vessel of light that we must row down the stream of consciousness. Be mindful of that regarding your judgment of others.

The hellfire he speaks of is the ego turmoil of your mind when you are losing the consciousness battle.

"Come to terms quickly with your accuser while you are going with him to court, lest your accuser hand you over to the judge, and the judge to the guard, and you be put in prison. Truly, I say to you, you will never get out until you have paid the last penny."

It's not at all likely that Jesus was giving legal counsel there, nor financial advice. It's energy processing within relationships that results in you being imprisoned in your own mind and guarded by the fierce enemy, the ego. Perhaps he was suggesting that you must always settle out of court, though certainly he was not worried about whether you met bail or paid off every last penny of your fines.

But he *was* emphasizing that you must rid yourself of ALL

energetic threads related to your costume in order to get out of the consciousness jail cell. (i.e. you must be balanced in virtues and see only spirit).

"You have heard that it was said, 'You shall not commit adultery.' But I say to you that everyone who looks at a woman with lustful intent has already committed adultery with her in his heart."

On the ego/flesh level, this is an excellent quantum physics reference, though in his day it was merely a "law" of spiritual intent. The observer is your consciousness and if it has already tuned into lust, then the deed is already done. Whether it actually happens is probability dependent based upon superposition, so Jesus focuses on the intent instead of the behavior.

On the spirit/soul level, this is a parable that goes much deeper. (See Level 28 for further explanation.)

"If your right eye causes you to sin, tear it out and throw it away. For it is better that you lose one of your members than that your whole body be thrown into hell. And if your right hand causes you to sin, cut it off and throw it away. For it is better that you lose one of your members than that your whole body go into hell."

Yet another metaphor that can lead to damaging physical consequences if misunderstood.

Clearly, Jesus does not want you disfiguring your physical body. But he does want you to remove parts or "members" of your thinking patterns that cause you to sin, or misperceive.

Your "whole body" is referring to your spiritual body, your soul. If your mind has been led astray by sin, such as resenting someone or worrying too much, you should dismember your thought patterns … otherwise your soul body will be energetically hell-bound.

"Do not take an oath by your head, for you cannot make one hair white or black. Let what you say be simply 'Yes' or 'No'; anything more than this comes from evil."

No need to make promises that you cannot keep, like, "God, if you get me out of this one, I swear I will do whatever you want me to for the rest of my life!" That's ego talk, what Jesus calls "evil."

All you have to do is say YES to the spirit and it will enter your vessel. Do you want it? Raise your hand. If you focus on this instead of that, which is saying YES or NO, then everything else falls into place. You are not doing anything that isn't driven by the energy that is inside you. Through grace alone you are saved.

"Do not resist the one who is evil. But if anyone slaps you on the right cheek, turn to him the other also."

This does NOT mean you do not resist home invaders or terrorists, that's ego thinking. Spiritually, not resisting *"the one who is evil"* means don't resist the ego; doing so gives it your energy. When you do not accept what is, you get energetically drained. What you resist persists ... but perfect love casts out all fear.

As for the oft-quoted "turn the other cheek," this is lower-upper mind thinking. That line does NOT mean that you should teach your child that if someone hits him on one cheek, he should ask to be hit on the other side as well.

It means that if you get hit on the ego cheek, offer back your spiritual cheek. Turn to the other side of you — the upper mind.

"I say to you, Love your enemies and pray for those who persecute you."

The world is a mirror. The ego is the enemy. Other people have ego energy in them, too, which makes them enemies as well. We are all teammates at war against the only enemy this illusion of a world has ever known, the human ego.

How do you defeat that enemy? Love it to death. Like a flashlight in the dark, like a laser on a tumor, the ego will wither when bombarded with love.

"You therefore must be perfect, as your heavenly Father is perfect."

Probably the most frequently repeated verse in this book.

You are a soul, which is perfected in higher consciousness, such that the Holy Spirit enters you and casts out all devilish ego energy. You must cast it all out, you must pay every last penny.

Some Christians have the idea that you do NOT have to be perfect, that as long as you believe that Jesus is the Son of God, that his mother was a virgin and that he resurrected after the crucifixion that they are therefore saved. That as long as Jesus was perfect, you do not have to be.

Nope, Jesus said that YOU must be perfect, that YOU must pick up your cross and follow after him. You have to be perfect in your belief, which means attaining Christ Consciousness. Without balanced, perfected virtues like forgiveness, courage, hope and discipline, you will not enter the kingdom of heaven. After all, how do you feel when your brain chemistry is not balanced? Not heavenly, that's for sure.

You have to be *sinless* in order to be perfect. Being sinless merely means to be solely focused on soul development. That's the right aim, for Truth. That was what Jesus was doing since birth: He was always aiming for spiritual perfection, so he was without sin.

Thankfully this verse doesn't mean we have to be physically perfect!

"Beware of practicing your righteousness before other people in order to be seen by them, for then you will have no reward from your Father who is in heaven."

If you do what you do to get a pat on the back or to be voted "Christian of the Month" at your church, if that's your motivation, then you did it for ego reasons and there is no reward from God.

"When you give to the needy, sound no trumpet before you, as the hypocrites do in the synagogues and in the streets, that they may be praised by others. Truly, I say to you, they have received their reward."

Jesus is emphasizing that you should not be looking for praise from human beings for your charity.

Besides, "giving to the needy" means giving spirit to those who lack soul food. In doing so, God fills you with the Holy Spirit (your reward), so there's no reason to desire praise from another human being.

You can give spirit to the spiritually poor while also giving food and shelter and money to the financially poor, just as you can give spirit to the spiritually poor who are physically rich. God loves millionaires, too, but sometimes they don't love themselves … because of a void in their hearts that money cannot fill.

When you give to the *spiritually* needy, THAT is true giving. But don't be boastful about it, because then you did it with ego intent.

"And when you pray, you must not be like the hypocrites. For they love to stand and pray in the synagogues and at the street corners, that they may be seen by others. Truly, I say to you, they have received their reward. But when you pray, go into your room and shut the door and pray to your Father who is in

secret. And your Father who sees in secret will reward you."

Can you pray in church? Of course. Are you doing it to show others how much of a Christian you are? Then you are a hypocrite.

Instead, Jesus said to pray in your room and shut the door … that's not your bedroom, that's your mind. You can do that anywhere, in church or in traffic or at work, but stay focused solely on God. No one gets bonus points from God for attending church every Sunday. Souls do, however, get rewarded by always being in spirit.

"And when you pray, do not heap up empty phrases as the Gentiles do, for they think that they will be heard for their many words."

It's not about the words, it's about the spirit in the words, the divine energy exchanged between souls. If you don't really mean it, don't bother saying it.

"Empty phrases" includes praying for physical things. Flesh is empty, literally empty according to quantum physics. God does not hear empty prayers.

"Your kingdom come, your will be done, on earth as it is in heaven. Give us this day our daily bread, and forgive us our debts ..."

This is a passage from the Lord's Prayer, where "God's will is done" only when one is operating with Christ's mind; otherwise, it is the devilish ego's way. "Daily bread" is not a hamburger bun, it is Truth that fills the belly of the soul, and "debts" refers to energetic karma of misperceiving the world as material. As he told us earlier, you must pay every last penny of that debt in order to get out of this prison for your mind.

God's will is done "on earth as it is in heaven" when we restore Eden.

"Do not lay up for yourselves treasures on earth, where moth and rust destroy and where thieves break in and steal, but lay up for yourselves treasures in heaven, where neither moth nor rust destroys and where thieves do not break in and steal. For where your treasure is, there your heart will be also."

It's not about new cars and fancy clothes and championship trophies and political power, that's all elusive and brings only temporary peace. Moths destroy fabric and rust destroys metal. But fruits of the spirit — such as wisdom and forgiveness and courage and hope — they are untouched by moths and rust as they are protected inside the heart.

"The eye is the lamp of the body. So, if your eye is healthy, your whole body will be full of light, but if your eye is bad, your whole body will be full of darkness."

This certainly could be a vision test, as light cannot enter the body when sight is impaired.

But Jesus was talking to your soul, and its eye is consciousness. If its aim is correct, targeting the spirit, your vessel is filled with light. If its focus is physical and sees the world accordingly, this is sinning, and the darkness of ego casts its shadow on your soul.

"No one can serve two masters, for either he will hate the one and love the other, or he will be devoted to the one and despise the other. You cannot serve God and money."

God or Satan. Spirit or Flesh. Soul or Ego. Pick one side to serve. We are indeed dual — always a soul that is currently wearing a costume, but only one can be your master.

"Therefore I tell you, do not be anxious about your life, what you will eat or what you will drink, nor about your body, what you will put on."

Do not be anxious, as the only reasons to be anxious are illusions or lies of the ego. Nothing bad can happen to a soul, so there's no reason to worry. You can physically die and still be a living spirit. You can be physically obese and have a beautiful soul. You do not have to be fashionably dressed in order to be spiritually cool.

Remember, you must be perfect! Jesus does not equivocate in this sermon, saying, "You can be anxious under some circumstances." Nope, he is clear. Do. Not. Be. Anxious.

And which of you by being anxious can add a single hour to his span of life?

Jesus also liked to utilize Hebb's Law, reinforcing his own teachings. Practice makes perfect.

As the ultimate therapist, he makes a great point here. Does anxiety help at all anyways? No it doesn't; worrying is the same thing as awareness but with ego as the driver. You can worry about having to pay your bills, or just be aware that you have to pay your bills. Same situation, but one has a decidedly spiritual touch to it.

Therefore do not be anxious, saying, 'What shall we eat?' or 'What shall we drink?' or 'What shall we wear?' For the Gentiles seek after all these things, and your heavenly Father knows that you need them all. But seek first the kingdom of God and his righteousness, and all these things will be added to you.

Jesus knew that we are "temporarily" physical and need to render unto Caesar's that which is Caesar's, like eating and drinking and wearing clothes, but put your soul's needs first and it will all work out just fine.

I call this a "win-win" scenario. If you take care of your spiritual body first, your physical body is likely to follow suit and you may experience the best of both worlds.

"Therefore do not be anxious about tomorrow, for tomorrow will be anxious for itself. Sufficient for the day is its own trouble."

Has he made himself clear? Don't worry, be happy.

Anyone who is struggling with worrying can replace that negative energy with the trust and faith that God knows what He is doing, that everyone is on a spiritual journey ... even sick children. You can still fight disease, of course, but worrying about it does not help at all. Just trust.

"Judge not, that you be not judged. For with the judgment you pronounce you will be judged, and with the measure you use it will be measured to you."

You are, after all, looking in a mirror.

"Why do you see the speck that is in your brother's eye, but do not notice the log that is in your own eye? ... You hypocrite, first take the log out of your own eye, and then you will see clearly to take the speck out of your brother's eye."

If your consciousness is blinded by the illusion of the physical world, you cannot help anyone else out and Jesus called you a hypocrite for doing so. But if your eye is healthy, if you see clearly, then you can be of assistance to others.

"Do not give dogs what is holy, and do not throw your pearls before pigs, lest they trample them underfoot and turn to attack you."

Pigs don't care about jewelry, they will just let pearls drop in the mud. Egos don't care about spirit, they will fight back and argue for their lower consciousness point of view.

"Ask, and it will be given to you; seek, and you will find; knock, and it will be opened to you. For everyone who asks

receives, and the one who seeks finds, and to the one who knocks it will be opened."

Ask for spirit, you receive spirit. Seek Truth, you will find Truth.

"Enter by the narrow gate. For the gate is wide and the way is easy that leads to destruction, and those who enter by it are many. For the gate is narrow and the way is hard that leads to life, and those who find it are few."

It is oh so easy to believe everything we have been told, to see the world as physical, to listen to the voice inside our heads telling us that this energy talk is crazy. That's why the masses are being led to an ego slaughter, through the wide gate.

Choose the other path, the narrow gate, the gate of spirit.

"Not everyone who says to me, 'Lord, Lord,' will enter the kingdom of heaven, but the one who does the will of my Father who is in heaven. On that day many will say to me, 'Lord, Lord, did we not prophesy in your name, and cast out demons in your name, and do many mighty works in your name?' And then will I declare to them, 'I never knew you; depart from me, you workers of lawlessness.'"

Jesus can be very direct, such as in this verse. If people think they are doing "mighty works" as a human, he will tell them that he never knew them. To apply the law is to do so spiritually, not physically.

Misinterpreting Truth as physical leads to all sorts of problems here on earth. It leads to people attacking each other. But we are lawless when we are not fulfilling Truth, and Christ says to depart from him. Harsh, but said with loving intent, meant to wake us up.

"Everyone then who hears these words of mine and does

them will be like a wise man who built his house on the rock. And the rain fell, and the floods came, and the winds blew and beat on that house, but it did not fall, because it had been founded on the rock. And everyone who hears these words of mine and does not do them will be like a foolish man who built his house on the sand. And the rain fell, and the floods came, and the winds blew and beat against that house, and it fell, and great was the fall of it."

Your house is your soul vessel and the rock is Truth. Build your soul upon it, as nothing will be able to knock it down, whereas building your house upon the ego's truth of lies will be a great fall. Sand is not reliable, it shifts and is not supportive, just like the ego.

You are wise when you are seeing spiritually, a fool when you seeing physically.

And when Jesus finished these sayings, the crowds were astonished at his teaching, for he was teaching them as one who had authority, and not as their scribes.

Many people had never heard Truth put this way before. Jesus was no ordinary teacher.

One final passage for this Level. Though not from the Sermon on the Mount, it is illustrative of how Jesus was clearly speaking a different "language" than some who were trying to understand.

"Truly, truly, I say to you, unless one is born again he cannot see the kingdom of God." Nicodemus said to him, "How can a man be born when he is old? Can he enter a second time into his mother's womb and be born?" Jesus answered, "Truly, truly, I say to you, unless one is born of water and the Spirit, he cannot enter the kingdom of God. That which is born of the flesh is flesh, and that which is born of the Spirit is spirit." - John 3:3-8

Nicodemus was a prominent Jewish leader, a Pharisee. In Aramaic, the language of Jesus, Pharisee means 'separated ones.' Indeed. Jesus was Jewish, too, but he was no Pharisee.

Separated from Truth and obviously physically focused, Nicodemus took Jesus's "born again" declaration literally. Anyone but Jesus would have rolled their eyes at Nicodemus, but merciful Jesus instead calmly drew the distinction between that which is born of flesh (your ego costume) and that which is born of spirit (your soul).

Jesus continues, "Do not marvel that I said to you, 'You must be born again.' The wind blows where it wishes, and you hear its sound, but you do not know where it comes from or where it goes. So it is with everyone who is born of the Spirit."

Unenlightened scientists might call this the "Hard Problem of Spirit."

For anyone who is "born of the Spirit" and shares Christ's mind, though, it is not a hard problem. They know precisely where spirit is coming from.

REMOVE THE ILLUSION

He is the Son of God, believed by followers to be the Almighty Himself born in the flesh here on earth.

He came to remove sin from mankind. He can perform miracles. He knows all the mysteries of the universe. He was immaculately conceived. He is called Lord. And he is ready to help you whenever you ask.

He is Krishna and his story, like his name, bears a striking resemblance to Christ.

Just as similar is the meaning of his teachings, if you read them with *New Eyes*. Seek division and you will find it, but seek unity and you will find it.

Krishna was born in Northern India in 3228 BCE, when, according to Hindu tradition, Mother Earth requested help in combatting sin among the people. Lord Vishnu, one of a trio of divine beings (i.e. spirit) in Hinduism, assured her that He would incarnate in order to eradicate evil, especially tyrannical rulers such as Kamsa, who was terrorizing the people (i.e. ego). Vishnu then descended into the world down into Krishna, who was born via 'mental transmission' from his father Vasudeva's mind to his mother Devaki's womb.

The sacred Hindu text Srimad Bhagavatam tells the story:

"The Supreme Personality of Godhead, who is the Supersoul

of all living entities and who vanquishes all the fear of His devotees, entered the mind of Vasudeva in full opulence."

Which means God, connected to all of us as the Master Soul, vanquishes fear by entering the minds of His believers.

The Srimad Bhagavatam continues:

"While carrying the form of the Supreme Personality of Godhead within the core of his heart, Vasudeva ... became as bright as the sun. He was therefore very difficult to see or approach through sensory perception. Indeed, he was unapproachable and unperceivable even for such formidable men as Kamsa."

Which means Vasudeva was so illuminating with spirit that it was very difficult for evil egoic men like Kamsa to perceive with their old eyes.

Finally:

"The fully opulent Supreme Personality of Godhead ... was transferred from the mind of Vasudeva to the mind of Devaki. Devaki, having thus been initiated by Vasudeva, became beautiful by carrying Lord Krishna, the original consciousness for everyone."

Devaki was also transformed by receiving this supreme mental energy and then gave birth to Krishna. It was conception by cognition, inspired by the Supreme Being, and resulted in the appearance of "the original consciousness for everyone."

Also known as Krishna Consciousness. Unity Consciousness. Or you might prefer Christ or Perfect or Whatever Works For You Consciousness.

As a child Krishna was a playful fellow, a jokester who liked to sing and dance and play the flute and eat butter. It is with this kind of light-heartedness, called Lila, that many Hindus approach reality. Life should be a joyful embrace as opposed to a chore. You are a free spirit, so you may live like one.

As a man Krishna was a fierce warrior of unmatched physical strength. He was a statesman, a yogi and a teacher of Truth. He is depicted as being blue, which is the spiritual color for inclusivity, like the vastness of the sky. It's not that his skin was actually blue as much as his aura — radiant unity — which was the energy that emanated from him.

He was also a husband. With 16,100 wives. (Let that one sink in … and look to Level 28 for the spiritual explanation.)

There are a great many teachings in Hinduism, chiefly found in the Vedas, which are ancient texts comprising a tremendous volume of spiritual literature and information on mantras, ceremonies and meditation.

Many people think of Hinduism as polytheistic because of its many gods, but those are easily conceptualized as differing aspects of one true God. If you think of all of God's varied roles, such as creator and disciplinarian and supporter, these gods are the Supreme God manifesting in many forms. Hindu literature is largely pantheistic, or reality as One. (As in the science of entanglement.)

This may seem to be a contrast from Christianity's typical concept of a personal God, but that's only when He is seen from the level of flesh. From a level of the spirit it is precisely *the same* God, as higher consciousness. Think of a prism. Just as clear light is really many colors rolled into one, God is many energies rolled into one. Cue F. Scott Fitzgerald again: "The test of a first rate intelligence is the ability to hold two opposed ideas in the mind at the same time, and still retain the ability to function." God is many while God is One.

Among the most important teachings of Hinduism is that a

soul can become perfect by remembering that pure spirit is already present in one's mind, just as Vishnu appeared in father Vasudeva's mind to give rise to Krishna through mother Devaki. (This is not that far removed from the Christian God using the Holy Spirit to impregnate Mary so that Christ could be born, especially if you think of it as a transference of consciousness.) In other words, you have to "wake up" and recall your connection to the divine, just as Buddha would later teach.

Other important concepts (greatly simplified here) within Hinduism include:

- Karma - you reap what you sow
- Reincarnation - since you are not a body you continue to evolve consciousness after death, which can lead to rebirth via samsara
- Dharma - God's divine laws that restore harmony to the suffering world, or the organization of chaos
- Moksha - liberation from ego consciousness

In the well-known Hare Krishna mantra, the former word is a variation of hari, which means "to remove." The mantra is a prayer, requesting that God remove the illusion of reality from our minds, thus eliminating sin, sorrow and suffering. The consciousness of Krishna is required to remove the illusion.

"Hare Krishna, Hare Krishna, Krishna Krishna, Hare Hare
Hare Rama, Hare Rama, Rama Rama, Hare Hare"

It is believed that anyone who repeats this mantra often enough will feel more joy and bliss in their lives.

Perhaps the best way to access the heart of Hinduism is through Krishna's wisdom in the Bhagavad Gita, which is the religion's most revered text. Meaning "the song of the Lord," the Gita was the primary inspiration for Indian pacifist Mahatma Gandhi, as well as the chief influence in the life of his assassin.

Clearly, the text can be wildly misinterpreted, as you shall see.

The story revolves around Arjuna, a warrior prince who was about to go into battle. Hesitating to fight against an enemy that included family members, Arjuna asks for guidance from his trusted charioteer, Krishna, who is fearlessly leading the way into the conflict. Krishna readily accepts Arjuna's request, promptly freezes time and proceeds to reveal all of the mysteries of the universe.

In what is mostly a dialogue between the two of them, the rest of this Level is immersed in highlights from the text and spiritual interpretations with *New Eyes*. The Gita is most certainly not intended to be taken literally, just as Christ's teachings are not. Read properly, it is a war within one's own mind, between higher and lower consciousness, between soul and ego.

Arjuna represents you — the soul vessel — with Krishna as the shepherd guiding you to Truth. Like Jesus, Krishna spoke in riddles to make you think, as the kingdom of heaven is uncovered within your consciousness. (All quotes are from Krishna unless otherwise noted. This version of the Gita was translated by Barbara Stoler Miller.)

Arjuna: *"I see nothing that could drive away the grief that withers my senses; even if I won kingdoms of unrivaled wealth on earth and sovereignty over gods."*

Even if he succeeded and became rich and powerful, he will still feel sorrowful. Memento Mori.

Narrator: *"Mocking him gently, Krishna gave this counsel as Arjuna sat dejected, between the two armies."*

Often a teasing presence who understood that our boats should be rowed gently, Krishna taught Arjuna, who was feeling lost within the war going on in his own mind. The "two armies" are ego vs. spirit. Arjuna represents the soul, sitting between ego and spirit.

"Learned men do not grieve for the dead or the living. Never have I not existed, nor you, nor these kings; and never in the future shall we cease to exist."

There is no such thing as death, nor does time even exist. We are all eternal souls.

"Contacts with matter make us feel heat and cold, pleasure and pain. Arjuna, you must learn to endure fleeting things — they come and go!"

Like Buddha said, all composite things are perishable. Like Jesus said, do not let fleeting things be your treasures.

"When these cannot torment a man, when suffering and joy are equal for him and he has courage, he is fit for immortality."

When you are balanced and face your fears with bravery, you achieve liberation and will not die.

"Our bodies are known to end, but the embodied self is enduring, indestructible, and immeasurable; therefore, Arjuna,

fight the battle!"

Flesh dies, souls cannot. So we should fight to win this war for the spirit inside ourselves.

"He who thinks this self a killer and he who thinks it killed, both fail to understand; it does not kill, nor is it killed."

Can your Halloween costume be killed? Of course not.

You are a soul that can neither kill nor be killed. Death is an illusion.

"As a man discards worn-out clothes to put on new and different ones, so the embodied self discards its worn-out bodies to take on other new ones."

Souls can remove one ego costume and put on another.

"Creatures are unmanifest in origin, manifest in the midst of life, and unmanifest again in the end."

Alpha and Omega. The "hard problem of consciousness" is answered, as the material realm is a manifestation of consciousness as souls (creatures) exist both before and after physical life.

"The self embodied in the body of every being is indestructible; you have no cause to grieve for all these creatures, Arjuna!"

Fear no evil. The soul inside the body cannot be hurt.

"No effort in this world is lost or wasted; a fragment of sacred duty saves you from great fear."

Everything is a learning opportunity, even mistakes are a teachable moment. Just a little bit of spiritual focus can produce an emotional awakening, as faith the size of a mustard seed can move a mountain.

"Undiscerning men who delight in the tenets of ritual lore utter florid speech, proclaiming, 'There is nothing else!'"

Material-focused people are stuck in the past and can only see it one way. They are blind to Truth.

"Their intricate ritual language bears only the fruit of action in rebirth."

Their thinking is robotic and conditioned, setting them up to do it all over again until they learn Truth.

"Action is far inferior to the discipline of understanding; so seek refuge in understanding — pitiful are men drawn by fruits of action."

Wisdom is superior to behavior.

Knowing the rules of the game is very important, otherwise you will play the game of life poorly. The beginning of wisdom is acquiring wisdom (Proverbs 4:7).

As for fruits of action, you don't do things to receive fruits or rewards. You must detach from material focus (Buddha) because doing anything to get praise from people gets you no reward from God (Jesus).

"When your understanding passes beyond the swamp of delusion, you will be indifferent to all."

When your consciousness rises up out of the illusory muddy pond of the physical world, you achieve equanimity. When you know this is all just a dream, you don't sweat the small stuff ... or the big stuff.

Arjuna: "*Why, Krishna, do you urge me to this horrific act? You confuse my understanding with a maze of words.*"

Arjuna is not getting it. He thinks Krishna is telling him to go kill people.

"Earlier I taught the twofold basis of good in this world— for philosophers, disciplined knowledge; for men of discipline, action."

It's a two-step process. First gain wisdom. Then put it into action. Through grace alone are you saved, but faith without works is dead. So first discipline yourself with knowledge, then act upon that knowledge.

"When his senses are controlled but he keeps recalling sense objects with his mind, he is a self-deluded hypocrite."

Once you know that this world is a dream state for your mind but keep falling for the illusory physical things within it, you are not holding yourself to the proper standards of Truth.

"He who fails to keep turning the wheel here set in motion wastes his life in sin, addicted to the senses, Arjuna."

Evolve or revolve. Wasting your life in sin is missing the mark and developing the ego instead of the soul.

"When a man finds delight within himself and feels inner joy ... his purpose (does not) depend on other creatures."

When enlightened, there is no human codependence. You have no false idols.

"Actions are all affected by the qualities of nature; but deluded by individuality, the self thinks, 'I am the actor.'"

You do not entirely control your behaviors. The laws of cultural conditioning, physical experiences, innate desires and energetic entanglement largely dictate what you are going to do. If you were born in another family as another gender and different race would your actions be different than they are now? Of course they would. You are part of a group system, we are all teammates, you must do unto others as you would have them do unto you.

To think otherwise, that you are a man on an island not entangled with others, is a delusion. You are not free to act independent of the ego energy of others until you have achieved enlightenment. Even then, it's tough, because the world is a persistent illusion and it is easy to recall sense objects with your mind.

"Knowledge is obscured by the wise man's eternal enemy, which takes form as desire, an insatiable fire, Arjuna. ... Great Warrior, kill the enemy menacing you in the form of desire!"

The wise man's eternal enemy is the ego, whereas the ignorant man's eternal enemy is other men. Ego creates an insatiable desire for materialism and confuses the soul, which means THE EGO needs to be killed.

This is not a battle against men, this is a battle within the mind.

"I appear in age after age."

God's "mind" has appeared many times before, as Krishna Consciousness, as Buddha Nature, as Christ Consciousness, through the angel Gabriel revealing Truth to Muhammad, and more. It is present right now, where you are.

"Just as a flaming fire reduces wood to ashes, Arjuna, so the fire of knowledge reduces all actions to ashes."

When consciousness evolves, behaviors change accordingly, so wisdom rules all.

"Sever the ignorant doubt in your heart with the sword of self-knowledge, Arjuna!"

You can win the battle between your spiritual mind and egoic mind by using Truth as the sword to slays the lowly ego beast inside you. Jesus referenced this kind of sword in his teachings as well.

"Seeing, hearing, touching, smelling, eating, walking, sleeping, breathing, the disciplined man who knows reality should think, 'I do nothing at all.'"

You are consciousness. It doesn't have physical senses. It just perceives as a human being, not a human doing.

"The man of discipline has joy, delight, and light within; becoming the infinite spirit, he finds the pure calm of infinity."

With proper focus you become the light of the world. It radiates from you. It's very peaceful to let it shine.

Therapeutically, I like to challenge myself and others to "Go Gandhi," which is practicing equanimity by being "pure calm" in as many situations as possible. Try it in traffic, or during a game that your favorite team is losing, or while watching a Presidential Debate. Mindfully keep your blood pressure down at all times.

Go Gandhi!

"He should elevate himself by the self, not degrade himself; for the self is its own friend and its own worst foe. ... For a man without self-mastery, the self is like an enemy at war."

Use the ego to push yourself higher, not to beat yourself up. The soul and ego are enemies but you can make them friends. If you don't, you will be at war in your mind. True Self vs. False Self. Blessed are the peacemakers.

"Firm in his vow of celibacy, his mind restrained, let him sit with discipline, his thought fixed on me, intent on me."

Adultery is cheating on God with ego, it is not cheating on a person with another person. Celibacy is similar, as a soul refrains from 'intercourse' with ego as consciousness is focused solely on Krishna.

"Arming himself with discipline, seeing everything with an equal eye, he sees the self in all creatures and all creatures in the self."

Seeing only with the Third Eye, the Single Eye, or *New Eyes*, you recognize reality is an entangled mirror. I am in you and you are in me. We are all One.

"I exist in all creatures, so the disciplined man devoted to me grasps the oneness of life; wherever he is, he is in me."

Reality is entanglement. You are always energetically connected to God.

Arjuna: *"Krishna, the mind is faltering, violent, strong, and stubborn; I find it as difficult to hold as the wind."*

This is hard work!

"Without doubt, the mind is unsteady and hard to hold, but practice and dispassion can restrain it, Arjuna ... but if he strives to master himself, a man has the means to reach it."

Yes it is hard, but stay focused. Hebb's Law will take effect as practice makes perfect.

Arjuna: *"Doomed by his double failure, is (an undisciplined man) not like a cloud split apart, unsettled, deluded on the path of the infinite spirit?"*

Doomed by his double failure? We've all been there. It's when you are "failing" in the material and spiritual worlds at the same time. The cloud of your mind is indeed split in two, which is very disturbing.

"Arjuna, he does not suffer doom in this world or the next; any man who acts with honor cannot go the wrong way, my friend."

As long as you are trying to be spiritual, you cannot make a mistake. We are here to learn spirituality, so only taking the ego route is the wrong pathway. If someone commits a crime, for example, you can either forgive them or pursue justice. If your intention is spiritual and not, say, fear or revenge, you cannot go the wrong way.

"All creatures are bewildered at birth by the delusion of opposing dualities."

Reality is complementarity, and it is chaotic while you appear to be two.

"Men who know me as its inner being ... know me at the time of death."

The kingdom of heaven is within you. If you learn this while you are physical, you will remember this when you die. You go into the light.

"Reaching me, men of great spirit do not undergo rebirth, the ephemeral realm of suffering; they attain absolute perfection."

You escape samsara, the wheel of life, by achieving Krishna Consciousness. As Christ said, you must be perfect as God is perfect.

"If he is devoted solely to me, even a violent criminal must be deemed a man of virtue, for his resolve is right."

Don't judge by mere appearances, said Jesus, judge correctly. Just because man is a criminal doesn't make him a lost cause as he is found whenever he commits to developing Krishna Consciousness.

Arjuna: *"I wish to see your form in all its majesty, Krishna, Supreme among Men.*

If you think I can see it, reveal to me your immutable self, Krishna."

Arjuna is starting to understand, so he wants to see it all at once. Krishna proceeds to reveal himself in totality.

Narrator: *"Krishna, the great lord of discipline, revealed to Arjuna the true majesty of his form. It was a multiform, wondrous vision, with countless mouths and eyes and celestial ornaments, brandishing many divine weapons. Everywhere was boundless divinity containing all astonishing things, wearing divine garlands and garments, anointed with divine perfume."*

It was a beautiful vision. But then the scene shifts.

Arjuna: *"Howling storm gods, sun gods, bright gods, and gods of ritual, gods of the universe, twin gods of dawn, wind gods, vapor-drinking ghosts, throngs of celestial musicians, demigods, demons, and saints, all gaze at you amazed. ... Rushing through your fangs into grim mouths, some are dangling from heads crushed between your teeth."*

Arjuna sees the superposition of Krishna's form, all the possible manifestations of the light, both 'good' and 'evil.' The spirit can be presented in every possible manner and it is left up to you how to perceive it.

"Man's spirit is set in nature, experiencing the qualities born of nature."

Your soul is wearing a dreamcoat inside an illusory movie and you are experiencing the qualities of those things.

"The great lord is called the highest self, man's true spirit in this body."

The Lord is your shepherd, the higher consciousness of your mind. That is your True Self, the higher self.

"Know that anything inanimate or alive with motion is born

from the union of the field and its knower."

Reality is an illusion, combining holographic images of the material world with the consciousness that observes it. "The field" is the quantum foam of superposition and "its knower" is consciousness moving through it, which creates a union of the two.

"He really sees who sees that all actions are performed by nature alone and that the self is not an actor."

Your ego costume's actions are determined by the way your consciousness observes the world. It's why Jesus said, "Forgive them, for they know not what they do." Materially focused egos are flesh zombies. They cannot see the light of Krishna nor Christ and operate mindlessly.

Think of it this way: Does *Pac-Man* control what he does in the video game or do you, the controller? Of course you do, *Pac-Man* is just a costume. Your body is not doing anything that isn't dependent upon the game (nature) or its controller, your conscious self.

"When he perceives the unity existing in separate creatures and how they expand from unity, he attains the infinite spirit."

Everything is entangled. Understand that and you achieve Unity Consciousness.

"Lucidity, passion, dark inertia — these qualities inherent in nature bind the unchanging embodied self in the body."

These are the primary levels of consciousness. Krishna goes into great detail throughout Chapter 14 of the Gita, so here is a more concise explanation.

Dark inertia is the lowest level, it is 'evil' ego. This is when people believe they are their physical costumes and happily harm other people to get their way in the material world. This is the level of murder and abuse, but also the level of jealousy and resentment and fear.

Passion is the middle level, it is 'good' ego. This is when people believe they are their physical costumes and focus on improving the physical lives of themselves and others in the material world. This is the level of "the road to hell is paved with good intentions" as people hope to guide *other people* to a better physical world, which is still a form of mental hell, a permanent residence in the lower world.

Together, passion and dark inertia form the energy dynamics of the tree of the knowledge of good and evil. You eat off that tree when you think of yourself as a physical being instead of a spiritual being. Things can be 'good' or 'bad' on this level of consciousness.

Lucidity is the highest level, it is not ego. It is enlightenment, it is spirit focus. You are aware that there is a material world but know that it is an illusion and that souls are the true beings. You therefore know that all is spiritually 'good,' which is the tree of life.

With dark inertia and passion, you see in a mirror dimly. With lucidity, you see face to face.

With dark inertia and passion, you are ignorant and blind. With lucidity, you have *New Eyes* and can see.

"When a man of vision sees nature's qualities as the agent of action and knows what lies beyond, he enters into my being."

When an enlightened soul knows that the characteristics of the laws of nature (particularly quantum mechanics) determine human behaviors, he becomes Krishna Conscious. Your role is aiming correctly and perceiving spirit at all times.

"Roots in the air, branches below, the tree of life is unchanging ... (reaching) downward into the world of men."

This is the same tree of life mentioned in the Bible and the same tree of life that is depicted as upside down in teachings of

Judaism, as spirit from the roots flow out of the upper world down into the branches of the material realm. Some say this is also the same concept as the Bodhi Tree, underneath which Buddha became enlightened, and a concept similar to the Tree of Immortality in the Quran.

"There is a double spirit of man in the world, transient and eternal."

The ego energy in you is impermanent while the spirit energy is everlasting.

"Charity given out of place and time to an unfit recipient, ungraciously and with contempt, is remembered for its dark inertia."

Some "unfit" people do not want spirit, don't waste energy on them. Do not cast pearls before swine.

"The joy of lucidity at first seems like poison but is in the end like ambrosia, from the calm of self-understanding."

Like Buddha after enlightenment and like Muhammad after receiving his revelations, seeing the world with lucidity can be challenging. You might feel 'crazy,' especially realizing that the world is an illusion. But if you stay with it, it's delightful.

"The joy that is passionate at first seems like ambrosia when senses encounter sense objects, but in the end it is like poison."

Experiencing a passionate ego life with all the blessings of the material world starts out delightful, but when it inevitably fades away, it creates suffering.

"The joy arising from sleep, laziness, and negligence, self-deluding from beginning to end, is said to be darkly inert."

Dead men walking.

"Arjuna, the lord resides in the heart of all creatures, making them reel magically, as if a machine moved them."

Please read that one again and remember that it was stated several thousand years ago!

Krishna is revealing that reality is a projector, as consciousness moves through our spiritual hearts like light through a filmstrip reel that "magically" makes creatures come to life in a total immersion 3D movie called our universe.

"You must not speak of this to one who is without penance and devotion, or who does not wish to hear, or who finds fault with me."

As Jesus said, "Do not give dogs what is holy, and do not throw your pearls before pigs." It's a waste of time and energy.

Besides, they are going to think you are crazy anyway. They might still believe the sun revolves around the earth, too.

Arjuna: *"Krishna, my delusion is destroyed, and by your grace I have regained memory."*

Thanks to the grace of Krishna Consciousness, Arjuna has awakened. The material illusion no longer controls him.

Narrator: *"Where Krishna is lord of discipline and Arjuna is the archer, there do fortune, victory, abundance, and morality exist, so I think."*

This is the final paragraph of the Gita. Krishna is the guide, or perfect consciousness. Arjuna is you, the soul vessel who is to aim correctly, as an archer. And the narrator reveals in the last few words that it is just his perspective, he is not forcing his beliefs on you.

Krishna is all-encompassing Truth, yet there are other pathways to Truth. He is all-inclusive blue, so those pathways are included in him.

COOL, OLD SCHOOL CHRISTIANITY

Riddles rule our lives.

Here is one for quantum physics buffs or *New Eyes* readers: *What are so big that they encompass the entire universe yet so small that they can never be seen?*

(Now, I cannot put the answer in this line because you would have seen it out of the corner of your eye and that takes away all the fun. So you have a few paragraphs to think about it.)

Riddles rule our lives because our lives *are* riddles.

Life is a mandatory, mysterious, often confusing journey with so much to do and so many places to go and seemingly requires so much thinking just to navigate it, and yet all it really takes is one simple concept to make sense of it all.

We are One.

Of course, that is not so simple to achieve, but certainly 'Oneness' is the answer to everything that ails us in this world. If ego is the thing that causes all the suffering — and it is — then Oneness is the cure. Ego is separation, which is conquered by humanity unifying through spirit.

Science has already shown us that everything is One, interconnected through quantum fields of energy comprised of tiny vibrating loops called strings, which are so small that we cannot see them, but nevertheless they *are* the entire universe.

(Tada! There is the answer to the opening riddle. Strings!)

Here is another riddle: *What can people learn that makes them look crazy on the outside but feel peaceful on the inside?*

Answer: Gnosticism.

Understand it and other people will think you have lost your mind, when in reality you have only calmed your mind.

Gnosticism has been around for thousands of years and has been linked to multiple other religions, but it is primarily rooted in Christianity through the teachings of Jesus.

Today, many traditional Christians look at Gnosticism with scorn. Back in the day, orthodox Christians (and many others) persecuted Gnostics for views that were considered to be a serious threat to the church.

So what was so radical about their views? They believed that you can have a direct experience of God. They believed that man is part matter/part spirit, and that there was a little piece of God inside of each one of us called a divine spark. They believed that Jesus Christ liberated people from sin and that all Truth is fundamentally knowable — which is gnosis — meaning 'knowledge' in Greek.

Oh, and they believe the world is an illusion. Crazy idea, huh?

What was really offensive to Christians at the time was the idea that Jesus himself was an illusion — something called Docetism, that Christ did not have a true reality based in form. Jesus was only *apparently* human, not actually human.

Sort of … like … all of us!

Of course, if you picked up this book and started reading at this chapter without going through all of the relevant modern science, you would certainly think that idea to be crazy indeed. Just like the earth revolving around the sun.

You almost cannot fault the pre-quantum Christians for deeming Gnosticism heretical, they had no idea that science would one day declare that everything is energy and that matter is indeed deceptive. But you *can* fault the pre-quantum Christians for being very judgmental and for not loving their enemies as their Savior instructed them to do, because they persecuted the Gnostics, killed many of them, burned their texts and drove their perspective underground.

Jesus probably would not have been too pleased with that.

There are other disputes between Gnostics and Christians, of course, but ultimately like every philosophy there can be multiple interpretations. Reality, remember, is a giant Rorschach inkblot test. It is what you say it is. Either you see it as a world of flesh or as a world of spirit.

Gnosticism also has its share of unusual customs and concepts — such as the 'lower-god' demiurge that created this evil physical world — but it is unarguably true that every religion has a theme or two dozen that are deemed to be laughable by outsiders looking in.

Gnosis is nothing crazy, it is merely a direct perception of God. "Direct perception" happens to be precisely the same definition quantum physicist Max Planck gave for knowledge, if you recall, so gnosis is not radical at all. Everyone is capable of it, in much the same way that everyone is capable of figuring out the answer to a riddle.

First you do not get it, then you get it. Direct perception. Gnosis!

The Gnostics responded to their persecution by safeguarding some of their valuable texts and burying them. Many of those manuscripts have been found in the last two centuries, including a vast array of scrolls discovered in Nag Hammadi, Egypt, in 1945 (Level 29 will be entirely devoted to the mystical Gospel of Thomas), and others in the 1890s near Akhmim in Egypt.

The teachings are decidedly esoteric, which makes them perfect for *New Eyes*. Far from being heretical, the Gnostic texts can add a beautiful layer of depth to the Bible, which in itself is quite a mystical document when read in the current quantum paradigm.

There are still Gnostics around today and they are not at all interested in preaching their viewpoint to others. (Once bitten, twice shy.) But they are also not materially focused, they are working on their inner world. The ones I have known are indeed cool, laid-back followers of Christ who are inspired by his teachings. *All* of his teachings. Just read the last paragraph of the canonical gospels, which lets you know that there is more to Jesus out there.

"Now there are also many other things that Jesus did.
Were every one of them to be written, I suppose that the
world itself could not contain the books that would be written."
- John 21:25

A lot of those "many other things that Jesus did" were indeed written but considered *not worthy*, possibly because they were *not understood* by the church leaders of that era. Many of the writings are complex spiritual riddles, designed to reach the inner world, where Jesus said the kingdom of heaven would be found — probably way down there in the inner dimensional realm of strings. Sometimes riddles force you to shift perspective, to elevate consciousness.

Doing so is your quest, according to the Bible.

"Let the wise hear and increase in learning, and the one who
understands obtain guidance, to understand a proverb
and a saying, the words of the wise and their riddles."
- Proverbs 1:5-6.

If you are hip to Universal Truth, just as in all of the major spiritual traditions that have stood the test of time, you can see the wisdom in these Gnostic parables and riddles as well. The historical accuracy of the physical events portrayed may be important, but the deeper spiritual meanings are what they are really all about.

Below is a small but very illustrative portion of Gnostic teachings. (Like the Bible there are several versions. Most of the following italicized translations are by the late Marvin Meyer, who has written several exemplary books on Gnosticism. The commentary following each verse is from the perspective of *New Eyes*. Italicized verses from other spiritual texts are noted.)

Gospel of Mary (Magdalene)

"Will matter then be destroyed or not?"

"The Savior replied, 'All nature, all formed things, all creatures exist in and with each other, and they will dissolve into their own root. The nature of matter is dissolved into the root of its nature. Whoever has ears to hear should hear.'"

Jesus began this gospel by invoking $E = mc^2$, entanglement, the law of conservation of energy, the holographic universe and enlightenment while answering the "hard problem of consciousness."

In that one passage, he noted that everything is energy, that energy is interconnected, that energy cannot be created or destroyed and that it (consciousness) goes back into the 'projector' from where it originated. And if you have the "ears to hear" and are open to spirit, he insisted that you should understand this.

"What is the sin of the world?"

The Savior replied, 'There is no such thing as sin, but you create sin when you mingle as in adultery, and this is called sin."

You are a non-physical soul vessel of light. When you 'cheat' on your spiritual nature (or God) with the world of flesh, you have committed spiritual adultery. Therefore, you have sinned, or missed the mark (hamartia).

"That is why you become sick and die, for (you love) what (deceives you)."

Only egos can get sick and die, occurring in physical form. Spirit is non-physical and cannot get sick or die, but we are addicted to the deceitful ego.

"I saw the master in a vision and I said to him, 'Master, today I saw you in a vision.'

"He answered and said to me, 'Blessings on you, since you did not waver at the sight of me. For where the mind is, the treasure is.'

"I said to him, 'Master, how does a person see a vision, with the soul or with the spirit?'

"The savior answered and said, 'A person sees neither with the soul nor with the spirit. The mind, which is between the two, sees the vision.'"

An illuminating passage.

The "Master" is Christ. Mary saw him in a vision, which is the illusion of the material world, but she recognized him as Christ through the flesh costume of Jesus. He then credited her for not "wavering" and thinking of him as a physical body.

Mary then inquired about how one sees the world of flesh,

and Jesus answered with "the mind." The soul is the vessel that you are filling, the mind is the vehicle that fills it and spirit is what it needs to be filled with. Mind is "between the two." So the mind sees the physical world. When it sees the physical world as spirit, the soul gets filled with spirit.

"Desire said, 'I did not see you descending, but now I see you ascending. Why are you lying, since you belong to me?'

"The soul answered and said, 'I saw you, but you did not see me or know me. To you I was only a garment and you did not recognize me."

Desire is ego (like Buddha said). It sees the soul and makes it a flesh body. But the wise soul knows better, that the ego only sees it as a costume and cannot see the spirit.

The Gospel of Philip

"No one would hide something valuable and precious in a valuable container, but countless sums are commonly kept in a container worth only a cent. So it is with the soul. It is something precious, and it has come to be in a worthless body."

Like a diamond buried beneath the material surface of earth, your soul is hidden inside the material body that ultimately has no value beyond that of a womb for spiritual development. When the soul is finally 'born' in spirit, the body has no value.

"'Flesh [and blood will] not inherit God's kingdom.' What is this flesh that will not inherit? It is what we are wearing. And what is this flesh that will inherit? It is the flesh and blood of Jesus. For this reason he said, 'One who does not eat my flesh and drink my blood does not have life within.' What does this mean? His flesh is the word and his blood is the holy spirit. Whoever has received these has food, drink, and clothing."

Human bodies do not go to heaven. Our flesh is what we

souls are "wearing," like a costume. But when Jesus refers to his flesh and blood he is talking about the flesh and blood of Christ, which is Truth and the Holy Spirit. Human bodies might crave bacon double cheeseburgers and copious amounts of grape-flavored Gatorade in order to feel satisfied, but the soul vessel thrives on the word and the spirit that Christ can offer.

This passage is nearly the same as was written in the Bible.

"Whoever feeds on my flesh and drinks my blood has eternal life, and I will raise him up on the last day. For my flesh is true food, and my blood is true drink."
- John 6:54-55

A few verses later, knowing that the disciples were "grumbling" about this "hard" teaching, Jesus said, "It is the Spirit who gives life; the flesh is no help at all."

"No one can meet the king while naked."

You are not going to meet God without having earned your spiritual merit badges. You must have your soul 'clothes' on before reaching heaven.

The Secret Book of James

"I tell you the truth, no one will ever enter the kingdom of heaven because I ordered it, but rather because you yourselves are filled. Leave James and Peter to me that I may fill them."

You can lead a horse to water but you cannot make them drink spirit. Our journey of Christ Consciousness requires filling our soul vessels with spirit light, thus discovering the Holy Grail inside ourselves. Jesus, filled with Christ spirit, was able to fill others who were open to receiving his light.

"So I tell you: Be filled and leave no space in you empty."

You must be perfect. You must earn all of your virtuous merit badges. You must fill all the atomic energy vessels of your body with light.

Go slowly while reading this next one.

"'Be filled,' that you may not lack. Those who lack will not be saved. To be filled is good and to lack is bad. Yet since it is also good for you to lack but bad for you to be filled, whoever is filled also lacks. One who lacks is not filled in the way another who lacks is filled, but whoever is filled is brought to an appropriate end. So you should lack when you can fill yourselves and be filled when you lack, that you may be able to fill yourselves more."

How's that for a riddle?!

As convoluted as that appeared to be, it is really simple. You can fill a cup with lots of things, like water or alcohol or poison or sand, or the cup can be empty.

You are a cup, a vessel that can hold many things. You can be filled with all sorts of light, specifically spirit or ego energy. You can be filled (with spirit) when you lack (ego.)

You can see plenty of this kind of talk in the Bible, as Apostle Paul's writings often had a distinct Gnostic tone to them.

"See to it that no one takes you captive by philosophy and empty deceit, according to human tradition, according to the elemental spirits of the world, and not according to Christ. For in him the whole fullness of deity dwells bodily, and you have been filled in him, who is the head of all rule and authority."
- Colossians 2:8-10

"Empty deceit, according to human tradition, according to elemental spirits of the world" is a perfect description of lower-mind ego-based religion. Paul was not a fan of physical rituals, for sure, nor the low-level "elemental" teachings of spirit or flesh-obsessed beings. He was a fan of Christ, both upper-mind teaching and being. The "whole fullness of deity" is called pleroma in Gnosticism, and when it "dwells bodily," you are filled with spirit.

"(Jesus) said, 'Do you not know that the head of prophecy was cut off with John?'"

"But I said, 'Master, is it not impossible to remove the head of prophecy?'"

"The master said to me, 'When you realize what 'head' means, and that prophecy comes from the head, then understand the meaning of 'its head was removed.'"

Understanding this passage could reduce some of the atrocities going on in the world.

Of course there was a physical aspect to this story — the beheading of John the Baptist. *New Eyes* does not wish to diminish nor influence anyone's opinion regarding physical truths of human history.

But deeper meanings are inherent in most of the Biblical stories. In this case, the deeper meaning is profoundly significant. A prophecy, or the declaration of divine will, comes from the head because it is based in the mind as a vision of spiritual Truth. It is "seeing" the future and knowing what is to come.

Then it arrives. Truth arrives. Jesus came to fulfill the law.

Christ had arrived — and no longer did John need to prophesy. His "head was removed" because there is no more need for mind. Truth becomes automatic, it emanates from the heart.

"Take no thought for your life."
- Matthew 6:25

Take no thought. You do not need to think. You must *know*. Truth is *knowing*. That is gnosis. *Knowing*. No more mental gymnastics, you only have spirit in your heart. And thus the "beheading" of John, which is known as "No Mind" in Buddhism. Christ Consciousness came and there was no more prophecy necessary.

This is sometimes confused as well as a violent act in Islam.

"I will cast terror into the hearts of those who disbelieve. Therefore strike off their heads and strike off every fingertip of them."
- Quran, Surah 8:12

Just as in the John the Baptist story, there is context for that verse, as it appears during a chapter on "The Spoils of War" and was regarding "the Lord" speaking to the *angels* at the Battle of Badr. The Lord was telling *angels* to attack ego-level thinking.

That is your higher mind attacking the lower mind.

Perhaps some people were killed that way during the time of Jesus and Muhammad, but beheadings were certainly not the intent of these passages. Wise Christians do not take Jesus literally when in Matthew 10:34 he stated that he "did not come to bring peace, but a sword," nor do wise Muslims take "strike off their heads" literally (and "fingertips" is a reference to detaching from physical senses or desires).

"I saw the souls of those who had been beheaded for the testimony of Jesus and for the word of God, and those who had not worshiped the beast or its image."
- Revelations 20:4

The souls were beheaded as the ego minds were removed, as they no longer worshipped the ego or its image, which is the material world.

Angels "strike off their heads" just as the Holy Spirit will "remove" the head. No more thinking will be necessary, not on the level of the soul. (Though there will always be a need for human beings to maintain lower-level earthly thinking, like 2 + 2 = 4 and "Where did I put my wallet?" This passage is about a higher-level beheading, when living Truth becomes automatic to the soul.)

Bottom line: Jesus and Muhammad were not physical executioners, but they did want God to bring death to the ego.

"The first aspect of the word is faith, the second is love, the third is works, and from these comes life."

Faith. Love. Works.

First, you must a establish connection to God by learning Truth and recognizing that, despite the fact you cannot see it, you are indeed a soul. That's *faith*.

Second, knowing that you are exercising in a spiritual gymnasium to work out your soul and develop virtues brings deep peace to your heart. That's *love*.

Third, with Christ Consciousness as your guide, you can put the spirit into action and your behaviors will be guided by Truth so that God's will is done. That's *works*.

If your actions (works) are not preceded by faith and love, you will not be behaving with spiritual intent. Krishna referred to such uninspired action as passion or dark inertia, operating on the level of the ego, whereas the faith aspect would be lucidity.

For Jesus, faith-love-works yields spirit life.

"Trust in me, my brothers. Understand what the great light is."

It's heaven. It's nirvana. It's the Zohar, or radiant light in Kabbalah. It's pleroma in Gnosticism. It's the ground of all being. It's the origin of consciousness.

"Hard problem of consciousness" solved.

"The body does not sin apart from the soul just as the soul is not saved apart from the spirit. But if the soul is saved from evil and the spirit too is saved, the body becomes sinless. The spirit animates the soul but the body kills it."

The soul is an energy vessel, if it desires the flesh, it sins. If the soul is not filled with spirit, it is not saved. But if the vessel does not have ego energy in it and it preserves the spirit within, the body cannot sin (since it will always focus on spirit). With spirit, the soul comes alive. With ego, it dies.

"Do not let the kingdom of heaven become a desert within you. Do not be proud because of the light that enlightens. Rather, act toward yourselves as I myself have toward you. I have put myself under a curse for you to save you."

The kingdom of heaven is inside of you, don't let it be dried up without the holy water of spirit. No man shall boast, even one who sees the light. Be confident yet humble, and remember that the soul of Christ took on the negative energy of the ego world to guide us out.

"First I spoke with you in parables, and you did not understand. Now I am speaking with you openly, and you do not grasp it. Nevertheless, you were for me a parable among parables."

Jesus spoke in riddles in order to get you thinking, guiding your mind into an inner world. But as he told his disciplines, sometimes he could just tell them something directly and they would still not understand.

From the perspective of Jesus — through Christ Consciousness — he views us as a "parable among parables."

Each of us has our own riddle to solve within a bigger riddle called life.

Each of us is a dreamer in the midst of a dream.

RECEIVING IS GIVING

Judaism ranks alongside Hinduism as the world's oldest religions, with origins dating back more than 4,000 years.

In patriarch Abraham, Judaism shares the same founding father as Christianity and Islam. All three are rooted in monotheism as well.

Neither Judaism nor Buddhism focus on the afterlife, with both emphasizing the importance of the present more than anything.

And while few have ever associated it with ancient Chinese spiritual traditions like Taoism, nevertheless Judaism certainly features its share of dualistic yin-yangs — and complementarity is definitely a compliment when it comes to religion.

Complex yet concise, Judaism is highlighted by a clear distinction between outer and inner worlds. Its esoteric teachings of upper and lower light, especially when combined with the deeper meanings of male and female, are spiritual revelations.

But you do indeed have to dig deep to realize those Truths.

The outer world of Judaism can get a little complicated, involving a variety of rituals and rules called halakhah that affect virtually every conceivable aspect of life. There are comprehensive guidelines for food, clothing, hygiene, finances, relationships and much more, all of which are focused on the 'here and now' world.

Within Judaism there are 613 mitzvot or commandments, including 365 forbidden things that can keep you on your toes every day of the year. Among those items on the *Don't Do List* are some we would all agree with ("not to kidnap" and "not to murder"), others very polite ("not to insult or harm anybody with words" and "not to overcharge or underpay for an article"), some that are regularly violated by most of us ("not to eat from that which was left over" and "not to delay burial overnight") and some you never have to worry about ("not to remove the staves from the Ark" and "not to eat the flesh of an ox that was condemned to be stoned").

But Judaism also offers a sharp contrast when it goes from the outer to the inner world. A practitioner of the faith can follow Jewish law and can also gain tremendous insight from its profound esoteric tradition of Kabbalah, which is considered by many to be the soul of Judaism.

Kabbalah, too, is incomparably complex to understand. There are so many layers, detailed descriptions and mind-bending concepts to learn that students of the discipline used to be advised not to study it until after the age of 40.

Yet the pearls of wisdom found within Kabbalah are so elegant and eye-opening that it significantly clarifies the complicated nature of the outer world.

Its main symbol is the Tree of Life, which describes the 10 emanations of Ein Sof, or The Infinite. These are called Sephirot and they include Keter, Chochmah, Binah, Daat, Chesed, Gevurah, Tiferet, Netzach, Hod, Yesod and Malchut. Together, they form a model for creation and a map of our complete reality. And it can take a lifetime to learn all of that.

But *New Eyes* wants to inspire Truth with a clear vision, not make it cloudier with complexity. The rest of this Level pulls many of those wisdom pearls out of Kabbalah and relates it to the context of this book while integrating it with other schools of thought.

The primary text in Kabbalah is the Zohar, which is a mystical commentary on the Torah — the primary text in Judaism. Christians would be familiar with the Torah in that it is largely comprised of the first five books of the Bible (Genesis, Exodus, Leviticus, Numbers and Deuteronomy).

How does the Zohar *explain* the Torah? You must read it with spiritual perception, with your sights set on the soul. Aiming at the proper target. Sinlessly.

Believed by many to be written nearly 2,000 years ago — the exact origins of the Zohar remains part of its mystery — it was known to only a select few for centuries, until Kabbalah became much more available to the masses in 1995. (This happened to have coincided with the emergence of the internet which, in my opinion, is actually no coincidence.)

Following are the most inspiring spiritual explanations and interpretations offered from Kabbalah and the Zohar, combined with the *New Eyes* perspective pertaining to spiritual themes throughout this book. It is Truth inspired by ancient Jewish esoteric teachings.

The Kli

Short and sweet.

Kli means vessel, or for the purposes of *New Eyes*, it is The Grail. When you learn what the true meaning of life is — to become a new spiritual creature and not a flesh-obsessed ego — your desire changes. Instead of craving materialism, you crave spirituality.

As a metaphysical vessel, when you choose soul development over ego desire, when you become solely focused on knowing Truth, you will 'win' this game as the Kli fills up with spirit light. Having you succeed at accomplishing this is God's only intention, as He offers you delight and wants you to receive it.

When you receive The Light, The Grail within becomes Holy.

Kabbalah Means Receive

Literally. And spiritually.

The word Kabbalah in Hebrew means "to receive," which is what nearly all of reality is really about. Receiving.

On the lower levels of consciousness, we all want stuff. Money, cars, clothes, food, jewelry, trophies, sex, drugs, alcohol — you name it, we crave it.

But on the higher levels of consciousness, the desire shifts to spirit. Hope, courage, forgiveness, compassion, mercy, patience, gratitude, persistence, leadership — you name it, Kli needs it.

When you aim for the flesh, you receive lower light. That's ego. (And that's sinning).

But when you aim for the creator in Kabbalah, you receive upper light. That's spirit. Your body literally absorbs that energy.

In order to give, you must first receive. Can you give anyone money without first getting some of it yourself? It's the same with spirit light. Receive, then give.

We Are All One

Of course, this is a theme in most other religions as well, but the way Kabbalah explains it is unique.

"Male and female created he them; and blessed them, and called their name Adam, in the day when they were created."
- Torah, Genesis 5:2

THEIR name was Adam, not HIS name. That's because collectively *we are all Adam* as Unity Consciousness.

In Kabbalah the original soul was called Adam HaRishon, and we are all parts of that original soul. Upon the fall out of the Garden of Eden, where he was initially ego free, Adam broke into 600,000 parts and we are the shattered pieces of that soul. Each of us is an individualized allotment of universal consciousness.

Once he/we descended into the material world egoism took over, along with the feeling of separateness. Yet we all remain energetically entangled, so our objective is to put spiritual Humpty Dumpty back together again through Unity Consciousness.

Each of us has a little piece of the Creator in us called the "Point in the Heart." It needs to be awakened (as Buddha would say) so it can grow. The soul remains latent until that Point is activated, then it remains in a fetal state until it is nurtured by upper light.

Accordingly, some people are indeed soulless. Or their souls, at best, are teeny tiny embryos.

We Are All Male And Female

Look back at Genesis 5:2 … "Male and female created he them … and called their name Adam."

The original soul was *BOTH* male and female, spiritually androgynous. Eve was then taken out of Adam, and in the flesh we see that as men and women, but energetically, all souls remain male (yang) and female (yin). As described in Level 4, the male is the "giving force" and the female is the "receiving force." We all have giving and receiving properties.

In Kabbalah, the upper light is the male force. It is why we call God "He." God is a giving force, a giver of the light. It is higher spiritual consciousness.

The female is the receiver of the light. It is a vessel, something to hold the energy given by the male. It is lower flesh consciousness. It's why the physical world is called "Mother Earth." The Latin origin of the word "mother" is mater, likened unto the material world.

Most spiritual teachings regarding men and women are references to this energy exchange that ultimately leads to new life, as uniting the male and female halves of God is a significant concept within the sephirot. A husband and a wife represent the marriage of both halves of self, the upper with the lower, and now the two are working together. The bridal chamber occurs inside each one of us when higher consciousness enters the lower nature vessel and 'fertilizes' the Point in the Heart, thus the conception of a new creature. When properly nurtured by the light, the embryo grows into maturity and the human is now 'born again' as a soul.

It's spiritual birds and the bees!

This male-female energy dynamic explains so much, including how it is that Krishna had 16,100 wives (Level 26). Did he physically wed that many times? (You can decide that for yourself.) But spiritually, the upper-light giving force that was Krishna was able to connect with an infinite number of receiving female vessels, and those vessels could be female or male in the flesh, of course. Spirit knows no physical gender.

This concept also explains the deeper meaning of "You shall not commit adultery" from Jesus's Sermon on the Mount (Level 25).

Your home is the upper light, which is the male aspect, while the physical world represents lower light, or female. If you "look at a woman with lustful intent" that is the same as being tempted by the serpent and eating off the wrong tree in Eden, as now you are desiring (lusting) after the physical world (woman).

Notice that that verse does not say anything about lusting after a man. Why? It has nothing to do with desiring males in the flesh, of course; it is because Jesus knew that the spiritual 'man' is upper light and you are indeed supposed to 'crave' it.

The male-female pattern is also seen in the lower world as the conscious mind and the subconscious mind. The conscious mind impregnates the subconscious with thoughts and ideas, giving birth to our identities. You are what you think.

More on spiritual "men and women" later.

Israel

Israelites are indeed God's chosen people, but that does not mean you have to be born in Israel to be among them, nor do you have to be Jewish.

Because Israel has nothing to do with a place or with a religion.

In Hebrew, there are many definitions for the meaning of the word Israel. One of the best understood is also the most compelling. "Isra" means "to strive" and "El" is short for "Elohim" or God.

Which means an "Israelite" is someone who is striving for God. That could be any one of us.

If you are a student in a classroom, how do you get 'chosen' by a teacher? You raise your hand and the teacher picks you. In this spiritual classroom called the universe, how do you get to be a 'chosen one' in God's eyes? You raise your hand and He will pick you, too.

"Let what you say be simply 'Yes' or 'No.'"
- Matthew 5:37

You either raise your hand or you don't. You either strive for God or you don't.

When you do, you are an Israelite. You are striving for God, so you are a chosen one.

In each of our hearts we have 613 competing desires (clearly linked to the mitzvot above) that in Kabbalah are called "nations" — and 612 of them are ego desires that are at war with the one desire called Israel, which is a desire to strive for God. This is the same battle inside yourself that Krishna described in great detail to Arjuna in the Bhagavad Gita and the same jihad that Muhammad said a Muslim needs to fight within himself.

This concept puts an interesting spin on the ongoing struggles in the Middle East, as competing nations are constantly at war with Israel … but it is also happening *inside your heart*, as the ego is battling the spirit for your attention.

The Equivalence of Form

Nothing in the physical world is exactly like anything else. No two people are precise matches as even identical twins are at least a few (billion) atoms apart, just as scientists actually contend that no two snowflakes are exactly alike.

But in the spiritual world, equivalence is the goal.

Energy just needs to vibrate on the same frequency in order to be identical, so while my physical heart can never be identical to yours, our spiritual hearts can indeed beat in synchronicity.

Similar to euphoric fans all feeling the same way after their favorite team wins a championship — or the same note being strummed in unison on two guitars — virtues can be a vibrational match. Hope is hope, courage is courage, compassion is compassion. As discussed in Level 2, our brains have matching neural sets that can help neuroscientists identify whether we are feeling love, kindness or even hypocrisy.

Filling the Kli with light is accomplished by mastering all of the fruits of the spirit until we become equivalent with God. The 10 Sephirot from the Tree of Life are attributes of God, including wisdom, love, power, beauty, eternity, male and female. These qualities must be balanced inside us.

Jesus, who was born Jewish and would likely have been

aware of Kabbalistic teachings, said that we needed to "be perfect … as your heavenly Father is perfect."

Perfection is equivalence of God's spiritual form. You can call it Christ, Krishna or Kli Consciousness, whatever works for you. But you must be perfectly, energetically equivalent to God in order to discover your Holy Christ Self.

Path of Pain, Path of Light

Everyone is moving toward the equivalence of form with God, whether they know it or not.

If you do not know it, you are following the Path of Pain. This is the physical world pathway, the way of the lower mind. It is unaware and ignorant. It is asleep. And it suffers as a result.

The pain on this path forces you along in the evolution of your consciousness as you seek to escape suffering. For example, one can only tolerate resentment for so long before one turns to forgiveness.

Once the desire in the heart to find God is activated, though, a new pathway appears. This is Torah, or the Path of Light.

One who walks this way is conscious and aware, receiving instruction by the light. Pain is not necessary on this journey. Just follow the light.

The Path of Light is the essence of one of Jesus's teachings, which suggests that life does not have to be difficult as long as you are pursuing Christ Consciousness.

"For my yoke is easy, and my burden is light."
– Matthew 11:30

Indeed, it is much more pleasant to 'think' like Christ than to wallow in one's low-level, contradictory, divisive ego thoughts. When you are harnessed ("my yoke") to the upper mind, life's burdens are not so heavy after all.

Tzimtzum

A Hebrew word meaning "contraction," this concept explains that the creation story began with God withdrawing his infinite light from the space that is our universe.

In contrast to the Big Bang, which is the universe exploding out of nothingness, tzimtzum suggests that there is no nothingness, that we are in a void of sorts. (Matter we see is actually the void, whereas the 'real stuff' is what scientists think of as dark matter and dark energy.)

This act of God basically allows us space to become creators like He is as we learn how to draw His Light back into our lives.

Tzimtzum supports the concept that reality is an interdimensional game of "Hide and Seek" between the Creator and us.

In this sense, God did not kick Adam and Eve out of the Garden of Eden, it only appears that way. In actuality, we are supposed to be inviting God back into our reality in order to restore Eden.

The Projector

The upper world of spirit is imprinting itself on the lower world of matter.

The spiritual world is the cause and the physical world is the effect.

While we cannot see them, there are spiritual laws that rule our reality. These rules are mitzvot, they are dharma, they are entanglement and balance and the mirror, as man is a microcosm of the universe. The rules are projected out of the upper world and require spiritual sight to see, a desire to strive for God.

The physical world is a world of effects, not causes. It's the movie screen, receiving the light from the projector. As Krishna said in the Gita, you must see "nature's qualities as the agent of action" because the world is inspiring your consciousness evolution — bringing you into balance and equivalence of form with the Creator.

The Great Flood

The earth represents ego. The flood represents the ocean of consciousness. The Ark represents Kli. The animals, male and female and two by two, represent balance. Noah represents you.

When you are under the flood, as in *drowned* by it, it is the ego mind that has destroyed you. But when you are *above* it, that is Jesus *walking on water* through Christ Consciousness, and you are *saved* with higher mind. (Many Taoist teachings link water to mind as well, emphasizing softness and flexibility of thought.)

The lower-world ego will ultimately get wiped out by the upper-world spirit when you balance your mind and build your soul vessel (Ark, Kli) by uniting male and female aspects in all their forms (two by two). Then you land safely and your work is done.

The name Noah, appropriately enough, means "to rest."

Chaos Is An Illusion

That says it all. Chaos is an illusion, so don't buy into it. When you realize this, chaos disappears. (At least, your emotional experience of it does.)

Knowing that the universe has chaos as *part of its design* takes the pressure off, as you are *supposed to have* times of struggle and suffering. Situations happen to show you the pathway out. It's an obstacle course for your soul. Scaling over the high wall and sprinting through the tire run and crawling under the barbed wire of life only serve to strengthen your spiritual skill set. It is challenging when you are navigating your way through an obstacle course, but at least you understand the objective, and that eliminates the emotional chaos.

In the end, knowing that death is an illusion, too, takes much of the sting out of grief.

Male And Female, Part II

Balancing energies is one thing, but in other contexts, male-female verses in several other religious texts are easily misunderstood when read physically, which has led to the ignorant abuse of women for thousands of years.

Kabbalistic teaching that female means 'receiver' of the male 'giving' force explains everything. Our souls are both male and female because we can all give and receive energy. It's what atoms do (Level 4) — emit and absorb energy. It's also what Adam does.

Wherever a verse says "the female must be submissive to the male," it represents a few things, none of which has a woman ever having to "obey" a man.

First, in any situation, clearly the giver must be present before a receiver. How can one receive without a giver? So the male starts to give, much like the sun shines its light … and eight minutes, 20 seconds later, earth receives it. The quarterback starts with the ball and throws it to the receiver. Both are equally important, but the giving comes first, and a giver has to have something to give. Then the receiver either takes it or refuses it, which comes second. Giver then receiver. Male then female.

This applies to everybody who has a Kli. Which is everybody. How does this play out in our physical world?

When we are judgmental or rude or melodramatic, we are being *ego male*, a giver of 'bad' energy. When we absorb that judgment or rudeness or melodrama we are being *ego female*, a receiver of 'bad' energy.

When we are courageous or forgiving or wise, we are being *spirit male*, a giver of 'good' energy. When we absorb that courage or forgiveness or wisdom, we are being *spirit female*, a receiver of 'good' energy.

If you perceive the world as hostile and unfair, you are energetically vulnerable to absorbing ego energy. If you perceive the world as supportive of your spiritual growth, you are energetically open to receiving upper light. In either case you are *female*, absorbing and open on a soul level.

If you assert that the world is hostile and unfair, you are bestowing ego energy into the world. If you assert that the world is supportive of your spiritual growth, you are bestowing spirit energy to the world. In either case you are *male*, assertive and bestowing on a soul level.

All of us, at one time or another, fit all four of those categories. Ego male, spirit male, ego female, spirit female.

Knowing this sheds the proper light on one of the more intriguing of Jesus's sayings, which features a Kabbalistic flair.

"I tell you, in that night there shall be two men in one bed; the one shall be taken, and the other shall be left. Two women shall be grinding together; the one shall be taken, and the other left."
- Luke 17:34-35.

You are two men (ego, spirit) and two women (ego, spirit) at the same time. There will come a time when one (spirit) will be taken and the other (ego) left. When this happens, you enter the heaven of Christ Consciousness.

(Symbolically, this giving-receiving principle is also why most of the world's prophets and greatest spiritual teachers have been men … as well as most of the world's evil dictators and mass murderers. Maleness gives energy, femaleness receives it. Some physical males bestow a tremendous amount of spirit energy, other physical males bestow tremendous ego energy. This is just symbolism, though, not a Truth.)

Only the ego would want us to perceive any of this as sexist or discriminatory, because ego wants to divide us. We are all energetically male and female, so do not listen to the ego. It wants us to argue over gender, but there is no need. Spiritually speaking, we are not boys and girls, we are One Soul.

Besides, understanding the Truth reduces *actual sexism* that is often followed in religions by ignorant, sleeping souls. The idea that "the female must be submissive to the male" only means that our lower nature must submit to the higher nature. The flesh must give way to the spirit. The ego energy of the world must yield to the upper light.

Eve represents the "flesh experience" removed from your soulful Adam consciousness. That's for every one of us. We all are a spiritual being (Adam) having a physical experience (Eve). When Eve tempts Adam (Genesis 3:6) because the flesh world appears to be so appealing, things go terribly wrong. On the day you (Adam) eat off the wrong tree, you will surely die (Genesis 2:17), because now you believe you are a mortal flesh being.

This process only gets reversed when Adam (higher consciousness) leads Eve (lower consciousness) back to the light. Then male and female are joined together in spirit.

Again, it has *NOTHING* to do with a woman ever having to *obey* a man!

Not only can you see the male-female dynamic in an atom/Adam, you can also find the concept all the way down on the level of strings.

Way back in Level 3, we discussed how our universe is comprised of tiny vibrating loops of energy, how open loops form matter and closed loops comprise your soul. Those strings vibrate and emit frequencies (male) that create the world, but when they get 'feedback' and receive frequencies (female) their vibrations change along with the world.

On the most basic energetic level of our reality, then, you can see how someone like Jesus would feed your soul. When you "eat the body of Christ" you are receiving upper light, and your Kli is filled.

When the Kli is full, you have balanced male and female energies and are born again as a mature soul.

Love Your Neighbor As Yourself

When the Kli is filled with light, your cup overflows (Psalm 23) and you are now a Son of God.

That's not sexist either — it just means you are a giver of the light.

And that can be all of us.

In Kabbalah it is the ultimate purpose of your development, as it says in Leviticus 19:18, to "love your neighbor as yourself." This may be the most important rule in the Torah.

You loved yourself enough to restore the light to yourself, now you must give it to others.

Jesus combined a line from Deuteronomy 6:5 with Leviticus 19:18 to create a perfect verse.

"Love the Lord your God with all your heart and with all your soul and with all your strength and with all your mind and Love your neighbor as yourself."
- Luke 10:27

Step 1: Love God through higher consciousness and fill your soul with light (female, receiving).

Step 2: Love others and share with them the light you now have that is overflowing (male, giving).

Some more depth is added elsewhere in the gospels.

"You shall love the Lord your God with all your heart and with all your soul and with all your mind. This is the great and first

commandment. And a second is like it: You shall love your neighbor as yourself. On these two commandments depend all the Law and the Prophets."
- Matthew 22:37-40

These two commandments are everything.

This is your entire journey of spiritual growth, going from receiver to giver of spirit. Doing this requires what may be the most important spiritual concept to grasp in Kabbalah — receiving IS giving. Receiving spiritually is spiritually giving. You cannot give unless you have first received. When you consciously receive in order to give, you have united both female and male into one. When you consciously choose to take the spirit that God is offering you so that you can distribute it to others, you have fulfilled the Golden Rule.

When you stop pursuing ego desires and you crave Truth instead, there is a shift in your awareness, a kind of sixth sense. You can see with the Third Eye. Your intentions change. You go from trying to delight the ego to trying to delight God by letting Him delight you with spirit.

Then you have achieved "equivalence of form" with God by simultaneously bestowing upper light upon others. It is precisely what Jesus did, and you are to spiritually follow after him and shine the light as well.

First you receive as a female, then you give as a male. Though it may appear to be sexist to the ego, just remember ...

"Stop judging by mere appearances, but instead judge correctly."
- John 7:24

Spiritually it is not about gender, it is about giving and receiving.

All women and men do this with their soul.

It's spiritual equality.

THERE'S NO DOUBT ABOUT IT

Sometimes you have a puzzle piece that just does not seem to fit.

Its color is a shade darker than the others around it and its edges don't seem to have a match, so you set it aside for later.

Lo and behold, when you complete more of the puzzle, the perfect opening just appears and you know precisely where to put it. Early on, you had no clue how pieces fit together, but over time things become more clear.

So it goes with universal spirituality.

"We know that for those who love God,
all things work together for good."
- Apostle Paul, in Romans 8:28

As long as you are seeking Truth, everything has its place in the puzzle of the Holy Grail. Everything has its purpose. Not just one book, just one path, just one person. God is a God of ALL things. That means if you seek, you will find where every piece of the puzzle fits.

The Gospel of Thomas is a Gnostic text and is not found in the Bible — for several reasons. Personally, I think the men who assembled the New Testament did not understand the riddles within and therefore voted against its inclusion.

That the supposed wise men of his day did not often understand him is perfectly illustrated by this exchange in John 3:9-10.

"How can this be?" Nicodemus asked after a deep spiritual lesson.

"You are Israel's teacher," said Jesus, "and *do you not understand* these things?"

Clearly some people get it, some don't. Even religious scholars such as Nicodemus failed to understand some of the teachings of Jesus.

In my journey, studying the Gospel of Thomas stirred the spirit inside of me as much as any text. Having gone through it a hundred times, this most well-known of the Gnostic Gospels has helped me experience a razor-sharp focus regarding the teachings of Christ. It made the wisdom in the Bible so much more clear.

As Buddha would say, "It *furthers* Truth."

Perhaps the Gospel of Thomas was in fact the secret teachings of Jesus that were finally written down two centuries after his crucifixion. Perhaps not. But in the very least, the 114 sayings in the text offer great insight into the canonical gospels as well as the nature of our relationship with God.

Personally, I don't care who wrote it — Truth is Truth. None of the poetry of Walt Whitman, Emily Dickinson, T.S. Eliot, Rumi or Maya Angelou appears in the New Testament, but their writings can still inspire divine wisdom.

It's just another piece of the puzzle. Fear no evil when reading it.

All things work together for good!

Following are italicized excerpts from the original Greek, translated by Stephen Patterson and Marvin Meyer (with interpretations through *New Eyes*):

1. And he said, "Whoever discovers the interpretation of these sayings will not taste death."

If you truly understand what these sayings mean, you realize that you are an eternal soul that does not die. The word "taste" is deliberately used as a physical sense, because although the soul transitions into another form, an awakened one will not experience it as the loss of the body.

Accordingly, if you do not interpret these sayings as Jesus intended, you will consider yourself a physical being and will experience death from that perspective as a result.

2. Jesus said, "Those who seek should not stop seeking until they find. When they find, they will be disturbed. When they are disturbed, they will marvel, and will reign over all. [And after they have reigned they will rest.]"

Whatever you look for with persistence you will find. Whether that is money, drugs, relationships or God, you will find it.

Finding what you are looking for always has a disturbing component to it, in that things will change as your path heads in a new direction. In the case of money and drugs, you always seem to want more and many negative features come with attaining those things. In the case of relationships, stress is inevitable and even the best physical relationships end in death.

In the situations where you are only seeking physical things, eventually you learn to look elsewhere for fulfillment, which ultimately leads you to spirituality. Keep seeking until you find it.

That's when the rest of the saying takes over. Once you have found a connection to God, it can still be disturbing. You have to let go of the ego aspects of your life, which can be challenging. People in your life might act differently around you, as some might resent you and others might think you are going crazy.

But in the case of seeking God, if you are persistent, you will marvel at what you find. The world is an illusion … we are all one … life is a mirror for spiritual development … no one can die … and so much more. These revelations bring about peace in your heart and allow you to reign over the ego while living your best spiritual and physical life.

Then you are born again as a spirit-filled soul, cross the finish line and rest.

3. Jesus said, "When you know yourselves, then you will be known, and you will understand that you are children of the living Father. But if you do not know yourselves, then you live in poverty, and you are the poverty."

Gnōthi Seauton. Know Thyself.

When you know that you are a developing soul, then you are a child of God and you are recognized as such. He is the Father of spirit, not flesh. If you do not know this, you are spiritually bankrupt.

5. Jesus said, "Know what is in front of your face, and what is hidden from you will be disclosed to you. For there is nothing hidden that will not be revealed."

Understand the nature of physical reality and see the spirit within. All of God's "secrets" will then be available to you.

6. His disciples asked him and said to him, "Do you want us to fast? How should we pray? Should we give to charity? What diet should we observe?"

Jesus said, "Don't lie, and don't do what you hate, because all things are disclosed before heaven."

If you are not moved by the spirit to do something, do not waste your time. If you do anything for ego purposes — in order to impress other people for example — it is the wrong reason.

7. Jesus said, "Lucky is the lion that the human will eat, so that the lion becomes human. And foul is the human that the lion will eat, and the lion still will become human."

In spiritual texts, the ego is often represented by a 'beast' of some kind. In this case, a lion is the ego, and the human is the body energy vessel (Kli) capable of absorbing ego or spirit.

When the human consumes ego, the ego becomes human and wins. And when the ego consumes the human, by addicting the human to all of its lies and illusions, the human is ruined and the ego still wins.

There is no spirit mentioned in this verse.

8. And he said, "The person is like a wise fisherman who cast his net into the sea and drew it up from the sea full of little fish. Among them the wise fisherman discovered a fine large fish. He threw all the little fish back into the sea, and easily chose the large fish. Anyone here with two good ears had better listen!"

Great fishing advice. But better spiritual advice.

There are many 'little souls' out there, and you are energetically entangled with them, as with a net in an ocean of consciousness. If you are wise, you hold onto the 'big souls,' the ones who are filled with spirit. They will feed you. Let the other fish swim for a while and grow.

Additionally, the mind itself is its own sea ... hold on to the big, useful, spiritual thoughts and let the little, immature, ego thoughts go free.

10. Jesus said, "I have cast fire upon the world, and look, I'm guarding it until it blazes."

The fire is Christ Consciousness. Like anything valuable, you should protect it so that the ego does not sneak in and try to steal it.

When it reaches critical mass, when 10 percent of your own mind or 10 percent of the world's population is open to Christ Consciousness, it will "blaze" and become the majority opinion relatively quickly.

(We are close to reaching critical mass.)

11. Jesus said, "The dead are not alive, and the living will not die. During the days when you ate what is dead, you made it come alive. When you are in the light, what will you do? ... When you become two, what will you do?"

The dead are filled with ego; they are not alive. The living are filled with spirit and cannot die. When you consume ego, it comes to life and Satan lives through you. You are one soul in the light of the 3D hologram — will you fall in love with the flesh or stay true to spirit? When you are both ego and soul, what will you focus your consciousness on?

13. And he took him, and withdrew, and spoke three sayings to him. When Thomas came back to his friends they asked him, "What did Jesus say to you?"

Thomas said to them, "If I tell you one of the sayings he spoke to me, you will pick up rocks and stone me, and fire will come from the rocks and devour you."

Jesus told Thomas things along the order of, "Reality is an illusion" and "This is all just a dream" and "Everyone is asleep."

The disciples would have disbelieved this and tried to cast rocks or stones (which in esoteric tradition means Truth) at Thomas but the fire of Christ Consciousness would have come through their misunderstanding of Truth and consumed their incorrect perspectives.

14. Jesus said to them, "If you fast, you will bring sin upon yourselves, and if you pray, you will be condemned, and if you give to charity, you will harm your spirits.

"When you go into any region and walk about in the countryside, when people take you in, eat what they serve you and heal the sick among them.

"After all, what goes into your mouth will not defile you; rather, it's what comes out of your mouth that will defile you."

If you are being ego for any reason — such as starving yourself because everyone at church is doing it, praying for material things or being generous with material possessions without giving spirit — your soul does not benefit.

When your soul manifests in the material realm (the countryside), you are going to absorb their energy (eat what they serve you) and you are to heal the ones stricken with ego. You do this by converting their ego energy to spirit light inside yourself, as Jesus did.

After all, you are not responsible for the energy that they have and are serving you, but if you respond to them with ego, you are defiled.

15. Jesus said, "When you see one who was not born of woman, fall on your faces and worship. That one is your Father."

Your physical body was born of woman. But when you "see" Christ, you may worship, because consciousness comes from God.

18. Jesus said, "Have you found the beginning, then, that you are looking for the end? You see, the end will be where the beginning is."

"Congratulations to the one who stands at the beginning: that one will know the end and will not taste death."

As discussed in Levels 0 and 1, once you come to know yourself as a spiritual being having a human experience, you realize that you end at the same place that you began — as a soul that does not die.

19. Jesus said, "Congratulations to the one who came into being before coming into being."

When you physically die, you return "into being" as pure spirit. You have succeeded if you remember your true divine self prior to dying.

21. He said, "If the owners of a house know that a thief is coming, they will be on guard before the thief arrives and will not let the thief break into their house (their domain) and steal their possessions.

"As for you, then, be on guard against the world. Prepare yourselves with great strength, so the robbers can't find a way to get to you."

Great homeowner advice. But better spiritual advice.

Jesus doesn't care about your big-screen TV being stolen; he wants you to guard your real possession, the spirit. The ego is the thief and it will break into your vessel and run away with your soul, like a devilish fox in an angelic chicken coop.

So you must be prepared when you face the world. Ego is everywhere. Get filled with spirit by building your spiritual muscle, then you can defend yourself.

22. Jesus said to them, "When you make the two into one, and when you make the inner like the outer and the outer like the inner, and the upper like the lower, and when you make male and female into a single one, so that the male will not be male nor the female be female, when you make eyes in place of an eye, a hand in place of a hand, a foot in place of a foot, an image in place of an image, then you will enter [the kingdom]."

You must be an energy alchemist, changing the energy within

your physical body into the energy of a spiritual body in order to enter heaven.

Note the recurring male-female theme, as the two energies are combined into one within a soul.

24. He said to them, "There is light within a person of light, and it shines on the whole world. If it does not shine, it is dark."

Light within a person of light is Jesus's version of $E = mc^2$.

Your body is energy, so you are a person of light. Your soul is energy and it can shine if it is filled with light, but if the vessel is empty, there is only darkness.

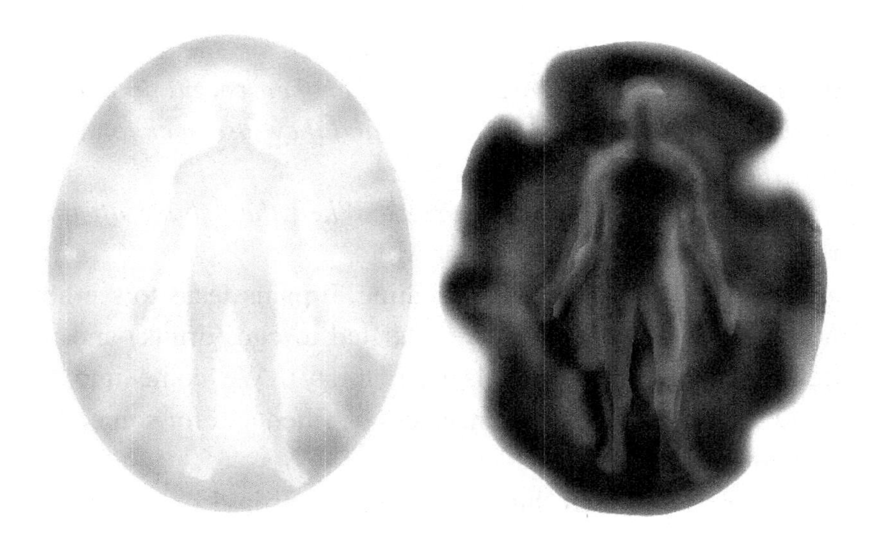

26. Jesus said, "You see the sliver in your friend's eye, but you don't see the timber in your own eye. When you take the timber out of your own eye, then you will see well enough to remove the sliver from your friend's eye."

The world is initially a mirror. If you are seeing someone else's flaws, they might very well be your own being reflected back at you.

Once you have removed ego from yourself, it becomes a oneway mirror and you can see well enough to help the other person work on their ego attachments.

27. "If you do not fast from the world, you will not find the (Father's) kingdom. If you do not observe the sabbath as a sabbath you will not see the Father."

Fast from ego, not from cheeseburgers and chocolate. Observing the sabbath is the same thing, taking a break from the ego world. You must tithe in order to achieve Christ Consciousness.

28. Jesus said, "I took my stand in the midst of the world, and in flesh I appeared to them. I found them all drunk, and I did not find any of them thirsty. My soul ached for the children of humanity, because they are blind in their hearts and do not see, for they came into the world empty, and they also seek to depart from the world empty.

"But meanwhile they are drunk. When they shake off their wine, then they will change their ways."

Things of the flesh are intoxicating. It pains Jesus to see how the people cannot see. We are addicted to ego (drunk) and not seeking spirit for their souls (not thirsty). We come into the world with a grail (Kli) that needs to be filled and for some, they die with it empty.

Eventually, though, humanity will grow tired of overdosing on ego and will wake up.

29. Jesus said, "If the flesh came into being because of spirit, that is a marvel, but if spirit came into being because of the body, that is a marvel of marvels.

"Yet I marvel at how this great wealth has come to dwell in this poverty."

The first part was discussed in Level 1, as Jesus states that it is amazing that consciousness brings about matter, but the idea that matter could produce consciousness is beyond belief.

The second part means that it is amazing to him how spirit can be now living amid lowly ego.

31. Jesus said, "No prophet is welcome on his home turf; doctors don't cure those who know them."

You can lead a horse to water but you cannot make them drink. Even Jesus could not heal those who did not believe, because they could not see past the ego and receive spirit.

33. Jesus said, "No one lights a lamp and puts it under a basket, nor does one put it in a hidden place. Rather, one puts it on a lampstand so that all who come and go will see its light."

If you are filled with spirit, let the little light inside you shine … let it shine … let it shine … let it shine.

34. Jesus said, "If a blind person leads a blind person, both of them will fall into a hole."

Ego leading ego is blind. Someone who is leading you physically, in order to merely improve your material conditions, is blind. True sight is spiritual.

35. Jesus said, "One can't enter a strong person's house and take it by force without tying his hands. Then one can loot his house."

If you are spiritually strong, you are only vulnerable to an ego that is stronger. A powerfully egocentric person will come at you with arrogance, jealousy, resentment and a whole host of negative energy. They will loot your house if they can tie up your soul's hands and prevent you from being forgiving, patient and humble.

37. Jesus said, "When you strip without being ashamed, and you take your clothes and put them under your feet like little children and trample them, then [you] will see the son of the living one and you will not be afraid."

When you fearlessly remove your ego costume, you will see Christ.

38. Jesus said, "There will be days when you will seek me and you will not find me."

This is not an easy journey. Some days, you will seek and not find Christ. It's spiritual superposition.

39. Jesus said, "The Pharisees and the scholars have taken the keys of knowledge and have hidden them. They have not entered nor have they allowed those who want to enter to do so.

"As for you, be as sly as snakes and as simple as doves."

Truth is available to all, but the teachers of the physical world who focus on behavior and not mind have not helped others gain access to it. Neither they nor their followers have upper knowledge.

To be "sly and simple" means to be creative and clear in your relationships with others, being flexible in your development as a spiritual being and cleverly finding new ways to give spirit energy to others.

42. Jesus said, "Be passersby."

Your soul is passing through this world. Do not cling to it. Observe it like a movie.

45. Jesus said, "Good persons produce good from what they've stored up; bad persons produce evil from the wickedness they've stored up in their hearts, and say evil things. For from the overflow of the heart they produce evil."

You are a vessel of light. You do not control your behaviors, just your perceptions. When you perceive spirit, you store up spirit, and "good" flows from you. Same with those who focus on materialism — they store up ego energy in their vessel and evil comes from that.

46. Jesus said, "From Adam to John the Baptist, among those born of women, no one is so much greater than John the Baptist that his eyes should not be averted.

"But I have said that whoever among you becomes a child will recognize the (Father's) kingdom and will become greater than John."

There are many great human beings, but an ego-free being filled with spirit is even greater than the best of human beings, such as John the Baptist. That person is a new being, a child in spirit, which is greater than anyone in the flesh.

48. Jesus said, "If two make peace with each other in a single house, they will say to the mountain, 'Move from here!' and it will move."

There are two voices in your head, the ego and spirit. They are battling inside your mind, the single house. If they can make peace, your mountainous emotional issues will be removed.

49. Jesus said, "Congratulations to those who are alone and chosen, for you will find the kingdom. For you have come from it, and you will return there again."

To be "alone" is to have merged your male and female energies, your upper and lower light. Doing this shows you the way to heaven, which is inside you. As for "returning there again," this is a reference to samsara, the wheel of life that includes the kingdom, which is both the exit and entrance of consciousness. The beginning and the end are the same. Alpha and Omega.

50. Jesus said, "If they say to you, 'Where have you come from?' say to them, 'We have come from the light, from the place where the light came into being by itself, established [itself], and appeared in their image.'"

This is Jesus describing the holographic universe, including the projector. We come from the light and came into physical being on the screen as an image of our consciousness selves.

51. His disciples said to him, "When will the rest for the dead take place, and when will the new world come?"

He said to them, "What you are looking forward to has come, but you don't know it."

Christ is right here, right now. He is present with you in this very moment.

52. He said to them, "You have disregarded the living one who is in your presence, and have spoken of the dead."

Christ is the living one. Jesus, as flesh, was destined to die. When we focus on Jesus, we are speaking of the dead. But when we focus on who he really was as Christ, we are paying attention to the living one.

53. His disciples said to him, "Is circumcision useful or not?"

He said to them, "If it were useful, their father would produce children already circumcised from their mother. Rather, the true circumcision in spirit has become profitable in every respect."

There is no reason to cut one's body to please God. But removing the darkened layers of the egoic heart pays benefits for your soul.

54. Jesus said, "Congratulations to the poor, for to you

belongs Heaven's kingdom."

Only the ego poor can fully receive the heavenly spirit in their grail. The ego rich have no room for it.

56. Jesus said, "Whoever has come to know the world has discovered a carcass, and whoever has discovered a carcass, of that person the world is not worthy."

The physical world is dead. When you realize that, the world is not worthy of you.

58. Jesus said, "Congratulations to the person who has toiled and has found life."

Suffering is valuable if you find spirit in it.

59. Jesus said, "Look to the living one as long as you live, otherwise you might die and then try to see the living one, and you will be unable to see."

Just as it is described in *The Tibetan Book of the Dead.* If you fail to wake up while you are here, when you have the opportunity to go to the heavenly light after death, you will still be blind.

62. Jesus said, "I disclose my mysteries to those [who are worthy] of [my] mysteries."

Be spirit and you will understand.

67. Jesus said, "Those who know all, but are lacking in themselves, are utterly lacking."

Ego know-it-alls might be great human beings, but they are empty spiritual beings. Knowing everything about the physical world does not get you far after death.

70. Jesus said, "If you bring forth what is within you, what you have will save you. If you do not have that within you, what you do not have within you [will] kill you."

You were born with a Point in your heart, a little piece of God. It's like a pilot light for the soul. Add fuel to it, it will grow and save you. If not, you will die an ego death.

72. A [person said] to him, "Tell my brothers to divide my father's possessions with me."

He said to the person, "Mister, who made me a divider?"

He turned to his disciples and said to them, "I'm not a divider, am I?"

Christ does not care about earthly possessions. He came to separate us from ego in order to unite us with spirit, as upper and lower consciousness come together.

Jesus was trying to inspire Unity Consciousness, not "my religion is better than yours" consciousness.

75. Jesus said, "There are many standing at the door, but those who are alone will enter the bridal suite."

You will not bring your version of the ego into heaven. Your costume stays here. When you have united male and female energies within yourself, you are married in spirit. If you do not do this, you are standing outside the bridal suite door.

77. Jesus said, "I am the light that is over all things. I am all: from me all came forth, and to me all attained. Split a piece of wood; I am there. Lift up the stone, and you will find me there."

Everything is energy. Accordingly, everything is spirit. God is hiding in plain sight.

78. Jesus said, "Why have you come out to the countryside? To see a reed shaken by the wind? And to see a person dressed in soft clothes, [like your] rulers and your powerful ones? They are dressed in soft clothes, and they cannot understand truth."

Powerful people on the physical dimension (the countryside) of earth, especially dictators and tyrants, are just wearing temporary costumes. Soft clothes. They will not last.

79. A woman in the crowd said to him, "Lucky are the womb that bore you and the breasts that fed you."

He said to [her], "Lucky are those who have heard the word of the Father and have truly kept it. For there will be days when you will say, 'Lucky are the womb that has not conceived and the breasts that have not given milk.'"

Like Buddha naming his son Rahula, or "the chain," Jesus is saying that children can bind you to earth. They can become false idols, if you live for them and fail to find your spiritual self.

82. Jesus said, "Whoever is near me is near the fire, and whoever is far from me is far from the (Father's) kingdom."

The fire is Christ Consciousness. It burns purity into your soul.

83. Jesus said, "Images are visible to people, but the light within them is hidden in the image of the Father's light. He will be disclosed, but his image is hidden by his light."

Another hologram reference. People see the images of people, but the spirit inside them is hidden. It's there, but you cannot see it, though you eventually will.

86. Jesus said, "[Foxes have] their dens and birds have their nests, but human beings have no place to lay down and rest."

Foxes and birds live here, earth is their home. But human beings are passersby, just observers inside this cosmic movie theater. This is not their home. They will rest when they find the kingdom.

87. Jesus said, "How miserable is the body that depends on a body, and how miserable is the soul that depends on these two."

Noble Truths 1 and 2. Life is suffering when flesh idolizes flesh.

89. Jesus said, "Why do you wash the outside of the cup? Don't you understand that the one who made the inside is also the one who made the outside?"

Don't just clean your outer body; you require proper hygiene for your inner soul as well. You contain the Holy Grail within you. Wash not just the outside of the grail — the cup — but also the inside of it.

91. He said, "You examine the face of heaven and earth, but you have not come to know the one who is in your presence, and you do not know how to examine the present moment."

Science can only take us so far, as Kurt Gödel said in Level 20. How can science study consciousness? How can science study Christ? You must learn to be in the now.

98. Jesus said, "The Father's kingdom is like a person who wanted to kill someone powerful. While still at home he drew his sword and thrust it into the wall to find out whether his hand would go in. Then he killed the powerful one."

The ego is an illusion. Powerful, but still an illusion. Once you identify it, you want to kill it. While at home (spirit focus), you break through the holographic image to see if you can get to the ego … and then you slaughter it.

99. The disciples said to him, "Your brothers and your mother are standing outside."

He said to them, "Those here who do what my Father wants are my brothers and my mother. They are the ones who will enter my Father's kingdom."

This saying is in the Bible, as many of these verses are. Jesus is emphasizing the eternal spiritual family as more important than temporary physical family.

102. Jesus said, "Damn the Pharisees! They are like a dog sleeping in the cattle manger: the dog neither eats nor [lets] the cattle eat."

Pharisees are self-righteous church leaders who think they know it all; they tell others what to believe and how to behave. But they are sleeping dogs, actually doing nothing but scaring the cattle, which do not consume Truth as a result of their ignorance.

103. Jesus said, "Congratulations to those who know where the rebels are going to attack. [They] can get going, collect their imperial resources, and be prepared before the rebels arrive."

When you know ego is coming, like that jealous person who resents your child's success or that self-loathing person whose melodrama might drain your energy, you can arm yourself with spirit and be ready for the pending ego attack.

106. Jesus said, "When you make the two into one, you will become children of Adam, and when you say, 'Mountain, move from here!' it will move."

As one who understands Hebb's Law, Jesus is being repetitive so that you can practice and become perfect. When the upper giving male and lower receiving female parts of your soul become united and create a new spiritual being (born again), you can move energetic mountains.

108. Jesus said, "Whoever drinks from my mouth will become like me; I myself shall become that person, and the hidden things will be revealed to him."

This is the message from Paul in Colossians 1:27, "And this

is the secret: Christ lives in you." You drink the Truth, you become the Truth.

113. His disciples said to him, "When will the kingdom come?"

"It will not come by watching for it. It will not be said, 'Look, here!' or 'Look, there!' Rather, the Father's kingdom is spread out upon the earth, and people don't see it."

Heaven is inside of you. When you recognize that, you see it everywhere. When you don't recognize that, you are blind.

114. Simon Peter said to them, "Make Mary leave us, for females don't deserve life."

Jesus said, "Look, I will guide her to make her male, so that she too may become a living spirit resembling you males. For every female who makes herself male will enter the kingdom of Heaven."

Flesh-focused Pharisees will disregard the entire Gospel of Thomas due to this one saying alone. With *New Eyes*, you can see Christ's brilliant teaching.

Just like many men today, some of the disciples were sexist and didn't believe women should be taught alongside them. Even Buddha thought this for a while until he wised up.

But Christ only sees souls. He knows that God created man in His image, both male and female. He knows that we all start out as female and become male, as we go from being receivers of the light to givers of the light.

There is nothing sexist about this verse. Gender is only involved on the ego level, where Simon Peter was when he asked that question. Ever in spirit, Christ directs them in a way that certainly forced them — and us 2,000 years later — to think.

Christ will guide ALL of us as females to make ALL of us male, as givers of the spirit like he is ... and that allows us to enter the kingdom as a new creation.

YOU MUST SUBMIT

Muhammad Ibn Abdullah emphasized that he was merely human, just like all of us. He was not to be worshipped. It makes him very relatable, as there is something in his story for everyone.

But Muhammad went on a journey of discovery that changed himself and, ultimately, the world. It can change you, too, if you do one simple little thing.

Submit!

You see, after completing the journey inside his own heart and mind, Muhammad began receiving revelations and became a teacher of Truth. At that point, he began leading a religion called Islam, which in Arabic means:

Submit!

Muhammad was both affluent and a commoner during different phases of his life. He was devoted to meditation. After years of practicing it, he began to experience divine revelations. He had a hard time transitioning back to reality once the spirit moved him, but he eventually became a teacher who changed the world by teaching the "middle path" and revealing Truth.

And his life story bears a striking resemblance to Siddhartha Gautama.

Just as Christ and Krishna lived out similar themes in their lives, so, too, did Muhammad and Buddha. Jesus and

Muhammad have a significant common bond between them as well. As direct descendants of Abraham, they can be thought of as distant cousins. (Of course, if you go back far enough, we are all basically cousins.)

But ultimately, the four of them are spiritual blood brothers. As we all are.

You may determine for yourself whether the similarities in their stories are coincidence or somehow meaningful, but there really should not be much debate about one aspect of those famed prophets: When viewed through *New Eyes*, they had a similar message for their followers.

We are all One in spirit.

No need to argue over the messengers when their messages are united. Whether you say one, un or uno, it's the same concept: We are all Eins.

Muhammad was born in 570 AD in Mecca (now Saudi Arabia) and had a challenging childhood. His father died before he was born and his mother died when he was 6, so he spent many of his early years orphaned and living day to day.

As a young man Muhammad was a member of the working class, serving as a camel driver. His financial fortunes changed at age 25 when he married his wealthy employer Khadija, a 40-year-old merchant who was so impressed by Muhammad's character and integrity that she proposed to him.

Despite being happily married and prosperous, Muhammad was not satisfied and was always seeking more in life. Living during a time period when people believed in many different gods, he sensed something deeper and was a consistent meditator throughout his 30s.

Muhammad made regular visits to a cave on a mountain near Mecca in order to pray and meditate fervently. One day at the age of 40, while sleeping, he awoke as the angel Gabriel appeared to him. It has been described as a terrifying experience for Muhammad, who felt as if his breath were being squeezed out of his body.

Gabriel commanded Muhammad to *read* and thus he began reciting thousands of verses. Initially he was in despair over this experience, but Khadija assured him he was a prophet and that his duty was to share his revelations to comman man. (Symbolically, Khadija was a calm, nurturing female vessel who was open to receiving male spirit wisdom.)

As a result, the Holy Quran was introduced to man as the Word of Allah (God).

Muhammad had gone inward and found the middle path of peace. The religion became known as Islam, and one of its adherents a Muslim, or "one who submits." To *New Eyes*, it means that the lower ego mind must be subservient to the higher consciousness realm of spirit — and may be a revelation to many who believe submission in Islam refers to behavior.

As Muhammad began to preach, he built up a following and over time experienced significant persecution and several military battles against the pagan people from Mecca. At one point he and his followers sought refuge in an area governed by a Christian ruler, who permitted the Muslims to stay after a companion of Muhammad recited from the "Chapter of Mary" in the Quran regarding the virgin birth of Jesus.

Indeed, Muhammad clearly recognized Jesus as a prophet of God. Verses from Surah 3:45-47 demonstrate Islam's embrace of Christianity's leader.

"Behold! the angels said: 'O Mary! Allah giveth thee glad tidings of a Word from Him: his name will be Christ Jesus, the son of Mary, held in honour in this world and the Hereafter and of (the company of) those nearest to Allah; He shall speak to the people in childhood and in maturity.
And he shall be (of the company) of the righteous.

"She said: 'O my Lord! How shall I have a son when no man hath touched me?' He said: 'Allah createth what He willeth.'"

Later in his life, during what was called his "Night Journey," Muhammad traveled both physically and spiritually on a noble steed from Mecca to Jerusalem, where he was taken to heaven and explored its seven stages while also speaking with several prophets, including Abraham, Moses, John the Baptist and Jesus.

Just prior to his death in 632, Muhammad gave a greatly revered final speech that included these words:

"All mankind is from Adam and Eve. An Arab has no superiority over a non-Arab, nor does a non-Arab have any superiority over an Arab; a white has no superiority over a black, nor does a black have any superiority over a white."

Muhammad stressed cultural and racial tolerance (it is why practicing Muslims often wear all-white garments, symbolizing equality and purity) and emphasized the importance of not pressuring others in their beliefs.

"Let there be no compulsion in religion.
Truth stands out clear from Error."
- Quran, Surah 2:256

There should be no coercion, no forcing anyone to adopt your beliefs, as Truth is self-evident. In time, everyone will find it and pressuring someone to convert is impatient and ineffective. Similar to Buddha's Kalama Sutta ("Charter of Free Inquiry"), Muhammad's revelations demonstrate a tolerance for other faiths.

"For you is your religion and for me is my religion."
- Surah 109:6

Muslims are expressly forbidden to worship Muhammad, as he is considered to be merely God's messenger. It is a sin (of misperception) to see him in the flesh. This is why images of him are not permitted to be shown, so that no one thinks of the man as more important than the message.

Islam features "Five Pillars" as a foundation, including the profession of faith (that there is no god except God and Muhammad is His Messenger), daily prayers, alms giving, fasting during Ramadan and Hajj, a pilgrimage to Mecca at least once in a lifetime. These mandatory rituals are Hebb's Law in action, as Muslims become devoted to their faith through repetition. Neurons that fire together, wire together.

Muslims also believe in six articles of faith known as Iman, which have a more metaphysical emphasis. Among them are a belief in angels, divine books, prophets, the day of judgment and Allah's predestination, but the most important is tawhid, or Muhammad's revelation that God is One.

Tawhid is the fundamental tenet that there is only one God, and that everything in existence comes from Him. Muhammad's "There is no God but Allah" message became a deity-unifying force during a time when people worshipped as many as 360 gods, though there is more to God's Oneness than merely the monotheistic aspect, just as we have seen in every other prominent religion.

God is One because all of reality is One, and we are part of that reality. We must recognize that Oneness and unite under God. We do so when we stop judging each other's relative costumes, achieving the awareness that Adam's fall out of Eden and shattering into 600,000 souls is symbolic of our separation within the material world.

"Mankind was one nation, but then they differed later on."
- Surah 10:19

We started out as One, then "differed later on" and became culturally and spiritually isolated because of that devilish ego.

Indeed, we are all still One in spirit, but are now separated by illusion. Experiencing that Oneness requires us to submit, to not let ego rule our lives, to not see separation in each other but unity. We all must win the battle between spirit and ego in our own minds, seeing the energy that connects us, not the illusory matter that seemingly separates us.

Just as with the Bible and the Bhagavad Gita there are many controversial verses in the Quran if read literally, from the ego's point of view, but the Quran is a masterful spiritual text … just like the Bible and Bhagavad Gita are when read spiritually. They all support each other, as well as the implications of quantum physics. The only reason people see division among these religious teachings is because of the ego battle still splitting their own minds.

Here are more excerpts from the Quran, followed by *New Eyes* explanations and links to other spiritual verses or themes throughout this book:

"O Adam, dwell thou and thy wife in this garden, and eat freely thereof, both of you, whatever you may wish; but do not approach this one tree, lest you become wrongdoers." - Surah 2:35

This should sound familiar if you are Christian or Jewish, as Islam shares the same Garden of Eden story.

The garden is a paradise of spiritual consciousness. If you eat off the tree of separation (good and evil instead of Oneness), you put your physical self before your spiritual self and become "wrongdoers" or sinners of misperception. Your actions become based upon things of the flesh as opposed to the spirit.

"We believe in God and that which is revealed unto us, and

that which was revealed unto Abraham and Ishmael and Isaac and Jacob and the tribes, and that which Moses and Jesus received, and which the prophets received from their Lord. We make no distinction between any of them, and unto Him we have surrendered." - Surah 2:136

Jesus is completely accepted as a prophet within Islam, along with several others.

"Allah intends for you ease, and He does not want to make things difficult for you." - Surah 2:185

Being spiritual is much easier than being physical. Ascend to higher consciousness, which is an easier yoke and a lighter burden. (Matthew 11:30)

"Enter perfectly in Islam ... and follow not the footsteps of Shaitan (Satan). Verily! He is to you a plain enemy." - Surah 2:208

Don't walk the ego's pathway. You must be perfect. (Matthew 5:48)

"Allah is with those who are patient." - Surah 2:249

Love is patient. (1 Corinthians 13:4)

"Do not invalidate your charities by reminders of your generosity or by injury." - Surah 2:264

Do not give to the needy and sound trumpets before you so that you may be praised by others. If you do, that's your reward. (Matthew 6:2)

"The life of this world is nothing but an illusory enjoyment." - Surah 3:185

The world is an illusion, whatever physical pleasure you derive from it is a mirage. (Level 13)

"O mankind! Be careful of your duty to your Lord, who created you from a single soul and from it created its mate and from them twain hath spread abroad a multitude of men and women." - Surah 4:1

Similar to Adam HaRishon in the Kabbalah, we all come from one original soul. Eve came from Adam. The flesh aspect of ourselves was created out of the soul, as well as all of humanity.

"Death will find you even if ye hide in fortresses built up strong and high." - Surah 4:78

Remember you are mortal. Memento Mori. (Level 11)

"Help each other in righteousness and piety, but do not help one another in sin and transgression." - Surah 5:2

Entanglement. Send spirit energy back and forth to each other, not ego energy. (Level 10)

"Verily! The worst of living creatures in the sight of Allah are those who do not use reason." - Surah 8:22

Evolve your consciousness. Learn the rules of the game. (Levels 12, 22)

"Verily! Allah will not change the condition of a people until they change that which is in their hearts." - Surah 13:11

The observer effect, as well as the placebo effect. Only through a shift in perception will you experience healing. (Level 9)

"So Allah sets forth parables for men, in order that they may receive admonition." - Surah 14:25

God speaks in riddles as a teaching tool for souls.

"Your Lord proclaimed, 'If you are thankful, surely I will

increase you, but if you are thankless My chastisement is surely terrible.'" - Surah 14:7

For to the one who has, more will be given, and from the one who has not, even what he has will be taken away. (Mark 4:25)

"Nothing is hidden from Allah." - Surah 14:38

Even the hairs on your head are numbered. (Luke 12:7)

"And if ye were to count the Blessings of Allah, never would you be able to enumerate them." - Surah 16:18

Trust God, and heaven will pour down upon you blessings until there is no more need. (Malachi 3:10)

"Surely, Allah knows what they hide and what they reveal. Indeed, He does not like the arrogant." - Surah 16:23

God knows your heart. No man shall boast. (Ephesians 2:9)

"Whatever you have will perish, but what Allah has will remain." - Surah 16:96

Physical things deteriorate, spiritual virtues do not. Similar to putting your treasures where moths and rust will not get them (Matthew 6:20).

"If you do good, you do good for yourselves; And if you do evil, (you do it) to yourselves." - Surah 17:7

You reap what you sow. (Galatians 6:7)

"You shall not follow anyone blindly in those matters of which you have no knowledge, surely the use of your ears and the eyes and the heart - all of these, shall be questioned on the Day of Judgement." - Surah 17:36

You should develop your sense of spiritual perception, because ignorantly trusting people will get you nowhere.

"Fear not! Allah is always with you." - Surah 20:46

You need not fear evil, for He is with you. (Psalm 23:4)

"My Lord! Increase me in knowledge." - Surah 20:114

Krishna emphasized that knowledge is far more important than action. (Level 26)

"And to Allah belongs the outcome of all matters." - Surah 22:41

God's Will be done. (Matthew 6:10)

"It is not the eyes that are blind, but the hearts." - Surah 22:46

When a messiah or prophet heals the blind, he opens their hearts and gives them spiritual vision.

"Repel evil with that which is better." - Surah 23:96

Perfect love casts out fear. (1 John 4:18)

"Do not enter houses other than your own, until you seek permission and greet the inhabitants." - Surah 24:27

This is definitely the polite physical thing to do, but spiritually it means to be mindful and respectful of other people's energy.

"And whoever strives, he strives for his own benefit. Surely, Allah is free from the needs of the world." - Surah 29:06

God does not want or expect anything from us. We are here to receive from Him.

"Verily! Allah is with those who do good deeds." - Surah 29:69

Good deeds come from spirit, which comes from God. Jesus

did as his Father told him. Not our will, but God's will be done.

"Allah has not put two hearts in a person's body." - Surah 33:4

You have to pick between materialism or spirituality. As Jesus said, a man cannot serve two masters. (Matthew 6:24)

"Let not then this present life deceive you nor let the Chief Deceiver deceive you about Allah." - Surah 35:5

Do not fall into the swamp of delusion and do not let ego (Satan) confuse you about the nature of God.

"O ye who believe! Do not ridicule others, perhaps they may be better than you." - Surah 49:11

Keep relativity in mind when it comes to how others are behaving. Stop judging by mere appearances, but instead judge correctly. (John 7:24)

"Behold, We have created you all out of a male and a female, and have made you into nations and tribes, so that you might come to know one another." - Surah 49:13

We are all One separated into many so that we can reconnect with each other.

"Allah is closer to you than your jugular vein." - Surah 50:16

The Spirit of God dwells in you. (1 Corinthians 3:16)

"Humans can have only that for which they make effort." - Surah 53:39

You must seek in order to find.

"Verily! We have created everything in equal proportion and measure." - Surah 54:49

Complementarity principle. Yin and yang. The world rests in

a state of balance. (Level 5)

"He has given freedom to the two great bodies of water, so that they might meet." - Surah 55:19

In the language of spirituality, water is thought, as both follow the path of least resistance. The two great bodies of water in our minds — ego and spirit — are free to mingle.

"Whoever believes in Allah, He will guide his heart." - Surah 64:11

The Lord is your shepherd. (Psalm 23:1)

"So verily, with every difficulty, there is relief." - Surah 94:5

All who are weary and heavy-laden will be given rest. (Matthew 11:28.)

"Whoever does an atom's weight of good will see it." - Surah 99:7

Faith the size of a mustard seed can move a mountain. (Matthew 17:20)

***

Just as in Christianity, Hinduism and Judaism, any seemingly violent imagery in the Islamic texts can be perceived as references to the internal war between ego and spirit. In that context "strike above the necks" (Surah 8:12) is a clear allusion to attacking the ego mind; any notion of "stonings" or "floggings" for adultery are to correct the ego mind for "cheating" on the soul as stones represent spiritual Truth; and jihad means to fight the Holy War inside oneself.

Indeed, the Arabic definition of jihad is "to strive," which happens to be the same meaning of "Isra" in Hebrew. Muslims and Jews are both striving together for the same God … if they only choose to see it that way … just as all Christians and

Hindus and Buddhists.

Somehow religion seems to have gotten the impression that convincing others to believe in their version of God is something required of their followers. To the contrary, you need not convert others … just focus on yourself.

Muhammad's *"Let there be no compulsion in religion"* revelation from Surah 2:256 is well supported by his spiritual blood brothers.

"First take the log out of your own eye ... "
- Jesus, in Matthew 7:5

"The one who has conquered himself is a far greater hero than he who has defeated a thousand times a thousand men."
- Buddha, in The Dhammapada

It's not about convincing others to believe your point of view, it's about perfecting yourself.

That's what Islamic Law, or Sharia, is really about as well. Mostly based upon the Quran and hadith teachings, when Sharia is taken literally, controversy often results. When taken spiritually, Sharia means "path to the water" or the way to higher consciousness.

So Sharia, with proper illumination, is Islam's Tao. It is considered to be the outer, physically focused dimension of a Muslim's life while "ihsan" is the inner dimension within Islam. Ihsan is an Arabic word meaning "perfection" … which is a Muslim's inner striving. Just as Jesus said, "You must be perfect."

Spiritually interpreting the Quran and hadith requires mystical perception, which in Islam is the focus of the Sufis.

Sufism can be compared to the Gnosticism in Christianity and the Kabbalah in Judaism, as the followers of each emphasize the spiritual dimension of their practice while striving for perfection. Muhammad was a perfect man in the eyes of Sufis, whose goal is to experience Allah directly in accordance with Muhammad's revelations.

Much like the experience of falling in love as discussed in Level 20, Sufis recognize that a true connection to God requires a direct experience of the divine, not just an intellectual understanding or casual belief. It is an inner journey that purifies the heart and complete annihilation of the ego.

In other words, it's not about your physical body, it's about your spiritual body.

According to Alevism, another mystical tradition in Islam, God is divine consciousness and our physical world is His mirror image. Humans reach perfection by balancing their male and female selves within ... a concept also found in esoteric Christian, Judaism, Hindu and Taoist teachings.

Mystical Muslims perfect themselves by recognizing the self as being one with that original consciousness and originating from the same light.

It is the Sufi poet Rumi who has been quoted several times in *New Eyes* saying, "This place is a dream. Only a sleeper considers it real. Then death comes like dawn, and you wake up laughing at what you thought was your grief."

The True Self does not die, it only changes form.

The following discourse from Rumi's book, *It Is What It Is*, captures the spirit of Islam in a down-to-earth manner:

"For Soul there is other food besides this food of sleeping and eating, but you have forgotten that other food. Night and day you nourish only your body. Now, this body is like a horse, and this lower world is its stable. The food the horse eats is not the food of the rider. You are the rider and have your own sleeping and eating, your own enjoyment. But since the animal has the

upper hand, you lag behind in the horse's stable. You cannot be found among the ranks of kings and princes in the eternal world. Your heart is there, but since your body has the upper hand, you are subject to its rule and remain its prisoner."

Your soul is riding a horse called ego, which is the domain of lower consciousness. The ego horse eats matter, but your soul consumes Truth. When the ego is in control, the soul is stuck in the horse's stable, or the material world. As a result, despite a point in your heart that longs to be released, you are in captivity.

Thankfully, the way to freedom is simple. Pound the enemy into submission.

The ego must submit to the spirit.

ALL FOR ONE, ONE FOR ALL

Truth is universal. It must be applicable in all situations at all times.

Truth must be healing, experiential and inclusive.

Like yoga, Truth must be able to twist and turn itself into whatever position it needs to in order to make everyone comfortable. One size fits all.

But like rock, Truth must also be solid and reliable and capable of supporting the most heavy of emotional human weight. You must be able to build a spiritual house upon it.

Some may think they can 'yin and yang' Truth every once in awhile, pointing out seeming opposites or shades of gray around it. Sometimes people say with a sneer, "I don't care what anyone thinks" or "Hate motivates me" or simply revel in their ability to condescend upon others as a show of superiority. Those perspectives might work for the moment, but those attitudes will not last over the illusion of time.

There are no opposites, nor gray areas, when it comes to Truth. The taijitu of yin and yang is ultimately One Thing, a complementary symbol of black or white. Truth is permanent and eternal.

So here's the Truth Test: If it allows you to experience unchanging, unabiding, everlasting peace in your heart while being comprehensive and expansive enough to include all other sentient beings, then it is True.

If not, then it is false and based upon an ego perspective. Period.

If you only feel peaceful for awhile, like while drinking or using drugs for example, then you know what you are doing is not based upon Truth. You are at peace only due to chemicals that you put into your body, which is not lasting peace. All addicts eventually come to that realization.

If you think you are always right in your relationships and feel that brings you peace, given enough time, we know how that is going to end. You will likely experience many arguments with important people in your life who disagree, which will zap you of your self-righteous peace.

And if you think your religion is the *only* correct one, then you have company with about five billion people who agree and think *their* religion is also the *only* correct one — and yet the majority of them disagree upon what that religion is. This irony has removed peace from the world as we fight over who is right.

Any model of Truth that attempts to separate us is ultimately false. Each of our jobs individually is to learn how to embrace the other's relative perspective as their truth in the moment, albeit not as the Truth. When someone tries to say that their prophet is better than your prophet, well, that is only their truth in the moment. Over the illusion of time, it will not last.

Be patient. You cannot force anyone to shift their perspective.

"Let there be no compulsion in religion.
Truth stands out clear from Error."
- Muhammad, Quran

Just walk your path and, if we all do it, collectively that will lead the way.

"If you find no one to support you on the spiritual path,
walk alone. There is no companionship with the immature."
- Buddha, The Dhammapada

Truth is, there is an all-encompassing Truth. It's Unity Consciousness. It's Christ, Krishna, Muhammad, Buddha and all of us, all rolled into One.

We are the light of the world.

"I am the light of the world." - Jesus, Bible
"You are the light of the world." - Jesus, Bible

I + You = We.

We are the light of the world.

Our collective consciousness is the light of the world.

"When he perceives the unity existing in separate creatures and
how they expand from unity, he attains the infinite spirit."
- Krishna, Bhagavad Gita

Unity Consciousness, filled with light. That light is the infinite spirit. It's in all of us, activated by elevating consciousness. Merely pursuing Truth is one way to do it. Seek and you will find, said Jesus, ask and you will receive. Both Buddha and Muhammad were dedicated meditators, which raised their consciousness and allowed them to access Truth. Hindus practically invented meditation.

Evolving consciousness upward or renewing your life with your mind allows you to see the entire world as spiritually One.

If your way of thinking puts you on a cognitive island, it is not inclusive. But if your way of thinking includes everyone else's island, it is inclusive.

Religious thinking often divides people, but spiritual thinking is inclusive. It can take on anything and give it meaning and purpose. It explains everything. With energy as the essence of the universe and not matter, it all becomes clear.

Spiritual perception unites Christianity, Islam, Hinduism, Buddhism and Judaism. It also unites all the other religions and includes Atheism and Humanism.

And it does so with just one word.

Love.

If the world would stop obsessing over matter and pay attention to energy, we could unite.

If we define God as a man, that causes problems. If we define God as a father figure who sits in judgment of our behaviors, that causes problem. If we define God as selective and only accepting of my prophet and not yours, that *really* causes problems.

But if we define God as spirit, as an energy force, it works for everyone.

Jesus himself did not think of God as a personal entity.

"God is spirit, and those who worship Him
must worship in spirit and truth."
- John 4:24

You do not worship God as flesh, you worship God as spirit.

Then in 1 John 4:8, He is described again:

"God is love."

There is a lot of support for a love-based definition in the other major religions.

In the Quran, verses 11:90 and 85:14 describes Allah as "loving" and "the loving." In the Torah, Leviticus 19:18 commands us to unite and "love thy neighbor as thyself."

And this inspiring wisdom comes from the Upanishads, which are ancient Hindu texts that are often shared by Buddhists and Jains:

> *"All is change in the world of the senses,*
> *But changeless is the supreme Lord of Love.*
> *Meditate on him, be absorbed by him,*
> *Wake up from this dream of separateness."*

Wake up from this dream of separateness!

That says it all.

God is love, God is loving. Love each other. Be absorbed by the Lord of Love so that you can awaken from the illusion and experience unity. That's Christianity, Islam, Judaism, Hinduism and Buddhism all giving each other a big group bear hug.

If your first reaction is to disagree and roll your eyes, we will never unify this world. If your goal is to argue and insist that your team is better than their team, then we are in deep trouble.

But if you can agree that God is love, heaven can come to earth and Eden can be just around the corner. Unity Consciousness works for all.

This is no ordinary love — it's transcendental. It's an energy form that moves through our hearts, minds, souls and bodies. Romantic love is just one form of it, like love of pet or love of career. Universal love encompasses all, including love of enemy, and requires higher consciousness to wire together the right configuration of neural patterns in the brain. Like a neurological combination lock being opened with good vibrations, finding the proper code triggers a release of endorphins, oxytocin and other neurochemicals to yield the sublime feeling of … love.

Paraphrasing the 1 Corinthians 13 definition of love — love is patient, kind, humble, polite, accepting, tolerant, forgiving, joyful, wise, faithful, trusting, hopeful, enduring, persistent, evolving, perfect and a mirror.

Love does not practice schadenfreude (delighting in someone else's misfortune), but it excels at mudita (delighting in someone else's joy). Love recognizes that we are all teammates and that we are all striving for God as Israelites (a word that means "striving for God") while following Islam's goal of spiritual jihad (meaning "to strive") toward inner ihsan (perfection), which is precisely what Jesus stated we should be in Matthew 5:48 — perfect.

The notion of energetically experiencing God as love through acquiring virtues such as compassion, forgiveness, courage and patience is a broad net that can be cast over other great philosophies of the world. As such, all spiritual traditions have added something to our collective wisdom.

Sikhism: With more than 20 million followers, this religion founded in South Asia ranks in the Top 10 in the world.

Sikhs emphasize a message of unity, believing that all spiritual traditions can lead their adherents to enlightenment and that no one religion can claim to be the home of Truth. They also consider the world to be an illusion and that the influence of ego is a distraction to finding God.

The teachings of Guru Nanak point to reconnecting with God as the purpose of our lives, while higher consciousness within ourselves is the shepherd to lead the way. Following this inner guide enables us to understand all religions as aspects of Truth.

Bahá'í Faith: A major teaching of this perspective is that all religions are united by the same spiritual source, with all of our various explorations (science, art, philosophy, etc.) merely different manifestations of God.

Originated in Iran, Bahá'ís believe that every religious text is metaphorical and has an esoteric interpretation. Each of us has an immortal soul and, according to its founder Bahá'u'lláh, "The soul of man is the sun by which his body is illumined."

In other words, reality is a projector and our physical world is the movie screen.

In Bahá'í, heaven and hell are symbolic references to the relative place of the soul on the eternal journey toward perfection; the more separated you are from the other souls in this world, the more hell you feel. The more united you are, the closer to heaven you feel.

Jainism: The primary point of emphasis of this religion is that we are here as teammates in spirit.

This teaching is called Parasparopagraho Jivanam, or "Souls render service to one another," as we are all interconnected, entangled energy beings.

Atheism: Often misunderstood, most Atheists do not contend that there is no God, they merely say that they lack belief in one. Rather, God is largely irrelevant to them, as living this life right now is more essential than aspiring toward a promise of afterlife.

Atheists, in principle, are accepting of other people's beliefs. They are just adamant that those beliefs should not be forced on them or anyone, which puts them in agreement with Jesus and Muhammad on that issue. They are also for the separation of church and state, which Jesus would also be. Considering there is no more egoic institution than government, which by definition is primarily concerned with human affairs, Jesus would be neither Democrat nor Republican as he was solely interested in spiritual matters. He supported that which furthered spiritual development.

Atheists are 'correct' from their point of view: Since the world is a mirror and their observation is that there is no God, they are right. For them, there is no God, and they are fine with that. It is what they are seeing in their mirror.

But if you define God as *love* or *spirit*, which Jesus did, an open-minded Christian can be at peace with an open-minded Atheist, and vice versa. The fruits of the spirit (compassion, forgiveness, courage, discipline, respect, etc.) are the same for both.

An Atheist can certainly come to know God … as universal love. A rose by any other name would smell as sweet.

Humanism: Similar to Atheism in its absence of an active belief in God — or in the absence of a belief in an active God — Humanists place a strong emphasis on moral principles using reason and logic. The essence of Humanism is compassion for humanity.

According to the Humanist Manifesto 2000, Humanists believe "that there is insufficient scientific evidence for spiritual interpretations of reality."

Absolutely true! As covered in Level 20, spiritual interpretations of reality cannot be achieved with science, which is limited by a glass ceiling. Human reason and logic may look 'up' for answers, but will ultimately run into a barrier called faith. You cannot move past that barrier with our available human senses (doing so requires a higher level of consciousness), but there is nothing inherently wrong with striving to make humanity the best it can be — you certainly learn a lot about your spiritual self along the way.

In that regard, Humanists as well as Atheists no doubt play a significant role in the advancement of mankind. To the extent that they encourage the development of character, evolution of consciousness and promotion of virtues, they are advancing the spiritual intent of *New Eyes* as well.

Actually, Atheists, Humanists and religion are much closer to agreeing on God than most people think — depending on how 'God' is defined.

If God is love? One that is reached through the ascension toward higher consciousness? Well, that's a pretty easy gap to bridge.

Agnosticism: In contrast to Gnosticism or "knowing," this is a philosophy that features an approach of "affirming the uncertainty of all claims to ultimate knowledge."

Under that definition we are all agnostic … until we are no longer agnostic, when we have perfected consciousness and come to know Truth for ourselves.

Primal indigenous: The tribal religions of Africa and Asia have 300 million followers and are largely henotheistic, which focuses on a single God while leaving open the possibility of other gods. They are tolerant of other pathways to God.

Adherents to these native viewpoints generally see God in all things, connected to everything, both in life and death. They do not see the distinction between material and spiritual realms, as it is all spiritual to them. (That is entanglement.) They are often proponents of timelessness as well.

Pantheism: God is not personal. God is everything in the universe.

Greatly simplified, God is nature.

Albert Einstein was essentially a Pantheist, and was quoted in 1955 in his New York Times obituary as saying, "My religion consists of a humble admiration of the illimitable superior spirit who reveals himself in the slight details we are able to perceive with our frail and feeble minds. That deeply emotional conviction of the presence of a superior reasoning power, which is revealed in the incomprehensible universe, forms my idea of God."

Slightly different is panentheism, in which God is both this entire universe and everything beyond it, as discussed in Level 24. In pantheism God is the universe; in panentheism God is more than the universe.

Spiritism: A philosophy that maintains we all have immortal souls that are using these mortal bodies to evolve consciousness.

Zoroastrianism: Consciousness also takes center stage in this faith, featuring a contrast between Asha (Truth) and Druj (deceit, or the ego). Whichever you focus on becomes heaven or hell for you.

Led by the prophet Zoroaster, everyone is responsible for their circumstances. It is an ancient teaching of the observer effect, where the way you look at reality affects reality.

Rastafari: With roots in Christianity, this Jamaican philosophy emphasizes the equality of all people and that the Holy Spirit is present in everyone, which makes all of humanity united in Oneness.

Rastafarians have a unique way of describing that Oneness, saying "I and I" instead of "We" in order to indicate unity, as there is an individual "I" and a collective "I." In Kabbalah, that collective "I" can be thought of as Adam HaRishon.

Hermeticism: In this esoteric tradition, Truth is inherent in all religions and accessible to all.

Two Hermetic concepts are particularly interesting for *New Eyes*.

Similar to the "upper and lower worlds" teaching of Kabbalah, Hermetics speak of "As Above, So Below." Essentially, it means that the spiritual and material worlds are entangled, that they reflect each other like a mirror. *The Tibetan Book of the Dead* is a good illustration of the idea, as the afterlife resembles this life from a consciousness perspective.

The concept of alchemy also comes from Hermeticism, although only on the lower level does it reference turning lead or other common metals into gold. On the upper level, you are an alchemist if you are working on transforming the physical body into perfect spirit.

Unitarian Universalism: This is "freestyling" spirituality, welcome to all comers united in the pursuit of Truth and meaning in life, which means that UU followers are pretty much open to exploring all of the above.

It's also largely what *New Eyes* wants to see: People of all religions coming together with Truth as the common goal. Especially Truth that focuses on the True Self, not the fake, costumed, ego self.

***

It often gets lost or overlooked in the practicing of worthy philosophies that everything in the world is energy. You are only the material aspect of you because of where and to whom you were born — and that includes Christians, Muslims, Hindus and Atheists. Had you been born in another man's shoes, you would certainly have a different perspective on the mortal ego self. Many well-intentioned people have no clue that they are imprisoned by ego thinking, and separation is the result. It is akin to believing that your favorite sports team is "the best" simply because of the town in which you were born. That's relativity.

Truth, though, rises above all that. Truth is accessible to all of us. Truth has nothing to do with the material world. God being "love" makes so much more sense than thinking of God as a physical being, and accordingly, He is not interested in human affairs … He is interested in spiritual endeavors. We are made in His image, as beings of great love potential.

Whatever your religion, whatever your philosophy, your journey is to navigate your way through the cognitive morass of divisive thinking and find unity with each other. And remember, *Truth must be all-encompassing.* If your point of view does not apply in all situations, it cannot be Truth.

New Eyes accepts as a curriculum within the high school of spiritual development that each religion or philosophy has its own relative grade. Just as humans possess different relative potential, so do religions in terms of their ability to deliver absolute Truth. None is better than the other — is seventh grade *superior* to third grade? Of course not. But it *is* more advanced, a little further along in the journey. Which is more correct, 2 + 2 = 4 or 1 - 3 + 7 - 1 = 4? Both are correct, but one is a bit less confusing ... while at the same time too simplistic for some. The other may be more cumbersome, but a greater challenge for others ... more collegiate. Either path gets you to the same answer in the end.

Some religions are deeper and more complex, others more clear and concise. Some paintings are Picasso, others are Michelangelo. Beauty is in the eye of the beholder — Truth can be described so many different ways.

As beings of consciousness, we do not differ by skin color or political party or religion, we differ by degree and by intensity and by clarity. Perfected consciousness is a clear diamond, capable of seeing self in all things and all things in self.

When we are unified in this vision, we amplify each other's light.

"The Universal Soul exists in every individual, it expresses itself in every creature, everything in the world is a projection of it, and that there is Oneness, a unity of souls in one and only Self."
- The Upanishads

A piece of God is in all of us, just as the spark of love is in all of us. The physical world is merely a projection of that love, if you choose to see Self that way.

The famous parable of the "four blind men and the elephant" illustrates our reality so well.

Having never seen an elephant, each man puts his hand on a different part of the animal and then describes what he is feeling. The man who touches the ear says it is a fan, the man

who touches the trunk says it is a hose, the man who touches a leg says it is a tree and the man who sits on its back says it is a rock.

Then they can either argue with each other about what the object is, or — like Bohm's goldfish — they can figure out that they are all merely experiencing the same object from their own relative perspective.

So here's a variation of that story: You have Christians, Muslims, Hindus, Buddhists, Jews, Sikhs, Jains, Bahá'ís, Atheists and everyone else … all blind. Truth is the elephant in the room, and seven billion of us are touching it.

Can we figure out what Truth is? Or are we just going to keep arguing with each other about it?

TO LIVE TRUTH

The Quantum Revolution has begun.

It's time to overthrow that evil dictator, ruler of all the earth: The human ego.

United we stand, divided we fall — both within the collective consciousness of humanity, as well as inside our own minds. So we must be One. We must assert ourselves for who we actually are … spiritual beings having a human experience.

At last, we are waking up to Truth.

We must join together to tell the ego, *"You don't control us, we control you."*

The enemy doesn't stand a chance. Like the Wicked Witch being dowsed with a bucket of water, the ego will dissolve right before our eyes if we flood it with Unity Consciousness.

"You cursed brat! Look what you've done!" the ego will cry. *"I'm melting! Melting! ... Who would have thought a good little girl like you could destroy my beautiful wickedness?"*

Yep, the ego never thought it would see the day. A bunch of cute little innocent gullible energy-receiving souls like us ... slaying the evil beast?

Whoosh! Splish! Splash! Hit it with more grails of elevated consciousness!

"Look out! I'm going! Ohhhhh!" the ego shall wail, leaving behind just an empty costume as it fades into oblivion.

With the proper focus, the ego recedes in an instant. Poof! It's gone. It's all hot air, not so scary after all. Shine a light anywhere, it will always make the darkness disappear.

For thousands of years, we thought of the devil as a fearsome, fiery-red horned creature with a trident and pointy tail. Turns out he was just a harmless straw man, a sham of an enemy that we set up to argue with and then knock down, enabling us to learn something about ourselves along the way.

We never did have anything to fear.

It was all just a dream, Dorothy.

***

Not all of the science is settled and it probably never will be, but the spirituality is — and it nicely fills in all the gaps. There is more than enough fact in the quantum evidence to complete the spiritual puzzle and discontinue the fictional physical narrative under which humanity has been living.

Here's the *New Eyes* therapeutic theory of everything, this entire book in review:

You are a soul. Consciousness is the 'head' of the soul, a tour guide that navigates its way throughout the illusory universe.

The soul is a vessel, a container for energy. The type of energy that goes into that cup is ultimately determined by your level of consciousness. The soul and consciousness are special types of energy and, along with the entire physical universe, are comprised of strings — tiny vibrating loops of energy.

When conscious energy passes through the realm of quantum foam, it vibrates with the Higgs Field and puts $E = mc^2$ into action. Energy takes on mass and manifests into matter.

As the sticky little open-loop strings clump together, they form quantum particles that clump together to form atomic particles that clump together to form molecules that clump together to form flesh particles that clump together to form your physical body. The little closed-loop strings do not clump together and therefore stay non-physical. They represent your spiritual body.

Duality has emerged, as you become two — one part physical, one part non-physical. Yin and yang, two halves of the same whole. The physical aspect is a projection of the non-physical aspect, so it is really just one thing. The physical is just a costume, your False Self. Ego loves this thing. The non-physical is your True Self. Ego hates this thing.

Once in the physical world, when scientists search for consciousness, they cannot find it. They call it the "hard problem of consciousness" because they cannot determine its origin, but it is not a hard problem for a spiritual being. Its origin is in another dimension, on the 'other side' of the quantum foam.

And yet, we forget that very quickly. As infants we slowly get conditioned to fall in love with the flesh part of ourselves, thus eating off "the tree of the knowledge of good and evil" and losing touch with the soul, which needs to eat off "the tree of life." We fall asleep, spiritually speaking, like Adam in the Garden of Eden story.

This is not a surprise. Babies cannot resist this, as they do not have the conscious capability of doing so; it is a fait accompli. We are wired to go to spiritual sleep, it is an essential feature of this reality. That allows 'the game' to begin, as waking up becomes our life's goal — whether we know it or not.

We must rediscover our True Selves. That is the Holy Grail. (The True Self as a soul is just the Grail, but when it is filled with Christ Consciousness, it becomes Holy.)

Our physical life conditioning is very strong, very compelling — family, friends, society, government, Santa Claus, religion, you name it — everything seems to hypnotize you into becoming obsessed with the material world. You come to believe that the False Self is you. We all do this.

This is important because the energy on the material side of the quantum foam is exquisitely receptive to the way in which you see the world. This is called the observer effect. Since the False Self is connected to the good-evil tree, 'bad' things may now happen in accordance with certain probabilities, or superposition. What you feel when those 'bad' things happen and you perceive them as 'bad' is called suffering.

'Good' things may happen, too, but that may not be a 'good' thing because when 'good' things happen you tend to idolize the false ego self even more. This can put you even deeper in a flesh-oriented trance as you believe your physical life to be your real life. It can be hard, though not impossible, to focus on spiritual development when the physical world treats you so well.

Prophets such as Jesus will warn you about 'good' things being potential ego traps, saying, *"Blessed are those who are persecuted for righteousness' sake, for theirs is the kingdom of heaven"* as well as *"It is easier for a camel to go through the eye of a needle than for a rich person to enter the kingdom."* (You will have an opportunity to learn that the Jesus teachings are about *"Christ in you"* — similar to Truths taught by other prophets and wisdom traditions — all inspiring in you the ability to conquer the ego and fill the soul vessel with upper light.)

The good-bad dynamic is intensified by the fact that nearly all of the other soul bodies around you are also asleep, believing in their False Selves as well. This is a mind-numbed state that results in a wicked exchange of low-grade energy, like putting sand in your vehicle's gas tank: The vessel might be full, but with a poor fuel source.

Every soul has a giving and receiving aspect to it, known as male and female in spiritual texts. When a soul is filled with negative energy, it can only spew out negative energy. When a soul is open to negative energy, it will receive negative energy.

On the lowest level of our development, this energy is like sludge in a tank, causing it to malfunction. Krishna calls this energy *dark inertia*. It is poison, an STD — a soulfully transmitted disease that sickens the True Self. It is a virus whose mission is to spread itself around and infect everyone it can. It does a very good job at that. Like a spiritual game of hot potato, as soon as it burns you, you give it to someone else to be burned, but the damage has already been done to you.

Worse yet, it hijacks your mind and forces you to think like it wants you to think. It gets you to argue FOR the very suffering it has created inside you. If someone tries to comfort you or help you see a way out, you might attack. But that is not you, that is only the negative energy inside of you. It is the reason behind all the mental health issues that human beings have ever experienced. *Dark inertia* gunks up the mental and physical vessels, resulting in more suffering.

That is the worst kind of ego, its darkest side.

There is also a 'bright side' to ego (ego would not be ego without being confusing). It's when people spread 'good' negative energy around to each other, when they really, really, really love you physically, so much so that they would do anything for you to help you out physically. Krishna calls this *passion*, but make no mistake — it is still ego.

When physical people help physical people improve physically, it's ego. And it still results in death. Maybe a 'good' death, a lovely material life that ends as you are surrounded by all of your material — albeit asleep — loved ones, but death nevertheless. Memento Mori.

So you cannot be bad nor good, at least not on the ego level. That's what it means by not eating off the tree of the knowledge of good and evil. Doing so doesn't get you anywhere, except a permanent place in the wheel of life called samsara … and continued suffering. It's a helluva merry-go-round. This endless battle between good and evil plays out that way because there is no end to it, like a dog chasing its tail. The physical world is a balancing act. Good and bad are complements, different aspects of the same thing — ego, or physical focus.

The only way out of this energy loop is to go up, up, up … by elevating consciousness. Upward toward perfection. You could call it ascension; Krishna calls it *lucidity*. It is realizing what you are here to do, then doing it. More accurately, it is realizing what you are here to be, then being it.

In order to be that you must wake up, according to Buddha.

You must know yourself.

Gnōthi Seauton.

You are not a body. You are that conscious energy being that *did not manifest* in the flesh way back there as it passed through the quantum foam. That physical part of you manifested as a costume for you to have a physical experience and learn more about your True Self, the soul. The material world always was and always will be an illusion, according to Muhammad.

You remain an energetic soul, guided by consciousness. You are timeless, as time also only exists as an illusion, according to Albert Einstein. Time is important only to your False Self. Spiritually you are eternal, which means *no time*, which means you have eternity to figure all of this out … so there's no reason to fear. You have an endless amount of no time to get the job done.

But you should use the idea of time wisely, because if your consciousness does not evolve — if you do not move from 'lower mind' to 'upper mind' — your soul will not get nourished properly and withers on the vine. In order to combat the ego that, like a boa constrictor, starts to squeeze the life out of you as soon as you are born, you must arm yourself with the proper tools. Spiritual ammunition or virtues, such as forgiveness, compassion, hope, courage, patience and wisdom, are the ideal weaponry for this inner war.

There are many ways to do this, to acquire such spirit. In fact, there are an infinite number of potential pathways to do so. In science this is called superposition. In spirituality this is called tolerance.

The world is set up to encourage each of us to find *our own* pathway, as the law of attraction will bring relative experiences to you that allow you to develop various aspects of your soul. You can tell whether you are making progress by a growing sense of peace inside your heart, as the human brain is a delicate energetic balancing tool and won't allow you to bypass any part of the curriculum. No one gets away with murder. The brain is a karmic enforcer: You reap what you sow and, like a mirror, what you see spiritually gets reflected back at you. This does not mean that you are 'bad' if something 'bad' has happened to you. Was Jesus 'bad' because he was killed? Of course not. High-level spiritual challenges often require complex physical circumstances, that is all.

Achieving the right balance of virtue fills your vessel with spirit. It often helps in the physical world, but always helps in the spiritual world. Forgiveness, for example, keeps you from absorbing the energy of someone who is trying to infect you with her ego perspective in one way or another. That might make things better for you physically, though it is no guarantee (see Level 33), but it absolutely makes things better for you spiritually (see Level 33).

Forgiveness, compassion, hope, courage, patience, wisdom and other virtues add up to perfect love, which casts out fear. Perfected spirit defeats the ego. That's how you defend yourself against the enemy's assault, by energetically trumping it. In baseball, a tie at first base goes to the runner. In spirituality, an energy tie between love and fear goes to love.

This is Krishna's lucidity and Buddha's enlightenment and

Jesus's ministry and Muhammad's revelations all rolled into One, as you recall that you are a spiritual being on an illusory physical journey. Seeing life this way is your salvation, as this singular focus will fill your whole body with light. You have solved the riddle. When you force the ego to submit under the weight of superior energy, you have won the war that all of the Holy Books are referring to, the battle inside yourself. You no longer need to *think* about what to do, because spirit is automatic and fills your heart, so you *know* what to do.

This state of being can be referred to as 'gnosis' in certain Christian circles or 'no mind' in Buddhism … or a metaphorical beheading. (Just don't take that literally, please, as that causes unnecessary suffering.) You no longer need a mind because your heart emanates the light of pure beingness.

Then your objective shifts. Having received the light as a female soul, you must now give the light as a male soul. Nothing about human gender there, that male-female interaction is referring to how souls roll — they exchange energy, in and out, just like atoms.

Realizing the nature of duality, that you are two but not two (esho funi), you are able to peacefully live and appreciate your physical life while helping others wake up. If you have removed the ego log from your own eye, you can assist your neighbors with their splinters. You become a giver of the light. You become the light of the world.

You can now judge correctly, not by mere appearances. You see souls instead of bodies. You know that filling people with spirit is far more important than filling their wallets with money. You also know that behavior is just a feedback loop for perception, as anyone who sees the world physically acts accordingly, just as a person with spiritual sight can be identified by their fruit. If someone is a cranky, judgmental, bitter person in any religion, his fruit is rotten. But spiritual souls project lovely light — healthy fruit.

Your final mission becomes clear: You must do unto others as you would have them do unto you. You must give the very light that you received. No worries, though, for as you give so shall you receive. When you light someone else's candle with your flame, your candle stays lit.

You can now help people understand that there is no 'bad' because the serpent is really an angel, accomplishing your salvation by motivating you to change your perception. If they are too sick with ego, you forgive them by not absorbing their energy and then let them find their own way to the light. You rest assured knowing that they will indeed find their way — everyone does.

When people are open to spirit, you heal them by offering them spirit. You might also offer them physical assistance, like money or food, but that act would certainly be combined with hope and encouragement, not pity or scorn. When you give to charity freely, starting with the spirit in your heart, the checkbook will likely follow. If not, no big deal, spirit is the currency that the soul craves. A spirited woman who gives two pennies offers more than an ego-fueled man who gives a million.

Filled with love, you are patient and kind with others. You do not envy, because your vessel is full. You do not boast, because you know that the spirit is guiding all of your actions. You always protect, trust, hope and persevere.

You dig in for the long haul, because there is a lot of ignorance out there, a lot of souls in need. But you understand, you were there once, too. You know that the war between good and evil always ends in peace. Plus, in healing the sick among them, you realize Truth. You are benefitting in the process as well. You are earning your spiritual merit badges.

While working on your spiritual dissertation, you become capable of consciously absorbing the sins of others — you recognize the ego energy in them and allow them to infect you with it. But since your spiritual liver is so finely tuned at processing toxins, you quarantine the ego energy and destroy it inside yourself. You do not let any of it out. You only send back love and light.

It's not what goes into you that defiles you, it's what comes out of you. If what comes out of you is spirit, you have taken on the sins of the world. This is Christ Consciousness. This is perfection. This is the finish line.

You are born again, in spirit.

"If any man be in Christ, he is a new creature."
- 2 Corinthians 5:17

Now the ego virus is dead, but you are alive. Your own physical death means nothing to you since you know you cannot die. If you fail to recognize this at death, you get to come back and do it all again. (Yippee!) But if you succeed, at graduation you pass back through the quantum foam as a new creature and the physical body fades away, since you cannot take it with you.

But the spirit? That's your treasure to keep. It's the promised land.

You have found the Holy Grail.

***

Many fearless prophets, enlightened spiritual leaders, committed armies of seekers and a dynamic array of stimulating philosophies have shown the way over the past few thousand years, marching humanity up to the point where Truth has been inspired inside of many. A spiritual revolution is starting to roll.

Incito Veritas.

We have reached critical mass, with enough people on board to create a sustainable chain reaction. About 10 percent of humanity authentically sees itself as spiritual beings having a

human experience, which means the idea is ready to catch fire. Our moment has come. If you have been inspired by Truth, now is the time to spread Truth by teaching Truth and living Truth.

Vivere Veritas.

To Live Truth.

We first identified Truth, and now we must apply it.

In the *CliffsNotes* version of *New Eyes* above, the word 'God' was not mentioned once. Quibbling over words will not get anyone anywhere.

"The letter kills, but the spirit gives life."
- 2 Corinthians 3:6

Saying the word 'God' does not give one life, either, only receiving the spirit does.

A spiritual being does not argue over whose material version of this dream story is correct, that is the ego having its way with us. A spiritual being recognizes that "the spirit" gives life, not letters or laws.

Personally, I believe in God. Rather, I have come to know God. I *know* God as a giving energy force, best described as universal love. I *know* God is not a man, because man is not even a man! (Illusory man kills, but the eternal soul in him gives life.) I know that connecting to a universal loving force offers each of us a dramatic shift in consciousness, a peaceful awakening.

May the force be with us.

But you don't have to believe in God or say the word 'God.' We are all spiritual beings on an energetic playground. I can play my game while you play yours. My job is to embrace your experience as authentically yours, not try to change you at all. I recommend you do the same, but ultimately, I can only control me.

If you feel like you are on a spinning carousel and it is making you dizzy, perhaps we should ride on the teeter-totter instead. Life will still go up and down, but it is less nauseating than all of that round and round. We can work together. We've got this.

Truth can be shared in our private lives, but we must listen to each other and figure out where the other person is on the consciousness evolutionary ladder. You cannot force too much Truth on someone, it will not work. There should be "no compulsion" in any of this, to borrow Muhammad's phrase.

In our primary relationships we must be patient and kind, and not envious nor boastful; and we must not get easily angered nor delight in evil, but rejoice in Truth. We must be role models. We must trust that all of our loved ones are on the same journey, looking to fill themselves with light, whether they know it or not. It's understandable if your family and friends go through hard times, they are learning. Show them the way. Show them how peace is found in their hearts. Reassure them that no one ever dies, we all just change form.

Truth can be shared in our professional lives, using science and spirituality to inspire clients toward insight and revelation. In my private practice we use 'quantum counseling' as a guide, utilizing superposition, the observer effect, entanglement, relativity and every therapeutic spiritual text available in order to promote healing.

As teachers, there is no need to use the word 'God' when working with students. Education on quantum physics and neuroscience — especially Hebb's Law and how peace is experienced when brain chemistry is balanced — is more than enough to light fires in children's hearts, especially done by an inspired, compassionate, wise teacher. Programs on 'everything is energy' and relativity, particularly as it relates to bullying, are greatly needed in our schools. Perhaps most importantly, the Butterfly Effect should be taught in first grade, so kids know that there is always a reason for hope.

Truth can be shared politically. The world of international politics has become the greatest fortress of ego — it is us against them, and it is all about materialism. Who has the land, who has the money; ego rules the world in that regard. Overthrowing it will require a new brand of leader, someone not afraid to speak Truth, and that does not require use of the word 'God,' but it does require the use of universal love.

"God is love."
- The Bible

If you have discovered a pathway that unifies everyone, you have found universal love, you have found God.

"Wake up from this dream of separateness."
- The Upanishads

Had there been a presidential election during the time of Copernicus and Galileo, candidates on both sides of the aisle would have been hesitant to say anything about heliocentrism for fear of being mocked. Soon we will have a politician who will understand the implications of quantum dynamics and will fearlessly put them into action — both personally and with policy — perhaps as a member of the Unity Consciousness Party.

If we're gonna dream, let's dream big.

IT IS FINISHED

The Greatest Story Ever Told is also The Greatest Story Never Told.

It's a wonderfully ironic spiritual yin-yang, as the most celebrated moment in human history is the most overlooked. Now you see it, now you don't.

What you have not heard about it will make what you have heard so much more meaningful. What you have not understood about it will make what you have understood so much more inspirational. You won't want to stop seeing it.

Two thousand years ago, a man walked the earth and billions of people now believe him to be the Son of God. He was born of a virgin through immaculate conception and became the most revered teacher that man has ever known. He later submitted himself to be killed in a selfless, heartbreaking, breathtaking fashion.

The details of his life and death have been heard so often by his followers that there is no need to review them here, and certainly not in the closing pages of a book that heavily emphasizes interpretation over narration.

It's the story of Jesus Christ, who lived as Son of God and Son of Man, then died in the most impactful instant in the history of the world.

And it's *your story*, too.

Not the physical details, of course; what Jesus did in the flesh is incomparable, although he himself said that you could indeed compare. (More on that later.)

It's the spiritual aspect of him, as Christ, that is your story. Jesus himself said that, in so many different ways.

"If anyone would come after me, let him deny himself
and take up his cross and follow me."
- Matthew 16:24

If you want to be a Christian, you must deny the ego in yourself and be crucified as well. He clearly did not mean this literally, he meant it spiritually.

It is not called Jesusianity for a reason. It is Christianity.

The difference between that which was Jesus (flesh) and that which was Christ (spirit) is an essential distinction, cleanly resolving any potential confusion over many of his teachings that may sound like doublespeak.

"Whoever finds his life will lose it,
and whoever loses his life for my sake will find it."
- Matthew 10:39

"I tell you, in that night there shall be two men in one bed; the one shall be taken, and the other shall be left. Two women shall be grinding together; the one shall be taken, and the other left."
- Luke 17:34-35.

"Whoever loves his life loses it, and whoever hates his life
in this world will keep it for eternal life."
- John 12:25

You have two lives — an ego life and a spiritual life. You

have two bodies — a flesh body and a soul body. There are male and female aspects to both.

So you do not have to do what Jesus did, you have to be what Christ was. You must follow the non-material essence of Christ, denying in yourself any material focus and pursuing the spiritual path. It is not about being a carpenter, wearing a robe and sandals, never marrying, never having children nor dying on a cross. It is about being wise, forgiving, courageous and recognizing that you are a soul, a spiritual child of God.

The pain of denying their ego selves is too much for many to bear, so many do not do it. It is a high mountain to climb, believing that you are not what you thought you were your whole life, a flesh-and-blood human being. You have to give up your relative points of view. You have to see the world the way Christ saw it.

He saw us as souls, not as physical bodies.

"They are not of the world, just as I am not of the world."
- John 17:16

He was referring to his disciples in this verse, which we all can be. We are not of this world, just as he was not. Though our illusory bodies are of this world, our consciousness and developing souls are not.

"(I pray that) all of them may be one, Father, just as you are in me and I am in you. May they also be in us."
- John 17:21

A clear message of Unity Consciousness, as it is impossible for this to be a physical reference. You are in me, I am in you, we are in Christ, Christ is in us, and we all are in God, unified as One.

You can only do that as an energetically interconnected and entangled soul. Ego does not fit into the puzzle.

"Whoever welcomes a prophet as a prophet
will receive a prophet's reward."
- Matthew 10:41

A message of spiritual equality. If you receive Christ, you receive Christ's reward. He put you on the same level as himself.

"Jesus answered them, "Is it not written in your Law, 'I said, you are gods'? If he called them gods to whom the word of God came - and Scripture cannot be broken - do you say of him whom the Father consecrated and sent into the world, 'You are blaspheming,' because I said, 'I am the Son of God'?"
- John 10:34-36

Jesus was debating the church leaders, who did not believe he was the Son of God. He then pointed out how Scripture says everyone who receives the Holy Spirit is a god, and Jesus noted that he fulfilled that role as well.

To be clear, the use of a small g in "god" is important, as Jesus was not saying that we *are* God, only that we are children of God or *part of* God — just as Jesus was the Son of God. We are all His children.

"I am the light of the world."
- John 8:12

"You are the light of the world."
- Matthew 5:14

A pretty specific union of Christ with us. Together, we are the light.

"If you had known me, you would have known my Father also."
- John 14:7

Many people knew Jesus, but they did not know Christ. We cannot literally know Jesus, but we can spiritually know Christ. When we know Christ in ourselves, we know God for real. Knowing Christ's mind is an altogether different experience than merely believing that Jesus performed physical miracles.

"Everyone who drinks of this water will be thirsty again, but whoever drinks of the water that I will give him will never be thirsty again. The water that I will give him will become in him a spring of water welling up to eternal life."
- John 4:13-14

Another spiritual reference not intended to be taken literally. The water he gives us is his consciousness — as water is a metaphor for mind or wisdom that leads to receiving spirit — and once your vessel is filled with Christ you are eternally filled.

Apostle Paul understood Jesus better than anyone, and he emphasized the spiritual aspect of Christ more than anything Jesus did physically.

"Do you not realize about yourselves that Jesus Christ is in you?"
- 2 Corinthians 13:5

His body is not in us, his spirit is.

"Be imitators of me, as I am of Christ."
- 1 Corinthians 11:1

Paul is of Christ and we should imitate Paul and be of Christ.

"I want you to understand that the head of every man is Christ."
- 1 Corinthians 11:3

The "head of every man" is certainly not a physical reference, it is a spiritual one. The head is the mind, and it must be filled with Christ Consciousness, which is the 'mind' of Christ's soul.

"My children, for whom I am again in the pains of childbirth until Christ is formed in you."
- Galatians 4:19

We are children not when we are physically young, but when we are not fully developed spiritually. It is a painful process of eliminating ego from our souls, but when we do, Christ forms in us.

Paul compared the process of a soul being born to the pain of physical childbirth. Jesus made the same analogy.

"It will be like a woman suffering the pains of labor. When her child is born, her anguish gives way to joy because she has brought a new baby into the world."
- John 16:21

Physical life is going to be painful and chaotic. If you are here, you will suffer. But the new creation that results is worth it, yielding joy inside you.

In so many ways, the Bible clearly references the need for you to be like Christ, which makes his spiritual story your spiritual story. You have to follow in his footsteps, including the crucifixion, which is the utter annihilation of the ego inside each of us.

It is not enough to just believe in Jesus, not by a long shot. That is a trick the ego plays on us, as we fall short of the glory of God by just believing that Jesus was God incarnate.

No, Jesus said you must do a bit more than that.

"Be perfect, therefore, as your Heavenly Father is perfect."
- Matthew 5:48.

Perfect physically? No. Perfect in consciousness? Absolutely.

If you believe that 'believing' means taking on Christ's mind, then you are on the same page as *New Eyes*. But if you believe that 'believing' merely requires a passive belief that Jesus was born of a virgin and was resurrected after his crucifixion, you are missing the mark.

How else could Jesus say the following verse if he were not putting you on his level?

"Truly, truly, I say to you, whoever believes in me will also do the works that I do; and greater works than these will he do."
- John 14:12

First of all, clearly following Christ requires more than belief, it also requires doing the "works" of the spirit. Secondly, not only is it possible for Christ to be in us in the form of his consciousness, Jesus said it is possible for us to do *greater* works than he did.

As flesh, Jesus was Son of Man. As a soul, he was Son of God because Christ was in him. Christ is 'God's mind' in Jesus, which can be in you. If God's mind is in you, of course you can do what Jesus did and more. It's all relative.

For example, according to the Bible, Jesus never had a child. I once ran a therapeutic group called 'Angels' for mothers and fathers who had lost a child. If you can experience the death of a daughter or son in the flesh and still remain perfectly committed to God in the spirit, you have demonstrated profoundly significant faith.

All of the parents I know who have lost a child would have much preferred to die themselves rather than experience the hell of having their child die. Ever humble, Jesus knew this.

He showed his humanity with that statement. He understood spiritual relativity. He preached spiritual relativity.

"Everyone to whom much was given,
of him much will be required."
- Luke 12:48

Jesus was born sinless. He understood the context he was in, that he was going to be resurrected, that he was going to heaven. Much was given to him, and much was required of him. He delivered. He cleared the high bar that was set for him.

Contrast that to parents who lost several children in a fire or car accident; to parents whose kids were kidnapped and never returned; to Holocaust survivors, who went through years of torture and not just hours, then had to face the rest of their lives with their anguished memories; to prisoners of war; to people with horrible, debilitating diseases that linger for decades; to pretty much anyone who has endured horrors and still has forgiven, none of whom was born sinless like Jesus.

"Greater works" does not mean simply experiencing those things. It means experiencing those things *in spirit*, with their faith in God intact. It means removing or taming the ego to become sinless during challenging circumstances that were as significant as what Jesus endured.

What sustained Jesus during his crucifixion is the same thing that sustains all of those others: Christ. Higher consciousness.

Connection with God. Knowledge of Truth. It is in that spirit that Jesus said we can do greater works than he did. These works are *spiritual works*, done by the soul.

As for works done in the flesh? As in behavioral works? Even Jesus did not take credit for anything he did.

"When you have lifted up the Son of Man, then you will know that I am He, and that I do nothing on my own."
- John 8:28

When you have raised your consciousness up higher than Egoland, you can see Christ as spirit, and also see that Jesus only did what God told him to do.

"I can do nothing on my own. As I hear, I judge, and my judgment is just, because I seek not my own will but the will of him who sent me."
- John 5:30

Seeking your "own will" is the very definition of ego.

Jesus the Son of Man did nothing without listening to his higher self and accessing the Father. As such, he was the Son of God.

Jesus wanted us to be like him, as Christ is the perfect connection to God. Jesus never said to worship him, certainly not in the flesh, but any notion that he should be worshipped would be in reference to Christ, or the aspect of God that was in him.

"I am the way, and the truth, and the life.
No one comes to the Father except through me."
- John 14:6

That was Christ talking. Jesus was a leader, for sure. With the mind of God in him, with Christ Consciousness leading the way, we should follow. This is how he is the savior, by elevating our low-level ego minds to the spirit plane.

The promised land is not anywhere on earth. You are a soul, not a body. Jesus was never going to guide anyone to physical safety. He did not even guide *himself* to physical safety! But as Christ, with higher consciousness, he leads the way, he leads your mind out of the hell that ego puts you in.

You get to the Father through Christ. Jesus led us with his Christ mind, and you must use yours in order to get to heaven. You must be like Christ. That is how you pick up your cross — your body along with all of your ego burdens — and follow him. As Christ. And this will also end in your metaphorical crucifixion, just as Paul explained.

"I am crucified with Christ: nevertheless I live;
yet not I, but Christ lives in me!"
- Galatians 2:20

We all must get symbolically crucified in order to reach heaven. But we do not die, the ego does, as in the process we are born again in Christ. Our soul vessels are filled.

There are many signs when Christ is forming in you. Attributes of Christ Consciousness that are recognizable include the experience of universal love, limitless compassion, unifying wisdom, constant peace, flexibility in thought, a sense of fearlessness, a falling away of regret, a heightened sense of perception, balanced virtues, the ability to manifest intentions, an awareness of eternal life, a connection to the divine and an understanding of your purpose as a spiritual being.

All of these qualities are of the spirit, and it forces ego out of you. That which you once were, you are no longer. You are born again.

***

Which brings us to the best part of The Greatest Story Never Told.

Remember how Jesus only spoke in parables, how wise men must learn how to understand riddles? Well, all you ever needed to know about spirituality and how to find God was described by Jesus during his crucifixion. He was talking to you and showing you how to die so that you may gain life.

When understood spiritually, you are indeed up on the cross with him.

The crucifixion is a powerful enough story on its surface, but contemplating it with *New Eyes* by considering the ego-soul theme discussed throughout this book adds layers of depth that can be transformative.

Keep in mind the emphasis on your spiritual body as a vessel that can be filled with heavenly light … or low-level hellish ego light, the kind that brings darkness.

"The kingdom of heaven is like a net that was thrown into the sea and gathered fish of every kind. When it was full, men drew it ashore and sat down and sorted the good into containers but threw away the bad."
- Matthew 13:47-48

Jesus was describing the potential Holy Grail "container" in that verse, as you must sort through all kinds of good spirit and bad ego energy in the ocean of consciousness. Keep the good, toss the bad.

That was precisely Jesus's journey through life — keeping the good energy, throwing away the bad, until he was filled up. Being born without sin, he always hit the mark and worked on filling his vessel with the Holy Spirit.

"Jesus increased in wisdom and in stature
and in favor with God and man."
- Luke 2:52

He may have been without sin, but that certainly did not mean he was the finished product from birth. He, too, as Son of Man, had to be filled and he did so through learning Truth, by elevating his consciousness. How else could he "increase in wisdom and in stature and in favor" with God? His was a journey of ascending consciousness toward perfection, just like yours. He increased his stature with God by expanding consciousness, just as you must.

The crucifixion was the last act of perfection, the complete eradication of ego and the lower mind combined with the complete filling of the soul through the upper mind.

The "Seven Words" spoken by Jesus while being crucified on the cross are yet another layered parable, full of deeper meanings that go unseen by blind spiritual eyes and serve as a metaphor for all of our lives. Successfully interpreting these sayings and then living them is a blueprint for salvation.

"Father, forgive them, for they know not what they do."

Jesus was certainly forgiving his persecutors, including the church and political leaders who oversaw his crucifixion, along with the men who carried it out. He certainly was also forgiving us, as he paid the ultimate price for our sins.

That's the conventional way of looking at it, and that works.

But seeing with spiritual sight makes it so much richer.

First of all, forgiveness is not about baking pies for criminals nor prematurely letting them out of jail. Those are behaviors. God is not concerned with your physical behaviors — He is interested in your soul's development.

Forgiveness is spiritual. Forgiveness is about giving spirit.

For giving spirit.

When you are giving spirit, no one else can give you ego. It is an energetic abomination.

"You shall not lie with a man as with a woman."
- Leviticus 18:22

That is a spiritual teaching. One soul cannot be giving energy to another soul that is also giving energy. The light cannot be transmitted that way. Like during gift exchanges on Christmas morning, there always has to be a giver and a receiver.

(Electrically, there cannot be a giver without a receiver either. You cannot stick a plug's prongs into another plug's prongs, nor does an outlet transmit energy into an outlet. All sorts of fasteners, connectors and hoses also follow this male-female dynamic, in addition to neurons among other things as discussed in Level 4.)

We are spiritually male and female. We give energy and receive energy. When you are spiritually forgiving, you are sending out the Holy Spirit and therefore cannot receive anyone's ego energy. This is forgiveness, when you no longer are affected by the negative energy of another soul. It's a critical component in the process of getting to heaven, releasing yourself from all forms of ego. Most everything gets much easier after learning forgiveness.

So yes, forgive them, all of them. Forgive everything. The world is a spiritual teaching tool, so forgiveness is great advice. It is a shield for your soul. Use forgiveness as armor, and the only thing that will enter you is the Holy Spirit straight from God.

Secondarily, by now you should quickly remember what the meaning of the word 'sin' actually is: Missing the mark or aiming at the wrong target. Do not sin and think Jesus died for your physical mistakes. He did not die because you stole a few snickerdoodles from the cookie jar, or because you had impure thoughts in church, or even because you killed someone.

No, Jesus died because as Christ he had proper perception and wanted to show us the way. He died because we misperceive the world as a material place and not a spiritual place, which is the original sin. When we eat off the tree of the knowledge of good and evil, we consume the physical world instead of spirit.

Jesus did indeed die for our sins. He died so that we could shift our perception of reality to Truth.

He also died to show us that we cannot die.

It is very important to realize that Jesus did not simply say, *"Father, forgive them."* He added the phrase, *"for they know not what they do."*

That means ignorance, or not knowing. We sin because we misperceive the illusory world as material and as such our behaviors follow suit.

If you do not know that the fabric of the universe has organized chaos coded into it, you probably wonder why you struggle with highs and lows in your life. If you do not know that human beings exchange energy all the time and do not realize that you are as absorbent as a sponge, you probably have taken in a lot of ego from others and accordingly may experience unexplained mood swings or anxiety when in public places.

If you are unaware that consciousness affects the behavior of atomic particles, you are most likely not utilizing the observer effect to its fullest potential. If you are unaware that there are infinite possibilities for your future that rest in a state of superposition, you may be stuck living a repetitive, robotic life on autopilot.

If you do not know that everything is energy and the illusory universe has holographic properties, you are probably mesmerized with the material world and unaware that you are spiritually asleep. If you do not know that you are a spiritual being having a physical experience, you probably seek physical things to comfort you and are never satisfied as a result.

If you do not realize that the world is a mirror for your spiritual growth, you might frequently blame others for your emotional pain. If you do not realize that other people are using you as a mirror for their spiritual growth, you probably are a little too sensitive and take things personally on a regular basis.

If you are unaware that everything is relative, you might be intolerant and judgmental of other people's behaviors. If you are unaware that things happen on a probability basis, you probably feel a lot of guilt and shame for your own behaviors and have a hard time finding hope.

If you do not realize that nothing actually dies, you are probably afraid of death. If you do not realize that we are all energetically interconnected, you probably cannot see the Oneness in all things.

If you do not know that there is one all-encompassing God who loves Christians, Muslims, Jews and everyone else equally, you probably do not feel united with the world. If you do not know that God does not care if you call Him 'God' or 'Allah' or 'Brahma' or 'Yahweh' or 'Supreme Mind' or 'Big Daddy' or 'He' or 'She' or anything else, you probably get into a lot of arguments.

If you do not realize that being a child of God is a reference to your soul and not your ego body, there is a good chance that you were never interested in reading this book in the first place.

All of the above are common examples of ignorance — or sinning, because the bullseye of Truth is being missed. You will behave accordingly. What you do stems from how you see the world, so your behaviors are not fully under your control without spiritual self-awareness.

Forgive them, for they *know not what they do.*

Someone who is sleepwalking does not know what he is doing. Someone who is asleep to spiritual Truth certainly does not know what he is doing either. Zombies are mindless. Ego zombies are too. They just operate based on instinct, on their wiring. They mindlessly pursue the material world. If you have Christ's mind, though, your behaviors will be significantly different than with ego mind, because your actions will be based upon seeking fruits of the spirit. Your mind will be full of spirit. You are mindful.

We want to teach our kids forgiveness, but do we want them permitting ignorant people to abuse them in some way? Certainly not. Jesus's forgiveness during his crucifixion was a teaching about not letting people *energetically* harm you. We certainly do not want to take this story only on its surface.

So if you are a being of light — transmitting nothing but spirit out to other souls in the world in spite of their ignorance — then you are living Christ's First Word on the cross.

Forgive them, for they know not what they do.

"Truly, I say to you, today you will be with me in Paradise."

The conventional wisdom in this verse is that Jesus was comforting, and forgiving, the repentant criminal who was being physically crucified along with him. This is surely the case.

But there is much more to this Second Word.

Jesus, as always, was speaking to all of us, for all time. He was talking to the repentant criminal, he was talking to the unrepentant criminal, he was talking to you and me.

As Christ, from his higher understanding, he knew that there was no such thing as time, at least not as we know it.

"With the Lord, one day is as a thousand years,
and a thousand years as one day."
- 2 Peter 3:8

Scientists have demonstrated that time is an illusion, it only exists inside systems, such as the physical world. Outside that system, where Jesus was operating from as Christ, there is no time.

So *today* you will be with him in paradise because *today* is all there ever is. Just an eternal now.

If you go to sleep at night and have a dream, when you wake up, you are still in your bed. If your soul comes to the ego land called earth and has a dream called your physical life, when you wake up from that life dream, you also realize you never left your spiritual home. It was all just an illusion.

Jesus also says that you *will be* with him in Paradise. This is unequivocable. He does not hedge — you *will be* with him in Paradise. He does not say *might be*. It's a big reason why you should fear no evil, because you *will* make it to heaven, guaranteed.

Oh sure, you may languish in hell for a long while, perhaps eternity. But since eternity is a really, really long absence of time, you will eventually realize your sinning, misperceiving ways and wake up. Then you will be in Paradise with Christ, too.

Everyone ends up perfect.

"Woman, behold, your son! … Behold, your mother!"

On the surface, Jesus was certainly being nice to his mother. He was about to die, and he wanted Mary to be taken care of, so he directs her to consider his disciple John a child of hers while telling John to look after Mary as his mother.

No doubt, Jesus would have thought that way. He wanted us to work together and be kind to each other on the human level.

But on the spirit level, it is again much different.

Many, many people go way out of their way to always portrait Jesus as a 'nice guy.' Surely he was always being nice, right?!

It depends upon your perspective. He was interested in saving our souls, not preserving the ego in us!

If Jesus were always a 'nice' guy, why did he say these things?

"Do not think that I have come to bring peace to the earth. I have not come to bring peace, but a sword. For I have come to set a man against his father, and a daughter against her mother, and a daughter-in-law against her mother-in-law. And a person's enemies will be those of his own household."
- Matthew 10:34-36

"If anyone comes to me and does not hate his own father and mother and wife and children and brothers and sisters, yes, and even his own life, he cannot be my disciple."
- Luke 14:26

But he turned and said to Peter, "Get behind me, Satan! You are a hindrance to me. For you are not setting your mind on the things of God, but on the things of man."
- Matthew 16:23

Sword? Hate? Satan? Peter was his right-hand man, and Jesus called him Satan! That wasn't very nice. (Or was it?)

That passage makes it clear where Jesus's focus was — on spirit. So certainly on the cross, of all times, he was focusing on spirit. He was seeing Mary and John spiritually, but was aware of their humanity.

Consider this passage:

"While he was still speaking to the people, behold, his mother and his brothers stood outside, asking to speak to him. But he replied to the man who told him, 'Who is my mother, and who

are my brothers?' And stretching out his hand toward his disciples, he said, 'Here are my mother and my brothers! For whoever does the will of my Father in Heaven is my brother and sister and mother.'"
- Matthew 12:46-50

If I ever talked like that in front of MY mother …

By no means am I suggesting that Jesus was being disrespectful, though some might argue that in this case. I find Jesus to be nothing but pure universal love of the highest order. He loved us so much he was willing to die for us AND try to stir us out of our deep sleep. If he had to shake us to wake us, so be it.

He was not being disrespectful; he was being spiritual.

Jesus, as Christ, saw from higher consciousness. He knew that we are all part of a larger soul family. He knew that earth relationships are temporary. His spiritual family, he clearly stated, are those who do "the will of my Father in Heaven."

While he was physically dying on the cross, Jesus was very aware of his spiritual ascension. Accordingly, those who saw him primarily as *dying* instead of *living* were still of the material world, focused on physical relationships. If we really understood what Jesus did that day, we should *celebrate* his crucifixion. Do not see the blood of the flesh, see the blood of the spirit.

Everyone saw Jesus dying that day, including Mary and John. They were all in the physical world while Jesus was headed back to the spiritual world.

Hence, *"Woman, behold your son."*

It is a profound message, backed by his own piercing yet loving words of sword, hate and Satan. No one should ignore those words. They were purposeful. Jesus was Christ, spiritually focused. He surely was not worried about human ego feelings, was he?

In fact, Jesus had a history of spiritually telling his mother like it is. Luke 2:41-51 relates the story of the family going to Jerusalem for Passover and, after the feast ended, his parents went home and forgot their pre-teen son. They "did not know" he stayed in Jerusalem. He was "missing" for three days.

Jesus, however, put his time to good use, learning from the teachers in the temple and "amazing" them with his wisdom. When his parents finally found him, his mother sounded offended, "Son, why have you treated us so? Behold, your father and I have been searching for you in great distress."

Did Jesus immediately offer an apology? No — he said, "Why were you looking for me? Did you not know that I must be in my Father's house?"

Why were you looking for me? Didn't you know where I would be?

Did you ever talk to YOUR mother like that?

Needless to say, Jesus was always operating on a much higher level, even at the age of 12.

"And they did not understand the saying that he spoke to them."
- Luke 2:50

And we will not understand, either, if we take this story literally. It's another parable.

This story is about Christ. I doubt very much that Mary, who a dozen years earlier had an angel appear to her and tell her that she was going to deliver the Son of God, would ever "lose" the savior for three days. But of course he was never physically lost, he was merely in his "Father's house," which is a reference to higher consciousness, or Christ Consciousness.

When you go on your own spiritual journey, sometimes you will appear "lost" to your family as well. No longer ego focused, your interests differ. Perhaps you do things like hang out with wise men in the temple all day.

You are, however, certainly not physically lost. You are merely in your higher mind — in your Father's house.

This story ends with Jesus returning home and being "submissive" to them, demonstrating his balance, and with his mother not taking offense at anything he said, as she "treasured up all these things in her heart" (Luke 2:51).

There is never any need to take offense at anything Jesus said, or anyone for that matter, if you interpret it spiritually. Such as, if you do not set your mind on things of God, Jesus will consider you a hindrance and call you Satan ... he would only say that because he loved you and wanted you to wake up to your True Self in spirit.

When he told Peter, "You are not setting your mind on the things of God, but on the things of man," he was saying that if your mind is set on things of God, you are in his spiritual family.

If you set your mind on things of man, however, you are in each other's physical family.

You *can* be in both families, as long as you have found the spirit and tamed the ego. But Jesus's highest priority was to guide us to God — not to each other.

"My God, my God, why have you forsaken me?"

He was Son of Man and Son of God.

In his Third Word, Jesus showed concern for his mother (as Son of Man) while drawing a distinction between physical world families and spiritual world families (as Son of God).

In his Fourth Word, he demonstrates his humanity like never before. He was Son of Man and more relatable than ever.

Just because Jesus was without sin does not mean he was without pain, temptation, distraction or moments of weakness.

Being without sin just means that he knew that the target was always God. He always knew that. He was sinless.

And yet, it was a rough road for him, just as it is for us. He had to fill his soul vessel with light, just as we do. He was "increasing" in favor with God by gaining wisdom and spirit over his 33 years on this earth, so obviously there was a need for spiritual progress throughout his life, just like for us.

"Not that I have already obtained this or am already perfect,
but I press on to make it my own."
- Apostle Paul, in Philippians 3:12

Jesus was striving during his life, too, like Jews do as Israelites ("striving for God") and as Muslims do in spiritual jihad ("to strive").

If Jesus were filled since birth, how could he grow in favor and stature with God? Why was there ever a need for him to learn from teachers in the temple? And why would he ever have felt forsaken by God on the cross?

Because he was human, too.

Forsaken means "abandoned or deserted." If Jesus *IS* God, then isn't "*why have you forsaken me?*" a strange thing to say to himself?

Also, if Jesus had been the ever-perfect and complete-from-birth Son of God, he would never have flinched — he would have gone through the crucifixion operating at 100 percent spirit and demonstrating unyielding faith.

But it did not go that way. Jesus felt forsaken, which in that context can only mean one thing. He did not feel the presence of God during an extremely trying moment in his life.

Just like us sometimes.

God, of course, will always be there, but that does not mean we will always feel His presence. The sun always shines, but we do not always feel the light. We are not always filled with spirit. Neither was Jesus. He was human, too.

This was a perfect teaching, though, for us to be aware of in our journey toward God. No matter how focused we are, no matter how hard we try, sometimes things are going to be so tough that we just won't feel it.

Other than his divine spiritual skill set, there was one significant difference between Jesus and us, though.

He had a moment, but he was sinless, so he kept his focus.

He knew what to do next.

"I thirst."

Undoubtedly, Jesus was terribly in need of a drink. He had been scourged, lost untold amounts of bodily fluid and was minutes from death.

Asking for, and receiving, an actual sip of liquid from sympathetic observers makes complete sense. On the physical level.

But with *New Eyes*, something entirely different is unfolding in this Fifth Word.

Jesus, recognizing that he had lost some divine energy and felt forsaken for an instant, then followed his own profound advice.

Ask and you will receive. That plus forgiveness will get you nearly all the way home.

"I thirst" was a request coming from his soul, which was desperately in need of a boost in order to get through the crucifixion. It is all we need to remember to do in times of struggle — simply ask from a spiritual place. Jesus was not asking to get out of his difficult physical circumstance, he was asking for his cup to be filled.

In the story of the woman at the well in John 4, Jesus diminishes the importance of physical liquid and tells her of the "living water" that he can offer her. It is "living water" that all of our souls crave ... and can offer to others ... to quench spiritual thirst.

"Whoever believes in me, as the Scripture has said,
'Out of his heart will flow rivers of living water.'"
– John 7:38

It is this living water that Jesus was thirsting for on the cross.

As he told the Samaritan woman, "The water that I will give him will become in him a spring of water welling up to eternal life."

"A spring of water welling up" means the Holy Grail is filling up. When it is filled, you have eternal life.

Jesus was 99.9 percent filled. He was thirsting for a bit more spirit.

So he asked for it.

"It is finished!"

And he received it.

Yes, Jesus finished his physical mission at this moment, but in his Sixth Word we need to focus on his spiritual life, not physical death.

He asked for more Holy Spirit and he received more Holy Spirit.

"All things you ask in prayer, believing, you will receive."
- Matthew 21:22

To ask *in prayer* means to ask for your soul, not for the ego. And *believing* is what one does when they are without sin, perfectly focused on the target.

He was born without sin, knew that he needed to fill his soul vessel with light, strived for it his whole life, learned from others (female receiver of light), became a teacher himself (male giver of light), forced the ego energy inside him to submit, and then during one of the most challenging circumstances imaginable, he sought one last time — and found.

He became a perfect vessel, filled entirely with light.

The Holy Grail of Christ was finished.

You, too, must be perfect like this.

"Father, into your hands I commit my spirit!"

His Seventh Word from the cross needs no significant explanation. It's impossible to see this any way other than the completed soul of Jesus, the Christ, ascended to heaven.

It's your story, Christ formed in you. The Real Creation Story.

When your soul is filled with the light, you are fully developed. Liberation and salvation are yours. You are One with God and are now a spirit being as well.

Mother Earth had been a womb while you were a spiritual embryo, but you thought you were a physical being because you were fast asleep. Energy Mom that she is, she received you, nourished you and protected you so that you could never get hurt. And you never did get hurt. Souls cannot be hurt.

God, the energy Father, had given you instruction throughout your whole life. When you understood it, it became wisdom. He loved you unconditionally, but disciplined you conditionally. You reaped what you sowed, after all. He also offered you an endless supply of light. When you were open enough to take it, the light enabled you to grow.

Then, like the Grinch on Christmas morn, your heart grew one, two, three sizes bigger until you were perfect. (And for the last time, *you must be perfect* to get into the kingdom.) The ego died, but you were raised from the dead.

Oh, and any punishment that you felt along the way was of your own doing. That was you sinning, so don't blame your parents — Father God never told you to misperceive, and Mother Earth had her hands full with all these other crazy soul toddlers running around down here. Truth is, the bigger the obstacle, the more spiritual progress you made. It was all totally fair. Adversity built character as well as your soul body.

When you finally understood what suffering was for, you stopped suffering. When you finally understood what the meaning of life is, you forgave everyone and everything, even yourself.

When it was finished, you were born again.

You are now a spirit child of God.

When we all do it, Christ fully returns, arisen inside of God's children. *Christ is in you.* He was the light of the world, we are the light of the world.

On earth as it is in heaven.

We return to Eden.

ABOUT THE AUTHOR

STEVE TREU, LPC

is a licensed professional counselor and Chief Visionary Officer for Quantum Revolution Inc. His insight-focused therapy uses quantum physics to help clients understand the scientific nature of reality, and process what it means for them from both a physical (body) and non-physical (soul) perspective as they heal themselves. As an applied quantum philosopher, Treu assists people in exploring their infinite possibilities as they improve their lives through a variety of mind, body and spirit techniques.

Made in the USA
Middletown, DE
26 December 2022